D1557813

Constructing Coleridge

Also by Alan D. Vardy
JOHN CLARE, POLITICS AND POETRY

Constructing Coleridge

The Posthumous Life of the Author

Alan D. Vardy
Hunter College and the Graduate Center
City University of New York

palgrave
macmillan

First published 2010 by
PALGRAVE MACMILLAN

Palgrave Macmillan in the UK is an imprint of Macmillan Publishers Limited,
registered in England, company number 785998, of Houndmills, Basingstoke,
Hampshire RG21 6XS.

Palgrave Macmillan in the US is a division of St. Martin's Press LLC,
175 Fifth Avenue, New York, NY 10010.

Palgrave Macmillan is the global academic imprint of the above companies
and has companies and representatives throughout the world.

Palgrave® and Macmillan® are registered trademarks in the United States,
the United Kingdom, Europe and other countries.

ISBN 978–0–230–57480–9   hardback

This book is printed on paper suitable for recycling and made from fully
managed and sustained forest sources. Logging, pulping and manufacturing
processes are expected to conform to the environmental regulations of the
country of origin.

A catalogue record for this book is available from the British Library.

Library of Congress Cataloging-in-Publication Data

Vardy, Alan D., 1954–
    Constructing Coleridge: the posthumous life of the author / Alan D. Vardy.
        p. cm.
    ISBN 978–0–230–57480–9 (hardback)
    1. Coleridge, Samuel Taylor, 1772–1834—Criticism and interpretation—
History.   2. Coleridge, Samuel Taylor, 1772–1834—Appreciation.
3. Romanticism—England.   I. Title.
    PR4484.V37 2010
    821'.7—dc21

                                                               2010023946

10   9   8   7   6   5   4   3   2   1
19   18   17   16   15   14   13   12   11   10

Printed and bound in Great Britain by
CPI Antony Rowe, Chippenham and Eastbourne

In memory of Jack Vardy (1928–2008)
and Robin Blaser (1925–2009)

Contents

Acknowledgements

This project began as a response to the various controversies over determining the 'true' Coleridge. Fascinated by Coleridge's practice of republishing fragments of his earlier works in new contexts, often for dramatically different purposes, I sought to understand the versions of Coleridge we have inherited as the products of historical processes, editing, textual production, current critical controversies, et cetera. In developing my thinking, and ultimately, in producing this study, I am deeply indebted to the Coleridge Summer Conference under the direction and leadership of Nicholas Roe and Graham Davidson. They have created a remarkable community of scholars, and they never failed to challenge my assumptions, broaden my knowledge, and sharpen my thinking. I am especially indebted to two colleagues: Fred Burwick for suggesting that I needed to know more about James Frederick Ferrier before I adjudicated the plagiarism charges and Nick Roe for a casual remark about the 'posthumous life of the author' which provided part of my title.

I am also indebted to the Professional Staff Congress of the City University of New York for their generous support of my research throughout the process with a series of Research Foundation grants, and to the Paul Mellon Foundation for a British Studies Research Fellowship that allowed me to consult the Coleridge family papers at the Harry S. Ransom Center at the University of Texas at Austin. The generosity of Hunter College President's Travel Fellowship program made it possible for me to present my research at numerous international conferences. Throughout the research process, I have been grateful for the kindness and expertise of the archivists, librarians, and staff of the following collections: the Harry S. Ransom Center, the Pratt Library of Victoria College, University of Toronto, the National Library of Scotland, the British Library, and the Berg Collection of the New York Public Library.

Paula Kennedy encouraged and supported the project at Palgrave Macmillan, and remained patient while I saw it through. I am also grateful to Margaret Vetare and Alison Powell for their assistance in preparing the manuscript for publication.

Alan Vardy
February 2010, Cold Spring, New York

Introduction

The broad goal of this study is to examine how authorial identity is formed. Coleridge presents a unique challenge in this regard, first, because his life and various public personae are rife with apparent contradictions, and, second, in that there are considerable stakes in determining which Coleridge prevails. Which Coleridge is dominant in itself is not a question that is or can be settled, and much of the focus of this book will be on the historical processes that constructed Coleridge at various moments both throughout his lifetime and especially in the first decades following his death. I do not mean to suggest that Coleridge was simply subject to blind historical forces, a kind of Althusserian nightmare.[1] Coleridge's agency, the exercise of his will, is at the centre of his philosophy, and his efforts to re-fashion himself were complex and sprang from his understanding of his capacity for, and growing faith in, self-reflection. The book begins, then, with an analysis of several of Coleridge's efforts at reinvention by examining them as the complex interplay of Coleridge the subject and specific historical events, which combine to form Coleridge the author.

Coleridge's public personae have always been contentious. In 1795, was he a principled Unitarian dissenter and pacifist, or an irrational and dangerous Jacobin pamphleteer? During the war with France, his safety depended on his ability to determine the answer. Self-creation in this early iteration seems synonymous with self-defence. At the other end of the historical spectrum, writing in the early twenty-first century, was Coleridge remarkable for his lack of industry and perseverance, the master of fragmented discourse, or does the appearance of the *Opus Maximum* in 2002 put an end to the myth of Coleridge the idler? Between these two points it is possible to construct many other Coleridges, each conditioned by historical circumstances. For example, examining the hostile public representations of Coleridge over the roughly fifty-year period ending in 1850 (one of the aims of this book) reveals a constantly changing set of rationales for public disdain. These caricatures include, in roughly chronological order: dangerous Jacobin, wasted genius, political apostate, mad metaphysician, opium addict, plagiarist, failed husband, abandoner of his children, sensualist, idler. The final version (circa 1850), constituted of the last four items, not surprisingly occurs as a negative construction of Victorian morality. That these constructions were highly contested becomes apparent when we consider an alternate list of laudatory Coleridges over the same period: Unitarian intellectual, true patriot, poet, Idealist philosopher, Tory sage, Coleridge the talker, guide to the development of a Christian character, father of American Transcendentalism, impetus of the Broad Church movement, originator of Practical Criticism, 'rational' theologian. As the furore surrounding the publication of Norman Fruman's *Coleridge, the Damaged Archangel* attests, this contestation continues. While both Fruman's moralizing and the fierce counter-attacks it provoked now seem out of proportion, they nonetheless indicate continuing over-sensitivity on both sides of the question of Coleridge's moral character. This book has no interest in this debate. If Coleridge plagiarized from Schelling (he did) that does not make him a bad person; if he was the single greatest influence on the development of Emerson's thought (he was) that does not make him a good person. The moral tone of this debate has been debilitating, and I hope to weigh the various facts without falling into the same pattern of moral judgement.[2] Editing Coleridge commenced at a time when his reputation was far from secured, and the array of defensive manoeuvres deployed by his literary executors, Henry Nelson Coleridge, Joseph Green, and James Gillman, and inherited by Sara Coleridge, condition the Coleridge we have inherited in turn by imbedding their strategies in the corpus itself. The magisterial *Collected Coleridge*, and Kathleen Coburn's conceptual framing, cannot be free of the executors' and family's influence. Even the ordering of the volumes, for example, determines Coleridge's reputation. The appearance of J. C. C. May's edition of the poems near the end of the process means that Coleridge the philosopher and theologian has been in the ascendancy for forty years. And, as noted above, the appearance of the *Opus Maximum* as the final volume has begun a currently ongoing process in which Coleridge the Anglican theologian demands equal space. In addition, critical trends tend to recover particular Coleridges as evidenced by renewed interest in *Aids to Reflection* as an essential text in Transatlantic Romanticism, or New Historicist interest in Coleridge the 1790s radical.[3] Given the sheer scope of the subject defined in these terms, I have chosen two specific periods on which to concentrate, judging them to be formative in a way others are not. The first covers Coleridge's efforts to shape his own public persona from the principled Unitarian patriot of the 1790s to the equally principled Tory sage of the 1820s, and the second (the main focus of the book) covers the efforts of the family editors to construct Coleridge in the first fifteen years following his death. Among those editors, I will focus particularly on Sara Coleridge who will emerge as the most significant single individual in the long history of constructing Coleridge.[4]

Two puzzles began this project, one from each end of the period concerned: Coleridge's redeployment of his radical pamphlets to argue that he had never been a radical, and Sara Coleridge's assertion of the 'consistency' of his political opinions in her Introduction to *Essays on His Own Times*. These apparently counterintuitive strategies have nonetheless largely carried the day, and the sage of Highgate and spiritual father of the 'clerisy' has largely displaced the idealistic primitive communist Pantisocrat in our understanding of Coleridge the author, regardless of whether we see this process as political apostasy or maturation. How Sara Coleridge came to make her claim, and whether it can be understood as valid, as opposed to simple subterfuge or dissembling, represents one of the main questions addressed in the final third of the book.

The family's posthumous editing and their other public efforts to secure Coleridge's reputation,[5] circa 1834–1850, constituted the textual body of Coleridge's works, and in determining how the various volumes appeared (the critical apparatus, Introduction, textual notes, appendices, et cetera) established interpretive parameters for subsequent readers and editors. The centrality of their work makes it the focus of the book, but Coleridge's propensity for self-fashioning needs to be understood in order to see how the executors were authorized in their acts of authorial creation. Furthermore, by exploring the shifting historical circumstances that conditioned Coleridge's self-created public selves, I want to make a larger claim about intellectual history—that rather than seeing it as a set of ideas transmitted over time, the example of Coleridge reveals that it can be better understood as lines of force, the inheritance of philosophical methods as much as ideas. The issues of dissemination and history will be taken up in earnest in the second half of the book, as Sara Coleridge self-consciously projects her father's theological and philosophical views into the future.

The first chapter focuses on particular moments in Coleridge's life where he felt compelled to represent himself to the public as a means to project a version of himself that accorded with his self-perception. Self-perception constitutes an important part of Coleridge's metaphysics. The conflation of the personal and the philosophical provides an intense sense of commitment in his philosophy, and simultaneously creates an extremely fragile personal psychology. Philosophy and psychology are difficult to disentangle in his thought, especially given his emphasis on consciousness and imagination. But, Coleridge's motives for reinvention were complex and various, depending on shifting contingent social forces and personal crises as much as on the desire for philosophical coherence. In 1802, for example, as a regular contributor to the *Morning Post*, Coleridge came to the attention of the *Anti-Jacobin Magazine*. They denounced his radical past as a Unitarian dissenter and radical pamphleteer in a devastating attack called 'Once a Jacobin Always a Jacobin'. Britain was at war with France; the Gagging Acts of 1795 were still in force, habeas corpus once again suspended. The article put Coleridge at risk for arrest without charge (without habeas corpus protection, he could be imprisoned without charge for six months) or a charge of sedition. Coleridge defended himself in the *Morning Post* in an article also called 'Once a Jacobin Always a Jacobin'. He argued that he had in fact never been a Jacobin, and that his dissenting past was principled and patriotic (a contested term then as now). What I find most interesting about Coleridge's article is its reliance on his own radical pamphlet of 1795, *Conciones ad Populum*. He carefully selected passages from the pamphlet as evidence that he had 'never been an adherent of the Jacobinical creed', in his phrase. He based his argument on the proposition that the Jacobins were atheists, and he was a principled and devout Unitarian. He left out the sections of the pamphlet where he advocated the wholesale levelling of classes, and by focusing solely on religion, protected himself from guilt by association. His definition of Jacobin, while doubtless accurate in its specificity, of course bears little relation to the way the term was actually deployed, by the *Anti-Jacobin* and others, as a general term of abuse for the entire range of reformers from those advocating the expansion of the franchise to rabid regicides. Coleridge's defence was clever rhetorically (he pointed out several Jacobinical tendencies of the Pitt regime) but ultimately disingenuous. For example, he vigorously defended the French Revolution up until the French invasion of Switzerland in 1798. I offer this example as an early instance of the pattern I am trying to sketch in this book— 'Coleridge' exists as a public construction, and revisions in any given historical moment entail careful forgetting and active rewriting of the personal and historical record. This rhetorical strategy becomes more complex once we realize that Coleridge did not leave well enough alone, and republished 'Once a Jacobin Always a Jacobin' on two other occasions, in the 1809 version of *The Friend* and again in the reprinted and expanded 1819 version. These two echoes served distinctly different purposes, as they occurred in very different historical and personal circumstances. It is in these subtle shifts that I locate Coleridge's self-fashioning. The chapter concludes with a brief section on Coleridge's most obvious act of reinvention, *Biographia Literaria*.[6] Rather than interrogate all of Coleridge's accounts of his political commitments in the 1790s, I focus on what may seem a relatively minor episode—the subscription tour in support of *The Watchman*. The *Biographia Literaria* account of the tour is self-mocking and punctuated by an actual punch line at his expense. The conversion of this piece of personal history into a picaresque vignette has interesting dynamics for Coleridge's creation of a post-*Biographia* self, and was singled out for sceptical analysis by both Hazlitt in his review and Joseph Cottle in his reminiscence written after Coleridge's death. Both critics rallied to the defence of Coleridge the radical, and defended *The Watchman* from trivialization at the hands of Coleridge the autobiographer.

Having established Coleridge's self-conscious efforts to recast his history and thus re-create himself, the book turns to the Coleridge family's inheritance of this task as they struggled to create a Coleridge palatable to their age. Chapter 2 examines their struggle to regain control over Coleridge's public persona and reputation immediately following his death. Fearing both scandal and hagiography, they set out to present Coleridge as the sum of his literary remains, as the Tory sage they, the executors, admired. The galvanizing event in this process was De Quincey's series of three essays on Coleridge for *Tait's Edinburgh Magazine*. Appalled by the characterizations of the loveless Coleridge marriage, Sarah Fricker Coleridge's lack of intelligence and sympathy, Coleridge's opium addiction, and, most famously, his various plagiarisms, the executors led by Henry Nelson Coleridge felt compelled to defend Coleridge against the charges. Family friend and self-identified Coleridge disciple Julius Hare rebutted the plagiarism charges in the *British Critic*, in an essay then reprinted verbatim in the body of Henry's Introduction to his edition of *Table Talk*. The personal family details, mortifying as they were, remained beneath the family's contempt, and met with official silence while De Quincey was derided in their private circles as 'ungentlemanly'. At the other extreme, the overly sentimental reminiscences of the great man that began to appear embarrassed them. Many were simple self-dramatizations: I knew Coleridge. The biographical sketch by James Gillman, one of the executors, could not be met with a critical public response for obvious reasons, but it exemplified for Sara Coleridge, Henry's wife and Coleridge's daughter, the need to gain control and stem the tide of unauthorized Coleridges.

The second important event in the immediate aftermath of Coleridge's death, besides publication of De Quincey's essays, was the publication of Henry Nelson Coleridge's *Specimens of the Table Talk of S. T. Coleridge*. Henry used the volume to construct his Coleridge, which the family then promoted as *the* Coleridge. Their efforts were not immediately successful, as reviewers were quick to point out that the speech attributed to Coleridge sounded nothing like him. In fact, the book presented a bit of a paradox, purporting to be specimens of Coleridge's famous dinner table conversation at Gillman's house, but actually containing none at all, not a single specimen. The brief notes that Henry recorded and then elaborated into the dated entries (some of the dating was fabricated) resulted from private conversations between him and his uncle in Coleridge's room at the Grove, Gillman's house. There are many reasons to believe that Henry's ventriloquized Coleridge was inaccurate or even parodic. Not given to self-knowledge, Henry was unlikely to have realized when he was propounding his own ultra-Tory cant and attributing it to his uncle. Critics on all sides registered extreme scepticism about the accuracy of many of the views attributed to Coleridge, especially concerning reform. Hartley Coleridge was among the most vocal, and I will suggest that his Whiggish reading of his father makes at least as much sense as Henry's Tory chimera. The *Table Talk* is also a special case in the posthumous contest to establish Coleridge's persona because of Kathleen Coburn's decision to include it in the *Collected Works of Samuel Taylor Coleridge* despite the fact that the author is clearly Henry Nelson Coleridge.

The third publishing event that set in motion the family's publishing strategy was the 1840 publication of James Frederick Ferrier's 'The Plagiarisms of S. T. Coleridge' in *Blackwood's Edinburgh Magazine*. Unlike De Quincey's eccentric account of Coleridge's genius, in which plagiarism appears as a fascinating character flaw nonetheless subsumed by the sheer scale of that genius, Ferrier's article detailed the borrowings from Schelling in passage by passage detail, leaving little doubt about the merits of the case. This created panic in the family for two reasons: they were completely unqualified to know whether the charges were true, and their best hope for answering the charges, Julius Hare, had been humiliated in Ferrier's piece over his attack on De Quincey. Hare was castigated as either unqualified or dishonest. This crisis redoubled the family's perceived need for a biographical account of the production of *Biographia Literaria* and a short biographical sketch in general. They debated whether the sketch should accompany a new edition of the poems or a new edition of *Biographia*, but Ferrier had forced their hand. Hartley had been their choice to write the biography, but he was now paralysed in the face of his inability to judge the plagiarism charge. In the end, the outcome of the crisis was the commencement of the sophisticated scholarly editing that has been the hallmark of Coleridge studies ever since—Sara Coleridge's edition of *Biographia Literaria*.

While it may sound ungenerous, the single most significant event in editing Coleridge was the premature death of Henry Nelson Coleridge. His strategies of dissembling and denial in response to controversy, his habit of hectoring perceived opponents from De Quincey to Cottle to their publisher William Pickering, his utter lack of qualification to evaluate Coleridge's debts to German philosophy, and his blinkered ultra-Toryism combined to make him the worst possible candidate to be the general editor of Coleridge's works. His death cleared the way for his brilliant widow to take over editorship, and she established an astonishingly high standard for subsequent editors. Her two greatest achievements were her editions of *Aids to Reflection*, which she had commenced during Henry's final illness, and *Biographia Literaria*, for which she had to master all of Kant, Schelling, and Fichte in German in order to adequately respond to Ferrier. Put simply, she was the only possible choice for the latter task, and there were very few people with a firm enough grasp of her father's adaptation of Kant in *Aids* to produce that edition either. *Aids to Reflection* had become the most important and widely disseminated of Coleridge's works, as evidenced by her use of James Marsh's Introduction,[7] and Sara used the occasion to publish her essay 'On Rationalism' as an appendix, and thus announce herself as a public intellectual in her own right.

Her intellectual bona fides were fully on display in her subsequent edition of *Biographia Literaria*. Her total mastery of Schelling in her notes to chapter twelve, for example, announced her as the most qualified person in Britain to judge the plagiarism question. Her complete facility with all the key German texts and the poignancy of her defence of her father's fragile psyche combined to make her response to Ferrier rigorous and eloquent in equal measures. Ferrier was sufficiently moved by her arguments and portrait to concede that his rhetoric had been unduly harsh and that Coleridge's eccentric composition practices probably contributed to the absent and insufficient attributions of Schelling's works.[8] In doing so, Ferrier was accepting one of Sara's key propositions about the transmission of ideas, and legitimizing the other intellectual achievement of her Introduction, her complex critique of Newman and Pusey. Sara sought to deploy her father's philosophical method and rationalism to engage in contemporary theological debates, and produced a nuanced Coleridgean critique of the Oxford Movement. In so doing she established the validity of her father's core beliefs and demonstrated their continuing efficacy. However, there were limits to her method, as witnessed by her next project, *Essays on His Own Times*.

Collecting and publishing her father's journalism presented obvious problems for the posthumous Coleridge her editing and Introductions had thus far produced—the philosophical sage, intellectual leader, and spiritual father of the hoped-for clerisy, the group where she wished to locate her own identity. Serious as ever about her task, Sara had to choose generous selections from her father's radical pamphlets and writing for *The Morning Post*, as well as his work for the *Courier*, which clearly squared more easily with the figure she was promoting. Rather than admit her father's often-strident radicalism, she attempted to deduce a set of core principles underlying all his social views. Encouraged in this by 'Once a Jacobin Always a Jacobin', she set about to establish what she called the 'consistency of the author's opinions'. The problems with her strategy were twofold. First, unlike her reading of Coleridge's theological goals, in which 1790s Unitarianism is largely irrelevant to her account of the philosophical model that commenced with the theological adaptation of Kant, she sought to subsume his early radicalism into ahistorical generalizations about his dedication to social justice. This attempt ended predictably in contradiction and deliberate forgetting, making her Introduction an impossible task. The second problem was also historical in that she could not recognize herself as an interpolated Victorian subject unable to fully comprehend the 1790s from a distance of half a century. Her lifelong circumstances of a sheltered childhood surrounded by the archly conservative Wordsworth and Southey circles, adulthood in the privileged Tory enclave of Regent's Park, marriage to an ultra-Tory, et cetera, combined to make her politically credulous. The predictable result was ideological blindness, but this is not to say that she should be pilloried for her failure. Such a response would be to misunderstand the force and nature of ideological formations. Furthermore, as a strategy to explain away political inconsistencies over time, her approach was the antithesis of her account of her father's philosophy and theology, in which his method was paramount in engaging a constantly shifting array of historically specific and conditioned ideas, from Emersonian transcendentalism to the Broad Church Movement to her projected critique of the Oxford Movement.

The final chapter looks at the material legacy of Sara Coleridge's work by analysing her conception of the Coleridge corpus as revealed in her negotiations with William Pickering. Henry was attempting to move from Pickering to Edward Moxon when he became too ill to complete the negotiations. He had infuriated Pickering with a combination of condescension and ingratitude, and things had reached a complete impasse. He had been motivated by envy over what he considered Wordsworth's more generous terms under Moxon, and wished to take advantage of this perceived largesse. Sara inherited this mess as well, and the tone of the letters changed accordingly. In the final days, Sara's replaced his scrawled hand and soon her voice, of necessity, replaced his. Pickering had all the cards, controlling the physical stock, and Sara made peace. Her relationship with Pickering was productive and justifies her decision. It is difficult to imagine another publisher agreeing to have *Aids to Reflection*, the most profitable Coleridge title, run to two volumes to accommodate Sara's two hundred and fifty page essay 'On Rationalism'. The critical assumption that the estate was unhappy with Pickering will not bear scrutiny; their unhappiness died with Henry. When Sara did move to Moxon just before her premature death it was for editorial differences over how the complete edition of Coleridge's works should be organized. She died without having been completely satisfied with a final organization. It was this work that Derwent Coleridge and subsequent editors inherited, and which provided the starting point for organizing the Coburn edition of the *Collected Coleridge*.

Kathleen Coburn's monumental standard edition owes more to Sara than to any other single figure. She also inherited the family's oversensitivity, and took loyalty to the cause of preserving and promoting Coleridge's reputation as a condition for editing. The 2002 completion of this project presents an opportunity to reflect on the historical processes driving the edition, and part of the purpose of this book is to provide the richest possible historical context in which to do so. As I said at the outset, despite the efforts of editors over a period of one hundred and seventy years, Coleridge's reputation is still contested, and responses to the J. C. C. Mays edition of the poems and the McFarland and Halmi edition of *Opus Maximum* have barely begun and ensure that posthumous constructions of Coleridge will continue.

1
'Once a Jacobin Always a Jacobin'

Coleridge first defended himself against the charge of Jacobinism in 1802, when, as a leading voice on the *Morning Post*, he came under increased attack from the *Anti-Jacobin*. But Coleridge's involvement with the *Morning Post* had placed him at the centre of the increasingly dangerous political climate considerably earlier, beginning in the first months of 1798. The original *Anti-Jacobin, or Weekly Examiner* was founded in 1797 precisely to counter the perceived liberal bias of the London press, and in particular the *Morning Post* and her sister paper the *Morning Chronicle*. Under the political direction of George Canning, then a junior minister in the Pitt government, and the editorial direction of William Gifford, the *Anti-Jacobin* set out to 'examine' the newspapers each week, and to check the spread of Jacobin principles. Coleridge was an obvious target of this examination. One of his first pieces for the *Morning Post* was a reprint from *The Watchman*, entitled 'Queries', which asked a series of inflammatory questions including:

1. Whether the wealth of the higher classes does not ultimately depend on the labour of the lower classes?

and,

6. Whether hungry cattle do not leap over bounds?[1]

The levelling implications of these questions were clear enough, and the proposed justification of a rebellion of the 'cattle' must have particularly enraged Ministerial circles. Coleridge's implicit threat to the ruling orders took the form of an instinctual response to oppression, and thus one that would naturally and inevitably occur. No appeal to reason would remove the desire to 'leap over bounds'. The uncontrollable realm of human feeling became contested terrain in the propaganda war, as each side attempted to use the fear of violence to their rhetorical advantage.

The first specific charge of Jacobinism against Coleridge came in early March 1798. The examiner section of the *Anti-Jacobin* was divided under the headings 'Lies', 'Misrepresentations', and 'Mistakes'. Under 'Misrepresentations' for 5 March, they attacked an article by Coleridge from the 24 February *Morning Post* which assessed the various political crises engulfing Europe including the invasion of Rome by the French army and the 'dying convulsions of the Swiss Republics'.[2] The editors of the *Anti-Jacobin* took particular offence to Coleridge's presumption in characterizing the British 'Public Temper' towards these events. They quoted Coleridge's opinion that: 'We read without emotion, that the Armies of France have entered Rome', along with their rejoinder:

> Where he found this 'insensibility' we know not, unless among the *Patriots* of the *Corresponding Society*.—For our parts, we have a very lively feeling of the transaction, which, for perfidity and inhumanity, surpasses whatever we have yet seen.[3]

This sneer at the lack of 'feeling' amongst radicals was coupled with a more pressing fear. With horror they noted that Coleridge had explicitly linked these European crises with conditions in Britain:

> In the midst of these stupendous Revolutions, the Nobility and Gentry, and Proprietors of England, Make NO EFFORTS to avert that ruin from their own heads which they daily see falling on other Countries.

This judgement provoked the charge of Jacobinism: 'Never, probably, in any period, in any Country, were such Efforts made, by the very descriptions of men this worthy tool of *Jacobinism* has pointed out as making no exertions.' Of course, the 'efforts' Coleridge had in mind were reforms, while the 'exertions' favoured by the *Anti-Jacobin* were those of the war policy. As a political slur the charge of Jacobinism did a paradoxical double duty. It accused the individual of excessive rationalism (considered to be a French disease), and tarred him with the violent chaos of the Terror. Coleridge's lack of 'feeling' made him a monster in the eyes of the editors, his 'insensibility' the sign of the dangerous ideologue. I draw attention to the details of this initial exchange because March 1798 was a telling month. The *Morning Post* had agitated against the corrupt Swiss Oligarchies, but that changed dramatically on

19 March with the French invasion of Switzerland. Coleridge could not defend French aggression, unless it was provoked, as was the case with Rome. So the assault on the Swiss republics, despite their corruption, could not be assimilated into his radical idealism, and precipitated the political crisis chronicled in 'Fears In Solitude', and 'France: An Ode', the latter of which was first printed in the 16 April *Morning Post* as 'The Recantation: An Ode'. Before this crisis Coleridge would have accepted being characterized as a Jacobin as part of the political game as it was played, but afterwards he felt the increasing need to distance himself from his earlier stridency, and to characterize it as youthful folly— excessive feeling. His sensibility distorted and betrayed his young and unformed intellect.

Coleridge's re-evaluation of the necessity of the war with France, and of his political beliefs in general, occurred during a time of increasingly bitter and personal attacks. Without the protection of habeas corpus, radicals had operated for some time under the threat of arbitrary arrest and imprisonment. Between 1798 and 1802 that political oppression intensified along with the emergence of Bonaparte in France. The successor to the *Anti-Jacobin, or Weekly Examiner*, the *Anti-Jacobin Review and Magazine*, used slander as well as the more direct engagement favoured by its predecessor. Coleridge and Southey were the clear, if anonymous, targets of an essay in the July 1800 issue entitled, 'The Literati and Literature of Germany', signed by 'An Honest Briton'. The essay recounts a story of two young Englishmen and their decline into Jacobinical vice:

I heard lately, too, from a friend, of two gentlemen, formerly well known at Cambridge, who, feeling the restraints of law and religion somewhat irksome, left the University and became philosophers. It seems these worthy men, finding the climate of England totally unfit for them, agreed with four others to go to America, and put their philosophy in practice. It was agreed that each of the six should engage a woman to accompany him, and that these women should be common to the whole. An actress, who acceded to this philosophical arrangement, was engaged for one; but the voyage to America failed, and the delicate lady remains, or at least remained some time, the mistress or wife of him who engaged her. Two of these gentlemen, who, it seems, were the projectors of this admirable colony for America, and who are writers for the Morning Chronicle and other publications of Jacobinical notoriety, came afterwards to Germany, to enable themselves, by acquiring the language and philosophy of this favoured country, to enlighten more compleatly the ignorant people of England.[4]

Here Jacobinism leads the young away from 'the restraints of law and religion' and into the dangerous realm of philosophical specula- tion and, eventually, into sensual degradation. Having one's youthful idealism reduced to a vulgar burlesque must, in part, have motivated Coleridge to set the historical record straight. In the spring of 1798, he felt betrayed by France but still in touch with his domestic political goals,[5] but by 1802, in a hostile political climate, he finally reconsidered and recast those goals.

On 21 October, 1802, in response to being targeted yet again by the *Anti-Jacobin*, Coleridge finally answered the charge and published the essay 'Once a Jacobin Always a Jacobin' along with a reprint of 'The Recantation: An Ode' and excerpts from 'Fears in Solitude' in the *Morning Post*. The thrust of his defence was two-fold: first, that the term 'Jacobin' lacked content, that it was 'a term of abuse, the convenient watchword of a faction',[6] and, second, that given the actual historical specificity of the term, he had never been a Jacobin. These two strategies are somewhat at cross purposes as they on one hand dismiss the charge as 'a term of vague abuse' used in Ministerial circles as one would 'use the word, *Whig*', while on the other hand they provide the historical detail necessary to legitimate such a charge. Coleridge lists the eight tenets of what he calls the Jacobin 'creed'. He uses the list rhetorically to point out that many active anti-Jacobins exhibit Jacobin characteristics. But, more significantly, he includes in the list the notion of levelling: that every citizen has the right to sufficient property to maintain them- selves (an edict against poverty), and furthermore that surplus property must not translate into greater political rights (more votes, a restricted franchise, et cetera). This belief was foundational to Coleridge and Southey's plan for Pantisocracy, but, surprisingly, it is introduced here, in his list of Jacobinical tenets, in an effort to disassociate himself from such extremism. He claims in his defence that:

As far back as memory reaches, it was an axiom in politics with us, that in every country in which property prevailed, property must be the grand basis of government; and that that *government was best, in which the power was the most exactly proportioned to the property*.[7]

Frankly, given the nature of the Pantisocracy scheme[8] and the political content of pieces like 'Queries' from earlier in his *Morning Post* career, this statement speaks to the fallibility of Coleridge's memory, but little else. Coleridge's political philosophy, at the time of composing *The Friend*, saw the right to private property as central to the constitution of civil society, but this was a later development in his thought, not a foundational tenet from the outset.[9] The true grounds by which Coleridge was not a Jacobin, and he was not, surface in the vocabulary that he uses to close his argument. He sees holding on to such radical enthusiasms despite the evidence of their failure as instances of sin. Jacobinism, in its extreme rationalism, leaves no room for the religious concepts of 'mercy' or 'repentance', and this absence of the reliance on God's love in the amelioration of the human condition is intolerable to Coleridge's devout Christian beliefs. At the time Coleridge made alliances where he needed to, but, after the fact, he can easily assent to the Ministerial prejudice against Jacobin ideology. However, resistance to ideology need not refer to a specific set of ideas, but rather describes the dangerous intellectual habit of constructing reality through a single lens, fanaticism, what Slavoj Žižek calls ideological 'quilting'.[10]

It is interesting that he did not foreground his profound religious difference from Jacobinism in his defence seeing that it was identical to his public dispute with Godwinian rationalism during the 1790s, and thus easily substantiated from the public record, unlike his clumsy falsification of his political views. Of course, the fact of his former radical Unitarianism may, in part, account for his reticence to argue the point on strictly religious grounds. Coleridge's developing Anglican orthodoxy made such a subject highly sensitive personally, and hardly helpful in attempting to convince others of his moderate political beliefs. The amount of historical detail necessary to attempt a defence of Unitarian beliefs in the 1790s exceeded the scope of a newspaper article, and he no longer felt any allegiance to those beliefs having concluded that they could not sustain his faith. As we shall see, the securing of Coleridge's religious reputation as an Anglican theologian becomes one of Sara Coleridge's goals in constructing her father's intellectual 'consistency' and posthumous influence.

When Coleridge revisited the charge, almost ten years after the fact, in *The Friend* of 1809, he chose to highlight the fancifulness of the Pantisocracy scheme in relation to Jacobin 'fanaticism'. While claiming that his early political beliefs were essential in the development of his mature moral being, he employed self-mockery to undercut the seriousness of those early commitments:

> when we [he and his fellow Pantisocracts] gradually alighted on
> the firm ground of common sense, from the exhausted Balloon of

youthful Enthusiasm, though the air-built Castles, which we had been pursuing, had vanished with all their pageantry of shifting forms and glowing colours, we were yet free from the stains and impurities which might have remained upon us, had we been travelling with the crowd of less imaginative malcontents, through the dark lanes and foul bye roads of ordinary Fanaticism.[11]

Following his return from serving the military governor of Malta, and the conservative political turn it precipitated, and in the midst of innumerable personal crises (estrangement from his wife, his feelings for Sara Hutchinson, the coolness of the Wordsworths), the time had come to dissemble and disassociate himself from radical politics once and for all—ten years of political commitment characterized as an adolescent folly. Pantisocracy became rhetorically equivalent to Jacobinism in its 'fanatical' blindness. The irony of this rhetorical performance is that it itself attempts to create a calm surface over the emotionally raw political chaos that necessitated those youthful commitments. 'Consistency' demands its own blindness, a new fanaticism for the old.

In the 1818 version of *The Friend*, Coleridge finally highlights the irreligiosity of the Jacobinical position, and moves closer to an accurate description of his original opposition to Revolutionary rationalism. This final revisiting of the charge of Jacobinism was occasioned by William Hazlitt's characterization, in the 3 January 1818 issue of *The Yellow Dwarf*, of Coleridge's extreme opinions during the time of Robespierre.[12] This shift in focus follows from the strategy employed to mount his defence. He submits as evidence his Bristol lecture of 1795, which he had published as the 'Introductory Address' in his *Conciones ad Populum*, also in 1795. His intention is clear enough; he offers his own radical thoughts and formulations from that period as a final proof that he was never a Jacobin. The original speech was one of extreme skill and cunning. He managed to draw a direct comparison between Robespierre's shameful practice of tolerating 'evil as the means to contingent good' (it is important to note that he left open the possibility that Robespierre's ultimate ends may have been just), and Pitt's practice of using 'inflammatory harangues'[13] to deform public opinion and incite violence. Coleridge's rhetorical performance hinged on his ability to make this comparison clear without naming Pitt, an act that, in 1795, would have constituted treason and risked prison. None of this matters to Coleridge in 1818, however. In republishing the speech he wants to emphasize a distinction he made between his own views concerning how public opinion could be shaped in the service of a meaningful political revolution, and Godwin's purely secular views of human perfectibility. He refers directly to 'the Author of an essay on political justice' who 'considers private societies as the sphere of real utility'. Godwin held that self-interest would be the mechanism by which human beings would manifest their inherent powers of reason and that the irrationality of absolutist politics would wither away. Coleridge, while agreeing with the proposition that 'the perfectness of future men is indeed a benevolent tenet', did not believe the mass of common folk would be afforded the contemplative leisure necessary for such a state coming to pass. As a result he claims that '*religion* appears to offer the only means *efficient*' to the task of transforming the natures of the poor and powerless. He offers the edict: 'Go, preach the GOSPEL to the poor'. 'By its simplicity it will meet their comprehension, by its benevolence soften their affections, by its precepts, it will direct their conduct, by the vastness of its motives ensure their obedience.'[14] In brief, then, Coleridge's republication of the Bristol lecture argued that he was never a Jacobin both on the grounds that he eschewed their unprincipled focus on the ends while employing evil means (a charge that makes Pitt a Jacobin), and, more importantly, he professed a deep faith in God's love as the only 'efficient' means of human amelioration. This difference from Godwinian rationalism provides the link between Coleridge's religious feeling and his political commitments. The two men shared identical political goals, but differed over how they were to be achieved. Coleridge claimed meaningful political change had to rely on the human capacity for religious feeling, while Godwin believed that the evolution of human rationality would displace the political absurdities created, in part, by the exploitation of the religious feeling of a gullible people.

In the political climate of 1818, what had been defensive evasiveness in 1802 and political reinvention in 1809 becomes a pro-Ministerial voice in opposition to the ongoing agitation for reform, a voice of the Tory establishment. Despite claiming that: 'the only omissions [from the original text of the 1795 Bristol lecture] regard the names of people', he disingenuously omits direct attacks on Pitt, the 'detestable Minister' who 'manufactures conspiracies'.[15] The result is the loss of the historical specificity of the original lecture and its original political significance. The cumulative effect, then, of Coleridge's repeated defences against the charge of Jacobinism was to erase the historical context of his views. His extraordinary range of views, from the belief that Robespierre's intended ends may have been just, to the defence of Tory resistance to universal manhood suffrage in 1818, is erased in favour of an abstract level of discourse in which all of his political views are made to exhibit coherence at the expense of the historical record.

John Wilson, writing as Christopher North, was particularly agitated by Coleridge's suppression of his public hatred of Pitt. In his review of *Biographia Literaria* for *Blackwood's Edinburgh Magazine* in October 1817, he ridiculed Coleridge's professed anti-Jacobinism and reminded the public of the author's attitude towards Pitt: 'he abhorred, hated, and despised Mr. Pitt—and now loves and reveres his memory'.[16] Responding to what he called Coleridge's 'multitudinous political inconsistence', he exposed what he assumed was subterfuge by noting the tenor of Coleridge's 'Slaughter, Fire, and Famine', which loaded 'the Minister with imprecations and curses, long, loud and deep'.[17] In defence, we might argue that the change in attitude was understandable in response to Pitt's leadership during the Napoleonic Wars, especially in light of Coleridge's service in Malta, but Wilson was having none of it. He drew the harshest possible inference from this shift, perceiving it as entirely self-serving, and concluded: 'that all good men, of all parties, regard Mr. Coleridge with pity and contempt'.[18] This from the Tory press, and from a former neighbour at that, must have hit hard. Wilson may have been score settling for the Southey circle over perceived slights against the laureate; Wilson's relationship with Southey was very close, and he readily forgave him the very attitudes towards Pitt that he damned in Coleridge in his review. More predictably, Hazlitt, writing on the other side of the party divide for the *Edinburgh Review*, was equally dismissive of Coleridge's newly discovered anti-Jacobin past in his review of *Biographia Literaria*:

> We shall not stop at present to dispute with Mr. Coleridge, how far the principles of the *Watchman* and the *Conciones ad Populum* were or were not akin to those of the Jacobins. His style, in general, admits of a convenient latitude of interpretation. But we think it quite safe in asserting, that they were still more opposite to those of the Anti-Jacobins, and the party to which he admits he has gone over.[19]

Less vehement than his attack on the republication of 'Once a Jacobin Always a Jacobin' in *The Friend*, Hazlitt nonetheless made clear that Coleridge's current politics were the product of apostasy, of 'going over', not consistency.

Another major goal of *Biographia*, besides political repositioning and the famous account of Wordsworth's poetry and poetics, was the promotion of the major intellectual project of Coleridge's life—the adaptation of Kant and German idealism to the service of his Christian philosophy. Of this, both Hazlitt and Wilson were openly dismissive.

Hazlitt's objections were philosophical; he considered Kant's philosophy empty and mechanical. He offered a devastating summary of what he took to be the impetus for Kant's theory of the mind: 'If he [Kant] cannot make good an inference upon acknowledged premises, or known methods of reasoning, he coolly refers the whole to a new class of ideas, and the operation of some new faculty, invented for the purpose, and which he assures you *must* exist, because there is no other proof for it.'[20] Having denounced Kantian philosophy as self-serving solipsism, 'absurdities that have not even the merit of being amusing',[21] he dismissed the subject from his review, and assured his readers that Coleridge's 'idol' would have 'few fellow worshipers' in Britain. Hazlitt's account was important in the creation of a critical commonplace that still has many adherents, that German metaphysics ruined Coleridge's mind and destroyed his intellectual and artistic potential. The result, for Hazlitt, was poignant, and his former dedication to Coleridge as a young Unitarian radical clearly conditioned his view: 'He might, we seriously think, have been a very considerable poet, instead of which he has chosen to be a very bad philosopher and a worse politician.'[22] Wilson was even more dismissive, presenting Coleridge's philosophy as beneath his consideration. To justify his dismissal, he offered the passage from chapter twelve describing the will as the 'primary ACT of self-duplication' out of context, assuming his readers would find it absurdly opaque.[23] With considerable hauteur, he evaded philosophy altogether, using the difficulty of the passage as pretext:

> We do not wish to speak of what we do not understand, and therefore say nothing of Mr. Coleridge's Metaphysics. But we beg leave to lay before our readers the following Thesis, for the amusement of a leisure hour.[24]

There is a certain irony in Wilson's assumption that he could dismiss philosophy that he did 'not understand'. In 1820, the Edinburgh City Council surprisingly elected him Professor of Moral Philosophy at the University of Edinburgh. He was the Tory candidate, and William Blackwood prevailed. The Whig candidate was Sir William Hamilton, probably the most qualified candidate in the English-speaking world. Against the odds, Wilson became an excellent and influential Professor; but, at the outset, his complete lack of qualification made him reliant on De Quincey, who wrote most of his lectures and whose views he simply mimicked. In a letter to De Quincey in summer 1820, his panic over his lack of 'understanding' is evident: 'What should I treat of in the

Senses—appetites and bodily powers? What are the books? and what theory is the true one? And your objection to Locke.'[25] De Quincey's source and inspiration for most of his philosophical views, and the origin of his 'objection to Locke', was, of course, Coleridge.

Having dismissed Kantian metaphysics as uninteresting, Hazlitt focused on one of Coleridge's few apparently straightforward biographical accounts, the *Watchman* tour. He reproduced a long passage, including the famous comic scenes Coleridge painted of his time in Birmingham with the 'Brummagem patriot', a figure of fun and condescension, and the worthy company of Birmingham Unitarians with whom he shared tobacco, ale, and stimulating conversation. I will return to this account below in the context of Cottle's competing and often-contradictory account, but Hazlitt did not challenge its veracity, barely commenting on it other than to register suspicion over its tone of good humour and fun. Instead, he recounted the '*Spy-nosy*' affair as a positive example of wit, thus intimating that the story was apocryphal: 'If this be not the highest wit in the world, it must be admitted at least to be very innocent merriment.'[26] He does not even entertain the notion that Coleridge's accounts of either the *Watchman* tour or the Spy-nosy affair are factual, and reviews them as amusing fictions. His objection to the passages as history—that they falsified Coleridge's commitment to radical politics by deliberately underplaying them—remained unstated until the end of his discussion where, as if reminding himself of past events, he described Coleridge's decision to write for the *Morning Post* upon his return from Germany. His devastating riposte to the tenor of Coleridge's autobiography was to expose it as a form of deliberate forgetting, a strategy which he delivered as a typically arch understatement reminding readers that the *Morning Post* 'was at that time not a very ministerial paper, if we remember right'.[27] Mockery and laughter masked a deeper anger, however. Hazlitt was enraged by Coleridge's obsequious apology and justification for 'going over' to the Tory cause so late. Coleridge argued that there was 'little wonder' that he hesitated in his conversion given the 'atrocious calumnies' that the Tory press had heaped upon him and other 'good men' of the political opposition. Hazlitt makes the obvious objection with utter venom:

> With us, we confess the wonder does not lie there: all that surprises us is, that the objects of these atrocious calumnies were *ever* reconciled to the authors of them; for the calumniators were the party itself. The Cannings, the Giffords, and the Freres, have never made any apology for the abuse they then heaped upon every nominal friend

of freedom; and yet Mr. Coleridge thinks it necessary to apologize in the name of all good men, for having remained so long adverse to a party which recruited upon such bounty.[28]

He expressed horror that any 'good man' would associate with these calumniating monsters, and deeply resented the implication that other 'nominal friends of freedom' would repeat Coleridge's action. Unlike Coleridge, Hazlitt had no interest in disowning his radical past; he was a Jacobin, and proud of it. Coleridge's offence was made worse by his apostasy, and his willingness to serve his new friends by: 'giving up [his] principles, and joining in the same venal cry against all those who did not become apostates or converts, ministerial Editors, and "laurel-honouring Laureates" like themselves'!

*

Another critical response to Coleridge's efforts to revise and forget the 1790s in *Biographia Literaria* took a more sober and disappointed tone— Joseph Cottle's *Recollections of S. T. Coleridge.*[29] Writing after Coleridge's death in 1834, the initial sting of publication had passed, but Coleridge's offence remained—his deliberate exclusion of Bristol and its complex intellectual and dissenter communities and their role in his development. Coleridge's account of *The Watchman* in chapter ten of *Biographia Literaria* barely mentions the Bristol intellectual milieu of which it was an expression and part. Instead it details Coleridge's subscription tour throughout England in support of his new enterprise and political goals. His commitment to those goals and excitement about the journal's potential led him to want the widest possible dissemination, beyond its local supporters in Bristol. In the *Biographia Literaria* account, however, the tour is presented as a series of comic anecdotes, culminating in the metaphoric destruction of the journal. The content and purpose of the enterprise are consistently underplayed and often mocked. Beginning the tour in Birmingham, he reports meeting with a city worthy who, upon being informed that the cost was '*only fourpence, Sir, each number, to be published on every eighth day*', observed that over the course of the year that 'comes to a deal of money'. Discovering that a subscription would commit him to reading thirty-two pages large octavo every eight days, he became horrified: '... that's more than I ever reads, Sir! all the year round. I am as great a one, as any man in Brummagem, Sir! for liberty and truth and all them sorts of things, but as to this (no offence, I hope, Sir!) I must beg to be excused.'[30] This is typical of Coleridge's entire account; he recalls another disastrous meeting where he became accidentally intoxicated with tobacco and ale, for example, with no actual account of political discussions. The reader might be surprised, then, when at the end of his 'first canvas' he returned to Bristol with 'nearly a thousand names on the subscription list'.[31] Coleridge immediately undercuts this evident success by claiming he returned 'half-convinced, that prudence dictated the abandonment of the scheme'.[32] It is difficult to take this alleged recollection seriously, and even a cursory glance at the first issue of *The Watchman* renders it absurd. Coleridge's political commitment and determination were unequivocal.

He proclaims the journal a failure, and it was, but his deliberate manipulation of the details of that failure is telling, as I will explain when I turn to Cottle's account. The pattern, though, is clear enough: a systematic disowning of the project by reducing it to youthful folly at best, serious political misjudgement at worst. The pattern culminates in the physical destruction of the journal in a hail of derisive laughter:

> Of the unsaleable nature of my writings I had an amusing memento one morning from our servant girl. For happening to rise at an earlier hour than usual, I observed her putting an extravagant quantity of paper in the grate in order to light the fire, and mildly checked her for her wastefulness; la, Sir! (replied poor Nanny) why, it is only 'Watchmen'.[33]

That this anecdote is apocryphal seems certain (why would Coleridge move unsold copies to Stowey?), but its function is clear enough: our laughter drowns out any trace of the journal or its politics. Just prior to this final denouement Coleridge had explained the failure of *The Watchman* as evidence of his unsuitability as 'a popular writer'. He ends with the somewhat glib assertion that: 'whatever my opinions might be in themselves, they were almost equidistant from all the three prominent parties, the Pittites, the Foxites, and the Democrats'.[34] His differences with the Pittites were fundamental (the 'Copy of a Handbill' parody from the first issue was a savage rebuke of Pitt), but, as we'll see, Cottle and the whole of Bristol associated Coleridge directly with Foxite policy, and the idea that Coleridge was not a Democrat is absurd— he was potentially one of the leading opposition figures in the West Country. *The Watchman* came into being, and readily found subscribers, following the success of his Bristol political lectures. Calling his views 'equidistant' from any party affiliation was disingenuous to say the least. The rhetorical purpose of this whole section of chapter ten seems to be a systematic denial of the significance of his political activities, and of his relevance as a public intellectual.

Cottle's recollections of these events are in agreement on several important points: the journal was a failure, and after the initial subscription successes, subscribers became disillusioned with what they took to be the journal's overly moderate tone. Cottle also recalls the concern of many of the author's friends as the project was launched: 'Of all men, Coleridge was the least qualified to display periodical industry',[35] a concern that Coleridge confirms with typical self-mockery in his account. However, their interpretation of key events is markedly different. Cottle emphasizes not the folly of the subscription tour, but its dramatic success. By his reckoning, Coleridge had three hundred and seventy subscribers before he left Bristol, not enough to support a journal with national ambitions, but a powerful local base nonetheless. He admits that: '[f]ew attended Mr C'.s lectures but those whose political views were similar to his own',[36] but, nonetheless, in Bristol he had an ideal base of supporters committed to opposition to Pitt's war. The tour, then, hoped to build support for a national effort that in many ways sought to extend the political and intellectual influence of Bristol, an ambition Cottle, not surprisingly, sought to publicly recover in his recollections. He recalls Coleridge's 'brilliant volubility',[37] and remarks on the inevitable success of the initial venture (even as he harboured doubts about its longevity). People enthusiastically subscribed: 'for who would not give fourpence every eighth day, to be furnished by such a competent man as Mr. Coleridge, with this quintessence, this concentration of all that was valuable, in Politics, Criticism, and Literature; enriched in addition, with Poetry of the first waters, luminous Essays, and other effusions of men of letters?'[38] Far from the bewildered outsider of the comic vignettes of *Biographia Literaria*, Coleridge emerges here as a potentially significant opposition voice.

Cottle was greatly aided in his account by his possession of the letters Coleridge wrote to Josiah Wade during the subscription tour. He introduces many of them into the record, as it were, to give a complex portrait of Coleridge on the road. An enthusiastic report from Birmingham presents Coleridge enhancing his reputation as both Unitarian preacher and political leader: 'Yesterday I preached twice, and, indeed, performed the whole service, morning and afternoon. There were about fourteen hundred persons present, and my sermons (great part extempore) were *preciously peppered with Politics*. I have here, at least, double the number of subscribers, I had expected'.[39] The nature of the politics is abundantly clear from his account of preaching in Nottingham. He decided against wearing his 'blue coat', fearful lest the local clergyman, the reverend Edwards, be accused, by the mixed audience of 'Unitarians, Arians, Trinitarians, &c.' of sticking 'a political lecturer in his pulpit'.[40] While shielding his host from direct association with his own Whiggish sympathies, Coleridge nonetheless concedes that his prudent fashion choice was necessitated by his 'sermon being of so political a tendency'.[41]

Neither were the politics of the tour without strategic sophistication. Writing to Wade on 7 January 1796, Coleridge described his stop in Sheffield and his decision to only send 'about thirty numbers', reasoning that any more might 'injure the sale of "The Iris"'. '[T]he editor of which Paper (a very amiable and ingenious young man, of the name of "James Montgomery")' was 'in prison, for a libel against a bloody-minded magistrate there'.[42] These vignettes are one of the great virtues of Cottle's book. The letter serves as a historical miniature: Coleridge briefly associating with James Montgomery in early 1796, and taking care not to damage another new publishing venture. Unlike the short-lived *Watchman*, *The Iris* became the leading radical reform journal in southern Yorkshire and remained so for the next third of a century. Montgomery, a poet and polymath, became the centre of Sheffield intellectual life, and through his association with the neighbouring Fitzwilliam Whigs, a leading voice for parliamentary reform in the region.

Clearly, this is a far cry from the otherworldly Stowey recluse 'equidistant' from all parties and factions Coleridge promoted in his account. Cottle states the case plainly in a footnote on Coleridge's political lectures: 'In all Mr. Coleridge's lectures, he was a steady opposer of Mr. Pitt, and the then existing war; and also an enthusiastic admirer of Fox, Sheridan, Grey, &c., &c.' In fact, following the abandonment of *The Watchman*, interest from the Bristol Unitarians in having so eloquent a spokesman enter the ministry was tempered by concerns about Coleridge's obvious partisanship. Cottle writes:

> The Unitarians in Bristol might have wished to see Mr. C. in their pulpit, expounding and enforcing their faith; but as they said, 'the thing, in Bristol, was altogether impracticable', from the conspicuous stand which he had taken in free politics, through the medium of his numerous lectures.[43]

Coleridge, in his account, challenged this public perception as a misapprehension of his actual views, and there is certainly an element of truth in his claims. For example, the perceived moderate political turn during the middle numbers of *The Watchman* accurately reflected Coleridge's pacifism and fear of social violence. His famous distinction concerning the pitfalls of political strategy: that reformers often made the mistake of 'pleading *to* the poor, instead of pleading *for* them'[44] revealed a consistent fear of demagoguery. Cottle noted the difference in strategy claiming one of the chief reasons the subscribers gradually fell away was the demand for 'More politics; and those a little sharper!'.[45] However, in the context of the passage in chapter ten concerning the Gagging Acts, Coleridge's distinction becomes a subtle distortion. Claiming that numbers two and three 'made enemies of all [his] Jacobin and Democratic patrons',[46] he created a rhetorical break with them. According to Coleridge, those patrons disapproved because:

> instead of abusing the Government and the aristocrats chiefly or entirely, I leveled my attacks at 'modern patriotism', and even ventured to declare my belief that whatever the motives of Ministers might have been for the sedition (or as it was then the fashion to call them, the *gagging*) bills, yet the bills themselves would produce an effect to be desired by true friends of freedom, as far as they should contribute to deter men from openly declaiming on subjects, the principles of which they had never bottomed.[47]

Coleridge's aversion to demagogues occurred in the midst of a crisis in the reform camp, as state oppression demanded a shift in tactics. The distortion in the passage is subtle. It appears to allow the inference that Coleridge supported Pitt's attacks on free speech. This is simply untrue. That Coleridge remained a convinced Democrat following the demise of *The Watchman*, becomes apparent in Cottle's descriptions of his subsequent auditions as a Unitarian minister.

Coleridge's Bristol friends arranged for him to preach in Bath, calculating that that was safer than in Bristol where his political views were notorious. Cottle accompanied him, and reminding his readers that 1796 'was a year of great scarcity, and consequent privation, amongst the poor', reported some anxiety that Coleridge chose as his text: 'When they shall be hungry, they shall fret themselves, and curse their king, and their God, and look upward! (Isaiah viii. 21.)'. Cottle's concern was legitimate as he makes clear: 'Mr. Winterbottom, a little before, had been thrown into prison for the freedom of his political remarks in a sermon at Plymouth, and we were half fearful whether in his impetuous current of feeling, some stray expressions might not subject our friend to a like visitation'—not the activity of a Ministerial apologist for the Gagging bills. In the end Cottle was relieved that Coleridge delivered a somewhat dull 'Lecture of the Corn Laws'.[48] The whole experience was disappointing; the congregation was meagre and several people left during the lecture. In the afternoon Coleridge delivered roughly the same text, leavened this time with a comic sidebar attacking the 'Hair Powder Tax'. The day convinced Cottle that, as a loyal friend, he could not 'entertain the wish to ever seeing [Coleridge] in the pulpit again'.[49]

For Coleridge's executors, especially Coleridge's son-in-law, the reactionary ultra-Tory Henry Nelson Coleridge, confessed Unitarian radicalism was at least as scandalous as opium addiction. Their contest with Cottle over which Coleridge would dominate in the public mind played out as part of a larger effort to determine the posthumous life of the author. Scandal and fear of scandal conditioned the family's early efforts to construct Coleridge's reputation and became a dominant influence on editorial decisions and the literary production of Coleridge's corpus. Lest they be accused of falsifying the historical record in creating the Tory sage of Highgate, their preferred Coleridge, they could assure themselves that they were following Coleridge's lead in *Biographia Literaria*. Their complex responses to the proliferation of Coleridges in the immediate aftermath of his death set the stage for ever more demanding constructions as they struggled with shifting historical circumstances. Out of this essentially defensive posture emerged the rigorous scholarly practices so characteristic of Coleridge studies. How this unlikely outcome occurred is the subject of the remainder of this study.

2
'Ungentlemanly Productions': De Quincey and Scandal

In summer and fall 1834, Thomas De Quincey began publishing a series of articles on Samuel Taylor Coleridge in *Tait's Edinburgh Magazine*. In the articles, De Quincey represented himself as the sole qualified reader of Coleridge's corpus and recounted his first meeting with the great man and their subsequent associations. He did not stop there, however, but went on to detail Coleridge's erratic personal history. He also asserted that Coleridge, his friend and mentor, had plagiarized the poetry of Frederica Brun, and, more importantly, the philosophy Schelling. The Coleridge family was shocked and dismayed. They responded by denigrating the notoriously erratic author of the article, and raged against the impropriety of what Sara Coleridge, STC's daughter, called De Quincey's 'ungentlemanly productions'. The family developed a complex strategy for limiting the potential damage of De Quincey's articles. The intellectual and personal stakes involved were equally complex. The family had a substantial financial stake in securing Coleridge's reputation as they set out to establish the value of his *Literary Remains*, and Henry Nelson Coleridge, in particular, was in the process of negotiating the value of his *Table Talk of Samuel Taylor Coleridge* with Murray. I shall return to the financial stakes when I discuss the family's dissatisfaction with Pickering in a subsequent chapter, but first I will outline the personal stakes involved, and then focus on the intellectual stakes brought into play by the accusation of plagiarism.

While the plagiarism charges strike modern readers as the most damaging, the family saw them as a small part of a larger view offered by De Quincey of Coleridge as an erratic genius who had abandoned his family—part of a pattern of personal irresponsibility. De Quincey's unflattering portrait of their family life, regardless of its factual basis, could not go unchallenged. Sara listed De Quincey's offences against propriety in a letter to her husband Henry Nelson Coleridge in September 1834. She denounced his mischaracterization of, among other things, the causes of her parents' 'estrangement': 'his [Coleridge's] want of domestic regularity', his 'being betrayed into opium', 'his eccentricity', '<u>her unintellectuality</u>', 'her want of tolerance', 'her jealousy of Miss Wordsworth', financial troubles, et cetera. Sara's anger became most evident in recounting the attack on her mother:

> He then launches out into a full tide of personality respecting my mother—he affects a great deal of candour & this & the superior style & tone of the paper will enable it to make an impression upon a class who are quite beyond the reach of more clumsy vulgar scandal. He exposes Lord Byron's malignant 'lie' in calling her & her sisters 'Milliners of Bath'—which he says implies worse than if he had described them as opera dancers.[1]

Rehearsing Byron's snub was one thing, but Sara clearly perceived the real risk lay in the dissemination of 'scandal' to 'a class' that had the influence to judge and subsequently damage Coleridge's posthumous reputation. The problem was De Quincey's very eloquence. His style made the slanders against her mother toxic; his capacity to delight with wit disguised what she took to be the vulgarity of his even broaching such a subject.

De Quincey's account of the marital difficulties fascinated because of its psychological plausibility. He appeared even-handed in his account, balancing the version of the 'forced' marriage (at Southey's insistence) he claimed to have heard directly from Coleridge, with an account from an unnamed 'neutral spectator' who claimed: 'that if ever in his life he had seen a man under deep fascination, and what he would have called desperately in love, Coleridge, in relation to Miss Fricker, was that man'.[2] The apparent generosity of the second version made matters worse, as it suggested that Coleridge dissembled about his true feelings, blaming Southey for his eventual unhappiness: '... his marriage was not his own deliberate act; but was in a manner forced upon his sense of honour, by the scrupulous Southey, who insisted he had gone too far in his attentions to Miss Fricker, for any honourable retreat'. The public spectacle of her mother taken on sufferance into the marriage was deeply upsetting for Sara, and for the family as a whole. De Quincey's account of the development of the marital problems during the intense production of *Lyrical Ballads* must have sown strife in the interconnected Southey, Wordsworth, and Coleridge households.

He summarized the circumstances that created the difficulties in the marriage, and offered an astute psychological account of their effects:

> A young lady [Dorothy Wordsworth] became a neighbour, and a daily companion of Coleridge's walks, whom I will not describe more particularly, than by saying that intellectually she was much superior to Mrs. Coleridge. That superiority alone, when made conspicuous by its effects of winning Coleridge's regard and society, could not but be deeply mortifying to a young wife.[3]

According to De Quincey the situation was made worse because it was innocent. Dorothy was 'much too kind-hearted to have designed any annoyance in this triumph, or to express any exultation'. How mortifying to feel bested by a rival who does not even recognize herself as such, and one who, according to De Quincey, 'had no personal charms'. Intellectual compatibility and profound interests in literature and scenery are innocent in and of themselves, but felt to the young wife at home with a baby (a detail De Quincey omits) like a source of estrangement, despite the absence of sexual charge. Coleridge emerged in this portrait as either insensitive or oblivious, if blameless. Not content with mere comment, De Quincey elaborated his account with anecdotes: Mrs Coleridge feeling usurped by Dorothy when she habitually arrived at Nether Stowey and took over the house (including borrowing her clothes if she'd been walking in the rain), the servants pitying her as 'an injured woman', or sneering 'at her as a very tame one'. The very detail of the portrait made it convincing, and ensured that Mrs Coleridge's public humiliation was complete. Whether De Quincey intended malice was the key question for Sara.

Sara felt frustrated that she had no means to correct the false impression of her mother. After all, the family could hardly respond. Such a move would create the open scandal they sought to avoid. Confined in this way, she could only address the subject personally, setting the record straight in her letter to Henry:

> My mother's unintellectuality was not the root of the mischief [in the marriage]—as far as it originated in her it was the want of sympathy produced by a mind not <u>unworthy</u> the partner of any man living as to its general power—she was not unintelligent like Lady Scott or Mrs De Quincey—but of a totally different essence from him—and a temper & disposition that had good points that extorted respect but did not conciliate—& weak ones which were peculiarly tried by the weaker points in his.[4]

This generous assessment of her parents' incompatibility offered a more balanced view, and made an unflattering comparison to Mrs De Quincey. Sara descended to De Quincey's level in repeating 'the epithet dough-faced' given her by a 'gentleman who knew her'. Her spite signalled extreme frustration, and a willingness to strike back at De Quincey tit for tat. He had started it, after all, with his prefatory comments about the marriage in which he admitted an animus:

> I, for my part, owe Mrs. Coleridge no particular civility: and I see no reason why I should mystify the account of Coleridge's life or habits, by dissembling what is notorious to so many thousands of people. An insult once offered by Mrs. Coleridge to a female relative of my own, as much superior to Mrs. Coleridge in the spirit of courtesy and kindness, which ought to preside in intercourse between females, as she was in the splendour of her beauty, would have given me a dispensation from all terms of consideration beyond the restraints of strict justice.[5]

For Sara, De Quincey's unwillingness to 'mystify' his account confirmed that he was not a gentleman, and the pettiness of his self-justification increased rather than mitigated his offence. It is difficult to know if his irony, decrying a lack of 'courtesy and kindness' in someone while pillorying them with an ad hominen attack, was intentional. Regardless, Sara could not have public justice without increasing the risk of scandal by re-airing the subject. Furthermore, she risked letting her emotion reduce her to De Quincey's level, as witnessed by her debased desire for revenge: 'some elegant anecdotes both of him & his Peggy might be furnished to that market [the vibrant magazine culture] by us were we as unscrupulous as himself'. The family had to hope that readers would consider the authorship, and read the essays as more evidence of De Quincey's public reputation as an erratic genius. Nonetheless, Sara had to admit that any family response had to negotiate a serious double bind: 'There are some things so well said by De Quincey that they ought to be quoted if his ungentlemanlyness in the article altogether did not render one averse to make allusion to it.'

Sara astutely observed that De Quincey's account of Coleridge's irregular behaviour held the potential of vindicating his own erratic career. Such behaviour signified genius in De Quincey's portrait, as it drew a direct comparison to the famous tableau in *Confessions of an English Opium-Eater* where he directs the reader to paint the scene of genius: his remote cottage, a decanter full of 'ruby-coloured laudanum' and 'a book of German Metaphysics placed by its side'.[6] This tableau could

equally stand for Coleridge (De Quincey demurred from including himself in the original scene, instead asserting that the objects attested to
his 'being in the neighbourhood'), a visible sign or even a synecdoche
for the author/genius. The Coleridge family needed to resist this reading but, as I say, found themselves in a difficult bind: De Quincey *was*
a genius, and by far the most brilliantly qualified contemporary commentator on Coleridge's corpus. In a subsequent letter to Henry, having
had a few days to reflect, Sara put the situation more generously:

> I bethink me that I have written too fiercely about the little Poppy-
> man in the first fuzz of my fury & though I would not even at first
> done him any harm I have done amiss in making such an elaborate
> picture of my wrathful emotions as rehearsing in fancy the retaliat-
> ing upon him. He is a man of genius & learning the finest metaphysi-
> cian, I should imagine, <u>now</u> living, & by nature & birth a thorough
> gentleman: indeed this he shews in his very transgression—there is
> an air of reluctance—a consciousness of something unworthy in the
> whole of his personal narrative. Indeed if he had a particle of coarse-
> ness in his composition the personality to which his moral weakness
> has forced him to have recourse would have burst forth in full glare—
> but he has performed an ungentlemanly thing in a gentlemanly
> manner—& had he merely said what he has published privately to a
> friend I might have thought him mistaken in some points but could
> not have taxed him with anything unhandsome.[7]

This symptomatic reading, De Quincey as a damaged child unable to
recognize the limits of propriety despite his 'genius', provided a way for
Sara to calm her original distress and anger and rescue the 'gentleman'
in De Quincey. In short order, she had come to realize that De Quincey
could not simply be attacked; they needed to find a way to recuperate
the scandal by ratifying De Quincey's ultimate estimation of Coleridge
as the greatest English genius of the previous half-century, while at
the same time limiting the damaging taint of personal weakness.
De Quincey's authority as 'the finest metaphysician' 'now living' could
potentially provide part of the foundation of Coleridge's posthumous
philosophical reputation. Displacing the scandal onto De Quincey by
focusing on the impropriety of parts of the essay ('an ungentlemanly
thing' marring an otherwise 'gentlemanly manner') instead of its content might allow them to recuperate an otherwise splendid estimation.
This seemed the obvious strategy. The scandalous aspects of the articles
could be characterized as more instances of De Quincey's manic need

to confess. However, the strategy bore risks. The family abhorred the accusation of plagiarism, for example, but approved De Quincey's contextualization of it as a minor quirk in a career of staggering genius. De Quincey insisted that his was a friendly intervention by an admirer, and necessary lest an unsympathetic reader discover the 'borrowings'. His strategy of placing the plagiarism in its proper context within Coleridge's work and career, quite frankly, made more sense than the course ultimately followed by the family under Henry's leadership. How they might disentangle the erratic, self-destructive De Quincey of their proposed caricature from the brilliant philosophical authority legitimizing Coleridge's intellectual career came to dominate their editorial decisions over the next few years, and I will discuss that process in detail below. At the beginning, the question that proved most troublesome was how to challenge the portrait of Coleridge's reliance on opium.

The problem of controlling which biographical details were published was not confined to De Quincey. In May 1836 the Coleridge family became concerned about the contents of Joseph Cottle's proposed volume of reminiscences of STC. Cottle intended to publish a letter written by Coleridge warning of the dangers of opium, a cautionary tale based on sad experience. According to Cottle, Coleridge gave him the letter, which he had originally sent to Josiah Wade, specifically for posthumous publication, and Cottle considered it his moral duty to honour the request. Thomas Poole who had journeyed from Nether Stowey to Bristol to read Cottle's manuscript had alerted the family to the letter's existence. Under the direction of Henry Nelson Coleridge, James Gillman wrote to Cottle to intercede. Threatening legal action on the basis that the letter was the property of the family, the tone and substance of the letter were astonishingly ill considered—ensuring not only its subsequent inclusion in the volume, but an angry harangue in the book's Introduction. The family's dealings with Cottle are instructive as they established a pattern of selectively suppressing facts, denial, and dissembling as they constructed the version of Coleridge they thought most palatable to the general public. Their antagonists in this process were not necessarily malicious, although there was some malice in De Quincey's account of Mrs Coleridge. Both Cottle and De Quincey felt that the way to secure Coleridge's reputation was to show the life as a complex interplay of genius and weakness, a strategy Henry, Gillman, and Green misrecognized as aggression. Had they been more astute they would have developed a realistic biographical context for the *Literary Remains* from the outset, rather than managing a succession of perceived crises as they inevitably lost control of the posthumous portrait.

As De Quincey had said, the details of Coleridge's life were 'notorious to so many thousands of people'[8] that such dissembling was futile.

The exchange of letters between Cottle and Gillman and Poole, who served as an unhappy intermediary, clearly demonstrate the pattern. The issue for Cottle was friendship, and what it meant to be Coleridge's friend, a subject he divided historically between the early friends in Bristol and Nether Stowey (himself, Josiah Wade, Poole) and 'those <u>New Family Friends</u>'[9] of the Gillman circle under the leadership of Henry Nelson Coleridge. Poole was in the unenviable position of mediating between these two groups. Alerted to the existence of the opium letter, the family first sent news of their concern to Cottle via Poole. Cottle did not set out to offend the family and was willing to a point to be sensitive to their feelings: 'determining, <u>as far as possible</u>, to make every sacrifice to the feelings of the Coleridge Family, not incompatible with <u>Truth</u>'.[10] The 'Truth' however could not be sacrificed, and his decision became simple with the arrival of the letter from Gillman. The hectoring tone and threat of legal action in the letter, its '<u>rude</u> and <u>ungentlemanly</u>'[11] nature, freed Cottle from any obligation to the family's feelings. Cottle found the idea of whitewashing Coleridge's life appalling—intellectually dishonest and misguided. Deliberate omissions created problems. How could readers make sense of Coleridge's career between 1802 and his final settling with the Gillmans if they were prevented from understanding the erratic nature of his life in those years? The question of publishing the opium letter rested on what Cottle believed to be a moral imperative and his duty as a friend. He believed he was fulfilling Coleridge's intention. His argument ran that only a full understanding of Coleridge's character would allow readers to make judgements about his work, and he upbraided Poole for losing sight of that principle:

> You seem to have entered heart and hand into the views of his more recent friends, and are labouring, in conjunction with them, to suppress Truth, & promote literary Falsehood; to <u>cheat</u> the <u>Public</u> with a <u>Life</u> of Coleridge, which is <u>no Life</u>. I will become accessory to no such temporizing conduct. Without concealing Coleridge's faults, I have done him <u>ample justice</u>, & have set an example of what Biography <u>ought to be</u>—a faithful exhibition of the Man, not stream of <u>undeviating Eulogy</u>: I regard <u>Traits of Character</u>, as of more consequence than even <u>Facts</u> themselves.

In disguising or concealing faults in the name of protecting 'reputation', the family risked losing Coleridge's 'character', and a true account of the mind that produced the work. On the vexed subject of Coleridge's letter warning against the evils of opium, he was unequivocal:

> And now I must speak one word about that Letter, which you wish me to suppress, in which S.T.C. makes a full confession of all the sins he had committed in drenching himself with Opium, and requires that 'after his death,' it might be made public 'as a warning to others.' This is the most <u>redeeming</u> Letter he ever wrote, and I should have thought that no friend to Coleridge's reputation would desire the withdrawment of a letter which so propitiates the Reader, and converts <u>condemnation</u> into <u>compassion</u>.
>
> Your argument against <u>publicity</u> as to his passion for Opium is also not <u>sound</u>: for fear, it seems, it should urge others to the same practice, from the perverse passion for <u>imitation</u>. On this principle, no Highwayman, no Forger, no Sheep or Horse-stealer should be punished, lest, thro' its notoriety, others should be stimulated to taste the sweet luxury of getting <u>hanged</u>!

Cottle's argument that disclosure would convert 'condemnation' to 'compassion' made abundant sense as a strategy, given that knowledge of Coleridge's addiction had circulated freely for over twenty years. His attack on the family's tortured logic (Coleridge's status as a moral leader would tempt others into immoral acts) indicated the fragility of the biographical fiction they sought to produce. For Cottle, it was 'the most redeeming Letter he ever wrote' precisely because in it he acknowledged and took responsibility for his own actions while warning others not to be seduced into following them. Placed directly into the public record, the letter had the potential to defuse the toxic rumours that swirled around Coleridge and opium, and, in Cottle's view, recuperate Coleridge's weakness via a positive assertion of character. Compared to the family's strategy, denial and active dissembling, this, in retrospect, seems a profound and subtle strategy in the posthumous construction of Coleridge's reputation. That they chose the opposite course, including their clumsy attempt to intimidate Cottle, was understandably met with contempt. Witness Gillman's attempt at indignation. Describing his surprise at the decision to go ahead and publish, he expressed shock that Cottle: 'was about to make a breach of private confidence, reposed in him in full faith by a friend revealing to him his sufferings, unconscious at that time of their real cause, but attributing them to the use of <u>Opium</u> which he <u>abhorred</u>'.[12] The mischaracterization of Coleridge's instruction to Cottle as a 'breach of private confidence' was galling

enough (assuming, as it does, bad faith), but the assertion that the letter should be suppressed because Coleridge had been mistaken about
the 'real cause' of 'his sufferings' was absurd, especially coming from
Gillman, Coleridge's physician who had spent many years administer-
ing his intake of laudanum. Cottle responded to Poole (now hopelessly
in the middle of the affair) with scorn: 'Mr Gillman, I see, affirms that
Mr Coleridge "abhorred" Opium! and that his bodily & mental sufferings did not originate in <u>this cause</u>! He might as well affirm that the
Sun's rays are <u>dark</u>'.[13] Cottle mocked the threat of legal action for, what
Gillman called, a 'betrayal of a confidence reposed in you by a departed
friend', recognizing a legal bluff: 'that property in Letters is <u>not</u> the property of the possessor, but where there is a Will, that of the Executor'.[14] No
action was taken. In a final postscript to Poole, Cottle put his position
concisely: 'Coleridge's Character, will only suffer from <u>concealment</u>, &
<u>false statements</u>, and will rise in proportion as <u>Truth is repeated</u>'.[15]

It is difficult not to side with Cottle in this affair. While his reminiscences were intended to set the historical record straight, as argued
in chapter 2 above, there was no personal animus, no score settling,
involved. The disagreement stemmed from a misunderstanding. Poole
believed that he had convinced Cottle not to publish, and the family
had hoped that he would give them his materials. Cottle had misread
Poole and taken his correspondence as encouragement.[16] The result
was the overreaction and empty threats of the executors, and their
general decision to try to limit the damage to Coleridge's reputation
through denial and dissembling. They would have done well to heed
Cottle's advice to be frank and complete in relating the details of the
author's life. The De Quincey affair, and subsequent scandals, especially
J. F. Ferrier's plagiarism charge in *Blackwood's Edinburgh Magazine* in
1840,[17] would have been easier to address had the executors been forthright from the beginning. However, history has sided with the family.
Their evident distress gained the sympathy of the reading public, and
contemporary reviewers accused Cottle of bad manners, even treachery.
Partly, this is attributable to that earlier understanding of the meaning
and purpose of literary biography. We now have greater tolerance of
an author's weaknesses. Writing in the *PMLA* in 1934, Warren E. Gibbs
summarized the history of the hostile critical response to Cottle's biographical sketches: '[b]iographies were still expected to be dignified,
moralistic, or instructive. To expose weaknesses of character would
naturally detract from the virtues of the subject; faults should lie bur-
ied with the dead.'[18] That Gibbs admits this consensus in 1934, almost
one hundred years after publication, demonstrates the success of the

Coleridge family in shaping contemporary opinion, and the subsequent influence of their defensive posture in constructing notions of respectability and reputation. This defensiveness has been the inheritance of subsequent editors, bequeathed from Henry to Sara to Ernest Hartley Coleridge to Kathleen Coburn. Whether it has enhanced or harmed Coleridge's historical reputation is one of the questions posed by the present volume. How much, for example, was Norman Fruman's relentless moralizing in *Coleridge, the Damaged Archangel* conditioned by a sense of grievance at discovering what he took to be a conspiracy at the heart of Coleridge scholarship originating in these early strategies of the family?[19]

De Quincey posed the opposite problem to Cottle. While Cottle felt it his moral duty to warn others against the use of opium, De Quincey sought to establish Coleridge's addiction as a shared experience conditioning both their geniuses. Sara quickly realized that De Quincey hoped to use the essays to vindicate his own opium addiction. Her initial response had been to dismiss the whole thing as simply self-serving: 'the Opium Eater's paper is all about himself & only an allusion to S.T.C. in a note'.[20] The essays gave her cause to lament the utter waste of De Quincey's prodigious talent. He had been her neighbour, and she retained affection for him and respect for his intellect. His offence was thus two-fold: 'De Quincey's article makes me despise him for his weakness in betraying his own passions & his [eagerness?] in getting his bread by scandal. It is finely written of course, his intellect is all there though put to base work, & consequently drawn with the expansiveness & luster that it might be'.[21] He degraded himself as a means to earn his living; and drawing Coleridge into the realm of scandal with him could only increase his notoriety in her eyes. Sara put it succinctly in a letter to Henry: 'How sunk must poor De Quincey's personal dignity and conscientiousness now be—since he can make his opium eating a mountebank habit to catch the eye of the public!'[22] Her sympathy and condescension would have been sufficient response had De Quincey not drawn Coleridge into his debased self-portrait. Nevertheless, she still managed to read the scandalous production as brought about by the economic necessity caused by addiction: 'De Quincey would never have penned for publication had he not been an opium-eater & a shameless one too—making a profit of the very shame which has reduced him to need such beggarly profits. But pity swallows up my scorn & indignation—though the pity & the indignation are both enhanced by appreciation of a fine mind thus degraded'.[23] The fact that the essays appeared in *Tait's Edinburgh Magazine* and not *Blackwood's* supports Sara's hypothesis. *Tait's* Whig politics were not in accord with

De Quincey's abstract Toryism, and he wrote for them periodically, whenever he fell out with John Wilson or William Blackwood,[24] and *Blackwood's* temporarily cut him loose. This practice highly amused Tait who referred to De Quincey as 'our Tory'. Sara's diagnosis of self-loathing provided a compelling reading of the essays, and allowed her to develop a subtle, nuanced account of De Quincey's psychological motives for simultaneously praising and damning his friend and mentor. The only way his own damnation could be ameliorated was by populating his hell with fellow geniuses. Sensual self-destructiveness thus became a sign of genius. The need to praise contained a competing need to tear down; the genius that so inspired simultaneously humiliated. De Quincey could construct his own genius by denigrating Coleridge, but only by first establishing Coleridge as the ultimate standard. Sara shrewdly described this element in the essays:

> [De Quincey wrote from] long suppressed jealousy & eagerness to prove how much he shares my father's subtlety though he does not equal him in creative & oracular power (he was always fretful that he could not get in a word during my father's dissertations) & how little my father was above him in moral energy strict uprightness—& lastly from utter recklessness respecting personal dignity—for had a parti-cle of feeling on that subject remained unwithered in his heart—he of all men would have been the last to venture on the personal affairs of another knowing how little his own will brook investigation.[25]

De Quincey's deliberate shamelessness threatened Coleridge's reputa-tion at the very moment the family was attempting to secure it through publication of the *Literary Remains*, and there was another potential association that they equally feared.

In discussing De Quincey's debased genius, they naturally enough made comparison to Sara's brother Hartley, the brilliant eldest son, similarly betrayed by personal weakness. An offhand comment by Sara to Henry is telling: '<u>He</u> [De Quincey] will indeed leave no work worthy of his powers. Even Hartley has thrown together some of his opinions in a more creditable form, & treated more worthy subjects than De Quincey has hitherto done'.[26] The phrase, 'even Hartley', says it all. Just as De Quincey suffered from comparison to Coleridge, so too did Hartley. Furthermore, like his famous father, and his potential rival, he was an opium addict. Any scandal concerned with dissipation clearly had the potential to engulf Hartley. The comparisons were obvious; Sara reported to Henry that Robert Lovell had expressed horror at the

De Quincey articles, and had then announced, unprovoked, that: 'he thought Hartley "eloquent in my father's style but wanting my father's learning"'.[27] The ease of Lovell's association gave cause for concern. Hartley, poet and essayist, represented De Quincey's natural rival, both as authoritative commentator on Coleridge's works, and in the self-destructive Oedipal economy Sara described. The naturalness of the rivalry made Hartley the clear family choice for a published response, even though Henry was the literary executor, and they started to discuss where they might place a biographical essay to set the record straight by challenging De Quincey's more provocative claims. For example, Sara felt strongly that the misrepresentation of her father's opium use needed to be challenged: '[De Quincey] has the unprincipled presumption to say that my father first took opium not for relief but for luxury—this he chuses to say and tries to believe from consciousness of his own weak self indulgence'.[28] However, the idea of Hartley penning the family riposte soon collapsed as new circumstances overtook them.

Hartley had never completely recovered from being dismissed from his Fellowship at Oriel College Oxford in 1820, which had precipitated a personal crisis that made him unfit in the eyes of the family for the task of defending his father's reputation. Not only was he psychologically in no fit state, the association of Hartley and his father bore enormous risks, and any suggestion that he could challenge De Quincey on the grounds of the latter's moral laxity became risible. Furthermore, the grounds for his dismissal made public disclosure dangerous not only for Hartley, but for the whole family enterprise. Dissipation and fraternizing with the students played roles in the dismissal, but the Wordsworth circle believed the more decisive factors were Hartley's decidedly Whiggish political views. The last thing the family wanted, especially the ultra-Tory Henry, was an opportunity for the press to rehearse Coleridge's radical politics, thus broadening the terms of the scandal beyond the personal. This was not the time for yet another round of 'Once a Jacobin Always a Jacobin'. The extended Coleridge circle were in general agreement in managing Hartley's disgrace, though Sara bitterly dissented in their too easy acceptance of its rightness:

As to the affair of his expulsion—Mr W.[ordsworth] as reported by Miss H.[utchinson] says that it was his opinions & habits previously formed which caused that event & that it was better for him on the whole not to have had his election confirmed. I know perfectly well that H.[artley] had begun to drink when he was expelled, but I believe it probable that he never would have taken to his strange habits of wandering if it had not been for the shock of that blow. I can't understand how it can be better that he should have lost the income when he might have enjoyed it at a distance. That his opinions in one sense were partly the cause of his expulsion I have no doubt nor ever had, & what strong feelings are excited by opinions on religion & politics in some of his expellers—I have had <u>other</u> opportunities of observing ... [29]

This unflattering portrait of Wordsworth more concerned with protecting his social position and Tory reputation than with Hartley's well being shows how fear of scandal and/or controversy could have a chilling effect on public discourse. Henry sympathized with Sara's sense of grievance that Hartley's dismissal was still the subject of tittle-tattle in the Wordsworth cirlce after fifteen years, but nonetheless supported the consensus: 'I take the same view of Hartley that you & Derwent seem to do, & I regret the harshness of Miss H.'s [Sara Hutchinson's] tone. She is terribly opinionated, & rather what your dear father called, goody. But it is better to take no direct notice of this; for after all, the Wordsworth's are the only persons upon whom we can rely for any superintendence of H[artley]'.[30] Hard enough to lose the Fellowship, Hartley found himself dependent on the Wordsworth/Southey circle as a result. Hartley's scandal eroded his authority; he could not attack De Quincey's public reputation without inviting scrutiny of his own. Furthermore, he was in no psychological state to undertake such an important task.[31]

Despite his descent into depression, Hartley remained the family's most eloquent, and intellectually best equipped, spokesperson. They still planned to have him write a biographical Introduction for a forthcoming volume of the *Literary Remains*, but there was disagreement on which volume. Hartley wanted to write an Introduction for the *Poetic Works* where he could dispute the charge that Coleridge was a 'metaphysical Poet' whose philosophy marred his poetry. This commonplace view (it still has adherents) needed to be challenged to secure Coleridge's rightful place as a poet:

I shall examine how far S.T.C. the Poet was influenced by S.T.C. the Philosopher and clear him from the imputation of being a metaphysical Poet. Undoubtedly in some of his early poems he did versify metaphysics, but then he ceased to be a Poet at all ... [32]

Hartley agonized over his failure to produce this essay for the rest of his life, and it became another sign of his weakness and failure. Henry believed that they needed to use Hartley's Introduction to challenge the most potentially damaging part of the scandal, the plagiarism charge. He planned a new edition of *Biographia Literaria* where the Schelling charges could be challenged directly, and he planned to rely on Hartley as the only member of the circle with enough philosophical background to perform the task. In the meantime, he arranged to have Archdeacon Julius Hare, a Coleridge friend and accomplished Germanist, place a comprehensive rebuttal of the charges in the 5 January 1835 issue of the *British Magazine*. Henry then simply imported Hare's arguments verbatim into his Introduction to the second edition of *Table Talk* then going to press. Hare's reputation was beyond reproach, and the stark contrast it made with De Quincey's notoriety formed part of Henry's rhetorical strategy. Furthermore, Hare could argue by simple contradiction, as there were few if any qualified readers of Schelling to adjudicate the matter.

Hare's rebuttal has numerous problems, but nonetheless served the purpose at the time. He began with the familiar attack on character, determining that De Quincey, whatever the facts of the case, was not a gentleman for broaching them; he declared: 'it indicates a singular obliquity of feeling, thus to drag them [the offences imputed to Coleridge] forth and thrust them forward'.[33] By entertaining the idea that the charges were genuine, Hare claimed rhetorical neutrality in the case while heaping further opprobrium on De Quincey for asserting that he was 'foremost of Coleridge's admirers'[34] while bringing the matter to light. Hare assumed bad faith, and argued that by bringing forward numerous trivial instances of similarities and minor borrowings 'lest any tittle that could tell against Coleridge should be forgotten', De Quincey betrayed an animus despite professing his admiration. Hare's astute reading made plausible psychological sense, but ran a great risk. By removing the trivial from consideration he focused on the substantial and most damaging charge, Coleridge's unattributed verbatim translation of Schelling in chapter twelve of *Biographia Literaria*. He began with a personal attack (inadvertently undermining his rhetorical position of neutral arbiter), deriding De Quincey for misidentifying the source in Schelling, and presenting this as evidence of 'an additional mark of audacious carelessness in impeaching a great man's honour'.[35] The charge of intellectual sloppiness would have held more weight had Hare not then proceeded to concede the central charge, thus rendering De Quincey's 'slip' a trivial point.[36] The ponderous syntax of his only direct defence from the plagiarism charge may have been an effort to hide the weakness of his position:

> [Chapter twelve] is a literal translation from the introduction to Schelling's system of *Transcendental Idealism*; and though the assertion that there is no attempt in a single instance to appropriate the paper, by developing the arguments, or by diversifying the illustrations, is not quite borne out by the fact, Coleridge's additions are few and slight.[37]

So De Quincey was technically mistaken, but the mistake was irrelevant to the case—hardly a ringing endorsement, or a devastating critique. Not surprisingly, this admission gave way to efforts to muddy the waters by arguing around the actual charge while admitting the truth. Coleridge plagiarized Schelling in assembling chapter twelve, and Hare knew it. The rest of his essay ignored the charge through the ingenious shift of topic to the specific details of the circumstances of De Quincey's charge, rather than its substance.

In attempting to explain the case, De Quincey was at pains to show that despite the prima facie evidence, some mitigation was allowable because of Coleridge's prefatory comments on the coincidence of his thought and Schelling's philosophical works.[38] Hare attacked the argument as inaccurate:

> Not a single word does Coleridge say about the originality of his essay one way or the other. It is not prefaced by any remark. No mention is made of Schelling within a hundred pages of it ... In an earlier part of the work,[39] however, where Coleridge is giving an account of his philosophical education, there occurs a passage about his obligations to Schelling, and his coincidences with him. This, no doubt, is the passage which the Opium-eater had in his head.

The 'error' became another instance of De Quincey's 'carelessness', but amounts to quibbling about the precise meaning of 'prefaced'. Hare then cited the passage from *Biographia* where Coleridge effusively praised Schelling, explained the coincidence of their thought, and generously advised the reader to consider any subsequent discovered similarities to be the work of the German:

> For readers in general, let whatever shall be found in this or any future work of mine, that resembles or coincides with the doctrines of

my German predecessor, though contemporary, be wholly attributed to him; provided that the absence of direct references to his books, which I could not always make with truth, as designating citations or thoughts actually derived from him, and which I trust, would, after this general acknowledgement, be superfluous, be not charged on me as an ungenerous concealment or intentional plagiarism.[40]

This passage famously wants it both ways—any discovered similarity with Schelling's thought should be assumed to be Schelling's property, even though it was not, in truth, because the similarity was purely coincidental. The note would make a fascinating preface to a specific passage of Coleridge's thought coincident with ideas present in Schelling, but Hare's opening rhetorical gambit (attacking De Quincey's accuracy) made that reading impossible by severing the note from the offending section in chapter twelve. He emphasized its distance of more than one hundred pages. Neither was the passage in question an instance of 'resemblance' or 'coincidence'; it was a 'verbatim translation'.[41] Hare simply ignored the meaning of 'verbatim', and either did not know the Schelling well enough to recognize the exactness of the borrowings or was actively dissembling. His subsequent defence of Coleridge's eccentric scholarly practices, unfortunately, points towards deliberate dishonesty. De Quincey's determination to make the status of the passage known was based on the fact that it was no coincidental 'resemblance'; chapter twelve could only have been composed with the Schelling texts present to translate. Letting Coleridge off the hook on the basis of his earlier note would have been intellectually dishonest.[42] Rather than follow De Quincey's lead by placing the plagiarism in broader philosophical and personal contexts, the family executors chose to deny the charge via Hare's intervention. This compounded the problem when the inevitable occurred and Ferrier published his detailed attack in *Blackwood's* in 1840. Their only defence was ridiculed in the most important philosophical publication of the day. The only way to address the plagiarism was to take De Quincey to heart and evaluate the material in light of a detailed understanding of Schelling, not to mention Fichte and Kant. This task eventually fell to Sara when she answered Ferrier in the Introduction to her edition of *Biographia Literaria*.[43]

Hare's essay eventually stated the obvious, if in an extremely contradictory form:

But, even with the fullest conviction that Coleridge cannot have been guilty of intentional plagiarism, the reader will, probably, deem it strange that he should have transferred half a dozen pages of Schelling into his volume without any reference to their source.[44]

Indeed. With all evidence supporting De Quincey, Hare turned to what has subsequently become the most popular excuse offered for the plagiarism, Coleridge's habit of keeping detailed notebooks as a means of synthesizing ideas. Coupled with Coleridge's 'notoriously irretentive' memory[45] this practice must have been the cause of the lack of attribution, especially as Coleridge had announced his willingness to give all credit to Schelling earlier in the work. Many critics have repeated this hypothesis since, despite its essential implausibility—how could Coleridge's 'irretentive' memory produce verbatim translations of Schelling's philosophy without having the texts before him? In the absence of Coleridge notebooks containing detailed unattributed translations from throughout Schelling's works, this defence cannot be taken seriously. The undeniable fact that it has been[46] points to the power of the defensive posture the family initiated. Its very success provided the originating act of what Fruman conceived of as a long Coleridge conspiracy.

The family, and Coleridge scholars, would have been much better served had they taken De Quincey's hypotheses seriously, that Coleridge's plagiarisms were a 'literary curiosity'[47] that could be explored in light of the enormous philosophical achievements that ultimately subsumed them. Only Sara had begun to come round to this view as she softened towards De Quincey, but unfortunately Henry carried the day. De Quincey's eccentricities were partly responsible for their decision to attack him. His evident dislike of Mrs Coleridge, and transparent efforts (to Sara at least) to use the occasion of discussing Coleridge to construct a public monument to his own genius could only cause suspicion. For example, Hare's attack on the incorrect identification of the Schelling volume was responding to an intentionally vague footnote: 'I forget the exact title, not having seen the book since 1828, and then only for one day ...'.[48] De Quincey feigned forgetfulness to show that not only was he the only qualified reader of Coleridge (no one else could have detected the plagiarism) and that the knowledge that made him so had been acquired in a mood of confident nonchalance. Lassitude seemed necessary to genius; correct footnotes were the province of small minds. Hare walked directly into this trap, spending much of his essay on the trivial failings he perceived in De Quincey's account, and moralizing about bad character. In the end, Hare presented himself as someone who had read Schelling, but not understood what he had read sufficiently to judge Coleridge's use of the material. Despite his final

pronouncement that, 'I readily acquit him of all suspicion of ungenerous concealment or intentional plagiarism',[49] this was not an inference
that could be made from the essay. The point had been made that
De Quincey was not a 'gentleman' for broaching the subject, but the only
possible inference on the matter of Schelling was that Coleridge had
plagiarized. That being undeniably the case, De Quincey had sought
to understand the case as part of a larger pattern in Coleridge's life and
work. The various minor cases of borrowings that Hare dismissed as
'tittle' were intended to establish a habitual pattern first made known
to De Quincey by Thomas Poole, Coleridge's oldest and dearest friend.
Placing it in the broader context of this 'literary curiosity' could mitigate
the serious matter of the Schelling plagiarism. A psychological account
of the origins precluded moral condemnation; Henry foolishly introduced moral stakes through his use of Hare's essay. His almost morbid
fear of scandal blinded him to the extravagant grandeur of De Quincey's
ultimate claim:

> Had then Coleridge any need to borrow from Schelling? Did he bor-
> row *in forma pauperis*? Not at all:—there lay the wonder. He spun daily
> and at all hours, for mere amusement of his own activities, and from
> the loom of his own magical brain, theories more gorgeous by far,
> and supported by a pomp and luxury of images, such as Schelling—
> no, nor any German that ever breathed … could have emulated in
> his dreams. With the riches of El Dorado lying about him, he would
> condescend to filch a handful of gold from any man whose purse he
> fancied … [50]

Coleridge's plagiarism became part of his casual mastery of Western metaphysics, a mark of his true genius. The aesthetic richness of the scene,
the 'gorgeous' products of a 'magical brain' supported by the 'pomp
and luxury' of supporting images, presented a stark contrast to the
chilly moralizing of Hare. De Quincey found the idea that plagiarism,
or opium addiction, denoted moral failure repulsive. The lassitude that
led to the practice of borrowing, and the use of opium that produced the
lassitude, were signs of Coleridge's genius, just as De Quincey's nonchalance about the precise source in Schelling was a sign of his own.

   For Henry, the other side of scandal was 'respectability', and he
set himself up as the final arbiter of social and intellectual propriety.
De Quincey was not a gentleman—period. Hartley's Whiggish opinions had also to be suppressed, as did Coleridge's, lest they occasion
a discussion of the great man's radical Unitarian past. The creation

of Coleridge's 'reputation' took on an unmistakable moral tone (from De Quincey's perspective completely presumptuous, even laughable), and 'propriety' became a posthumous editorial goal, despite its historically limited and localized meaning. The narrowness of Henry's Tory politics made him over-sensitive to the possibility of public scorn, and his social anxieties conditioned his goals in constructing Coleridge's posthumous 'reputation'. He set out to create the great Tory sage, a public figure beyond reproach, a project put at risk by De Quincey's psychological frankness. The immediate effect of these goals appeared in his *Table Talk* where he subtly distorted his original notebook entries to make some of Coleridge's views more palatable to what he conceived of as public 'propriety'—in fact the empty moralizing of a nervous, reactionary, and cosseted segment of the ruling class.

The question we must ask is whether the response to 'scandal' caused a distorted view of Coleridge's thought, and how pervasive that 'respectable' version became in guiding the family enterprise of editing the *Literary Remains*. Whether or not he intended it, Henry Nelson Coleridge's construction of 'respectability' constituted a narrow ideological field. Through a process Žižek would call 'ideological quilting',[51] Henry began to organize a complex and vast philosophical corpus into a coherent figure we call 'Coleridge', and his edition of *Table Talk* was the first opportunity to begin this process.[52]

3
'Henry's Book'

In October 1835 Derwent Coleridge wrote to his brother Hartley in the role of family peacemaker. Hartley had bruised the feelings of their sister Sara in his, perhaps too vigorous, attack on the veracity of her husband, Henry Nelson Coleridge's edition of 'specimens' of their father's *Table Talk*. Derwent struck a conciliatory tone, both admitting the merit of Hartley's view that: 'It [the volume] is, and could not but have been, fragmentary in respect to the conversation extracted—yet a succession of little wholes in respect of itself',[1] and defending the work on the grounds that it was clearly impossible to capture Coleridge's conversational brilliance. In this argument, the 'little wholes' that Henry produced had their source in Coleridge's talk, but inevitably failed in their task of accurate representation. The very nature of Coleridge's speech made it inimitable; Derwent described it thus: 'the heard gust of a corn-blowing wind, that came from I know not whence, and went you knew not whither—a stream, with an eddying surface, yet with an unchecked progression: the very substances broken and suggestive, rather than expressive and declarative'. To his mind Henry could hardly be blamed for failing to capture the 'unchecked progression', and he anticipated Hartley's likely objection to this defence: 'That such talk could be exhibited on paper, only in certain <u>artificial preparations</u>—more or less <u>qualified</u> by the virtue of the original, is self-evident,—and Henry's book must be read with this postulated allowance—you will say, why then do that at all, which could only be done so imperfectly?' This is an excellent question, even if rhetorically self-posed, and Derwent's response, in the form of another rhetorical question, speaks to the notion of posterity: 'are so many printed truths, so much just criticism, so much practical wisdom, to be wholly lost, because they came to us thro' an inferior medium?' In sum, Derwent's defence of *Table Talk* admits that it is an 'inferior medium', but presupposes that it is 'more or less <u>quali-fied</u> by the virtue of the original'. That the work is an accurate portrayal of Coleridge's views is assumed as 'self-evident', with only the slightest equivocation in the phrase, 'more or less'. In this assumption Derwent was deliberately refusing to engage Hartley's more serious charge that it wasn't the formal fragmentation that he objected to so much as the fragmentary and partisan account of Coleridge's thought created through the mediating consciousness of the volume's high Tory editor/author. I use this hybrid designation because, despite the subsequent reception of *Table Talk* including its inclusion in *The Collected Coleridge*, at the moment of its publication the two brothers were in agreement on the central point that the work was not their father's; they limited their debate to a discussion of the merits of what Derwent unambiguously referred to as 'Henry's book'.

Derwent closed the letter by reminding Hartley of Henry's sincere affection, upbraiding him for sending him anything 'which gives him pain', and risking family equilibrium. The siblings worked hard at maintaining a spirit of cordiality over the coming months, but nonetheless a fierce debate about the book raged just under the surface. Duly chastened, Hartley wrote to Henry early in the new year to apologize for any offence he might have given:

> what makes you think that I dislike your 'Table Talk?' I might have fears lest it should be Mali exempli—fears which Alsop has shewn not to be wholly groundless. I might tell Derwent that the book gave me no feeling of my father's manner which it does not pretend to, but the execution of the work I greatly admire, and Derwent well observes that it were sad indeed if so much excellent criticism, so much moral, religious, and political wisdom were to perish with the lips that uttered it.[2]

While acknowledging the merits of the work and repeating Derwent's justification for it, Hartley nonetheless maintained that vigilance was necessary lest inaccurate portraits of Coleridge proliferate. Alsop's reminiscence was one of a number of unauthorized works that threatened the family's control of Coleridge's posthumous reputation.[3] They were engaged in a contest to establish which Coleridge became dominant in the public mind, and Hartley tellingly saw Henry's book in this context, not as a recovered work. He was generous in stating that the book didn't 'pretend' to represent Coleridge's 'manner' given its disingenuous full title, *Specimens of the Table Talk of Samuel Taylor Coleridge*, something it decidedly was not. So in apologizing and setting the record straight about his admiration of the work, Hartley nonetheless asserted that the work was a partial list of Coleridge's ideas justified by the general principle that all such ideas should be preserved. The issue of their partiality would reappear as the focus of subsequent correspondence, but at this juncture family peace remained the focus. Again, it is clear that among the family members *Table Talk* was considered to be Henry's book, a biographical sketch, not a work by STC. This view is indisputable given the publication history; Murray published it, while Pickering held the rights to Coleridge's works. Henry's choice of Murray shows that the confusion over authorship was not entirely his doing, nor entirely deliberate. He may have hoped that the book be received as the work of STC, but recognized that he himself was the author. His motives are difficult to untangle and may not have been entirely clear to him. He sincerely believed that his conversations with the great man should be preserved for posterity (a proposition that Hartley conceded). He also had a simple economic motive; the contract with Murray was more generous than it would have been for a collection of reminiscences. The work was organized to claim authoritative status based on the shared authorship of conversation, yet everyone knew that Coleridge did not converse, but rather discoursed. The aphoristic style of the work paradoxically lent it authority as recovered nuggets of wisdom—paradoxically because there was wide agreement that that feature was what made it so clearly not 'specimens' of Coleridge's 'talk'. The final motive, and the most difficult to weigh, was his desire to use STC to lend authority to his own reactionary Tory politics. How much that motive influenced the first is the broad focus of this chapter.

Hartley's letter soothed the feelings of Henry and Sara, and she wrote later in January in an effort to cement the relationship: 'Henry was very glad of your long letter to him: "what a noble correspondent you have in your brother!" Might a spectator exclaim on seeing your second folio sheet follows its fellow-desk-mate so shortly—"Why don't you make a sheet every day!" was a stern aunt's speech to an industrious niece. I do not say why don't you write two folio sheets <u>every</u> fortnight, but thank you heartily for the treat we have received'.[4] Good humour and affection carried the day, but nonetheless Sara's letter continued her spirited defence of Henry's veracity and methods:

> That Henry has not only faithfully reported what he heard, but that he reported all he heard, as far as he could remember it on the subjects in question without picking or culling, I feel quite confident

both from my knowledge of Henry's character & conduct on other occasions, & from what I myself recollect of my Father's conversation. Besides I refer the objector to the Church & State & other works which my Father printed in his latter years. Has my husband printed anything as coming from him which is not accordant with the tone and substance of those deliberate productions?

She put her finger on the crucial question, and while vindicating the honesty of the approach, she nonetheless admitted that the material from which Henry, in her view, did not 'pick and cull' (a claim I will show to be untenable) may not have been broadly representative of her father's ideas:

Derwent says that my Father would naturally, from courtesy of his temper, [put?] forward the most Tory side of his opinions <u>to</u> a Tory. But the truth is, unless sincerity has to be sacrificed, my Father with all his ingenuity and subtlety, could not have seemed to agree with Henry on politics unless he had really done so in the main. The real truth is that I believe some of my husbands opinions on the Catholic Question, the Reform Bill, the Church, Political Economy, &c. to have been to a <u>certain degree</u> moulded by those of my Father—at any rate I think they took a more determinate shape from his—and I think it possible that Henry might have leaned a <u>little more</u> to the popular side had he not been kept from doing so by observing the position taken by a man of whose intellect and of whose disinterestedness he had the highest possible estimation.

So while on the one hand admitting the possibility that Henry sought confirmation of his own views in the conversations, and that STC may well have selected subjects and opinions to please his earnest nephew, she nonetheless denied that such events occurred, referring to her father's late prose works for support.

The idea that Henry was more moderate than STC is difficult to take seriously, but its rhetorical stance is necessary to her defence. Hartley was not the only person agitated by Henry's account of STC's views concerning reform. As Carl Woodring notes in the Introduction to his magisterial edition of *Table Talk*, Coleridge's old friends were especially upset by his purported attitude to the Reform Bill.[5] Henry Crabb Robinson made his distaste clear and offered an astute diagnosis of the likely origin of Coleridge's uncharacteristically partisan comments: 'It is quite provoking to see one of the profoundest thinkers and most splendid talkers of his age, as vulgarly orthodox—To think with the Wise and talk with the vulgar is an odious maxim of spurious prudence—C: cannot be said to talk *with* the vulgar, but he talked *to* them at least. And he was gratified by feeling and excited sympathy'.[6] Robinson's view contradicts Sara's assertion that Henry's 'orthodox' Toryism did not influence STC's discourse to him, and provides a compelling psychological account. Coleridge presented an extreme political view because he knew it would accord with the listener's, and result in 'excited sympathy'. The problem that Sara raised and then dismissed cannot be discounted by wishful thinking. Hartley was generous enough to assume that inclusion of partisan opinion unrepresentative of STC's views was down to Henry's naivety. Writing to his mother in May 1835 when the book had just appeared, he expressed his concern: 'I hope *Henry has been very, very, careful as to what he has recorded. Dear papa often said things which he would not himself have published: and I have heard him utter opinions both in Religion and Politics not very easy to reconcile with what he has published'.[7] In his view, his worst fears were realized; *Table Talk* included many of Henry's most extreme political views delivered back to him as an echo of his expectations.

For Sara and Hartley family affection trumped politics. As a result, Sara was careful to preface her defence of Henry's account of her father's Tory views by assuring Hartley that she respected his right to his Whiggish opinions: 'As to our differences in regard to politics they give me little concern except as to the different views it leads us to take of our dear Father's mind'.[8] Implicit here is the idea that Coleridge the political thinker was not yet fixed, and that they were engaged in a contest as to which politics were authorized as his legacy. The stakes were potentially high, and Sara was thus eager to confine them to the problem of individual perception lest they again disturb the family peace. Hartley's politics had isolated him in the family, and losing this particular debate conceivably could have exacerbated the problem by making him appear out of step with his father's views. Sara had noted this estrangement at the end of her letter in reference to the 'Ottery crowd': 'surely our vehemence in defending our own dearly beloved notions has not been taken by you as a reproach to yours. Of course we can have no imaginable right to find fault with your chusing to be in a minority among your relations'. His status in the 'minority' was still a sensitive subject in light of responses to his expulsion from his Fellowship at Oriel. In that instance, Sara had been his defender against what she took to be callousness in the extended family circle, their willingness to hide Hartley's 'opinions & habits' lest they proved embarrassing.[9] It was hardly surprising that Sara sought to limit the significance of political differences as a matter of individual choice, given the appalling short-sightedness and self-interest of the Wordsworths who feared Hartley's politics might disturb their conservative public image. She may have disagreed with Hartley's politics, but he had every right to them, and, more importantly, to attempting to vindicate them through their father's writing and conversation.

In this emotional context, it is clear that this was not merely a partisan dispute. Hartley sought to set the record straight by producing a broader picture of STC's political career and thought. Nor was Hartley a Whig apologist. His sense of independence was a frequent topic in the letters. Writing to his mother on 18 January 1835, the week before Sara's letter, he reconstructed what he took to be his father's final view of reform:

> But on this head, permit me to say, that my Father's opinions on many points of public import were considerably different during the years wherein I last conversed with him, from those which Henry has recorded. He admitted the necessity of a reform in parliament, and though I can never have imagined that he could have much admired little Johnny Russell's unprecedented piece of stupidity and blundering, call'd 'the Reform Bill', I thought that he would be thankful, as I am, for any thing that got rid of the idolized abominations of the old system, not as better in itself, but as necessary, transitory, and, at least, making room for something better.[10]

Henry's politics were derided as 'idolized abominations', and he made the fascinating claim that Henry's account was inaccurate not because it ignored STC's early political commitments, the focus of the complaints by Thomas Poole and Coleridge's Bristol circle, but because it ignored his late political views. In this reading, Henry's book was hampered by the poor luck of being largely confined to the zenith of Coleridge's Tory zeal in the early 1820s. According to Hartley he outgrew that belligerence, and developed a more thoughtful pragmatism about the necessity of evolutionary reform. Notice that Hartley, like many Whigs, considered the Reform Bill to be an unqualified disaster; STC's opposition to the Bill therefore should not be misrecognized as a partisan Tory stance.

Hartley presented the distinctness of his politics directly to Henry in a letter of 8 May 1836. On the occasion of the death of Sara Hutchinson, Hartley lamented the loss to the family, but did not forgive her coldness and disregard:

> Poor dear Miss Hutchinson, without a spark of malice in her heart, had, from the perfect faultlessness of her own life, a good deal of

intolerance in her head—and, yet, she could forgive in persons she liked [i.e. STC], much greater derelictions than she censured in those to whom she was indifferent! ... I believe politics had some little to do with this coldness. Not that she was so illiberal as to dislike people for differing from her own opinions, (she certainly and naturally liked them better when they agreed) but hers was eminently a one-sided mind. Had I been an out-and-outer, she could have understood it, but my mixture of old cavalier Toryism and German liberalism (for I never was, and never talked like a Frenchified Jacobin or Yankee republican) puzzled her, and she was rather shocked at my almost total disbelief in the existence of political integrity in any sect or party, to which, nevertheless, the time gives so much proof.[11]

Still smarting from the Oriel debacle, Hartley took the opportunity to clarify his politics for Henry while issuing this devastating rebuke of Miss Hutchinson, the very portrait of narrow-minded intolerance. Combining 'cavalier Toryism and German liberalism' in describing his political identity issued a challenge—there was another way to read STC's political influences. Toryism need not signify Henry's narrow reactionary views, and 'German liberalism', Hartley well knew, took Henry out of his intellectual depth.[12] The balance of this fascinating letter wed his politics to his father's by offering Henry a comprehensive rebuttal of the inferences to be drawn from his *Table Talk*, presenting an altogether different Coleridge. As a significant competing account, I quote the passage in its entirety:

I know not what induced me to teaze dear Sara with my politics in my last long letter.[13] I must have expressed myself ill, for nothing could be more remote from my intention than to accuse you of misrepresentation or suppression in regard to the public opinions of [undecipherable, but clearly STC]. All I said was, that his was a many-sided mind; that it had chanced that I had seen it under aspects probably less frequently developed in latter years, and though I well know that he never would have approved of the measures called reforms, and still less of the manner and spirit in which they have been carried, his conversation, when I was last in the habit of hearing him authorized me to think that he did[14] perceive the necessity of deep and vital changes, nor in servile compliance with the spirit of the age, (an odious phrase) but to approximate the practice of the constitution to its ideal and final causes—he certainly did hold, or I grievously mistook him, that though the government did work

well according to the money getting commercial principles of the
economists who assailed it, it did not work well morally, did not perform its duty to God or to the divine in man, did not supply those
demands of human nature which are at once rights and duties. He
did express strong indignation against the selfishness and short sight-
edness of the governing classes, a selfishness modified and mollified
indeed by much kindness and good nature—but not controuled or
balanced by any clear principles. He utterly condemned I know, until
his latest hour the system which considering men as things, instruments, machines, property does in effect make them so. Though he
never held that happiness is the legitimate end of human existence,
he thought comfort, competence, national free-agency, a kind and
paternal treatment of the Many, which alone can render a duteous,
filial loyalty possible—are the essential conditions of a healthy state
either of individuals or classes—I cannot moreover, help thinking,
that though at no time in his life a Jacobin or a revolutionist, he
was in his youth at the period to which my earliest recollections of
him extend a great deal more of a republican—and certainly, much
more of a philanthropist and cosmopolite than he appears to have
been distinctly aware of in his riper years—I recollect being somewhat startled and terrified at the exulting tone in which he spoke
of the French Revolution long after its true character had appeared.
He was as far as his nature allowed him to hate any thing—a king-
hater and a prelate-hater and spoke of Charles 1st and of Laud with a
bitterness in which I never did and never can sympathize. He also—
but read not this to Mama or Sara did, even when I was last with
him at Highgate, speak very harshly of the political subservice of
W[ordsworth] and S[outhey]—Indeed I am most happy to see by the
Table Talk, and by the testimony of his will that ere he deceased, his
heart was fully reconciled to those excellent men, from whom he
was for a while cruelly alienated by the ill offices of inconsiderate
tale-bearers, perhaps a little aggravated by the injudicious praises of
others, who dwelt upon their virtues in a way that sounded a great
deal too like an implied reproach of his merely corporeal infirmities.
There is, moreover, I am afraid, a jealousy in friendship as well as
in love—and W[ordsworth] certainly was apt to consider himself as
my father's only true friend. Many and many a time have I pleaded,
almost with tears, for my dear Uncle—and I think it very hard, that
I should have been represented to my mother as a detractor from his
moral and intellectual greatness, because I did not and do not admire
any of his laureate poetry—(except the epicedium on the Princess,

which is beautiful) nor agree with all his articles in the Quarterly. Entre nous, I think he has retained even in his ultra-toryism, and high-churchmanship, the fundamental error which made him, in the heat of youth, somewhat of a revolutionist—he expects a great deal more from positive institutions than God ever intended they should produce. You cannot make men moral or religious, or enlightened by law. Law has done its best, when it prevents the evil-disposed from being mischievous with impunity, and leaves no pretext for any man to take the law into his own hand. The first, not highest duty of a Government is to constitute and maintain the State, to defend the national existence and public honour—the second to keep the peace at home, to give security to person and property, to protect religion and morality from insult or oppression—the third, to promote the healthy circulation of property by a well-regulated taxation, and, as far as may be, to prevent individuals from growing rich by making or keeping others poor, to see that private wealth is not increased without a proportionate increase of public wealth. These I hold to contain the sum and substance of the duties of a state—out of which duties arise the just prerogatives of a state and the just obedience of the subject. No individual, no multitude or combination of individuals, be their rank education or usefulness what they may, have any right to set their private will, interest, convenience, humour, or opinion against the will of the State embodied in law—but the law should never represent the will, inclination, or interest of any individual, or any class, but should be the passionless exponent of practical reason. As to the distribution of powers and functions, it is plainly absurd to lay down any general rule or to assert the absolute unconditional right of any man or number of men to a legislative voice—but certainly, that does appear to me to be the best condition of society in which the citizen is never fully merged in the subject which gives every adult, not indeed direct political power but a political existence, a public character, which attributes to every man a something beyond his bare human being. It seems to me a great solecism to allot political privileges or franchises to any man from which others of equal rank, property, occupation, and execution are excluded—the effect, by the way, of the blundering ten-pound qualification—about the worst that could be devised.

This remarkable letter took Sara at her word and described a Coleridge predicated on Hartley's politics. In stating that STC was 'many-sided' he set out to limit Henry's Tory version by placing it in the much broader context of contemporary political philosophy. Liberated from Henry's partisanship, this Coleridge emerges as a rational gradualist, admitting the necessity of constitutional change. Hartley's distinction between 'reform' and 'change' shows a Coleridge suspicious of party politics and the reform camp, but one who nonetheless saw such change as inevitable, as the unfolding of 'the practice of the constitution to its ideal and final causes'. This compromise between Burkean organicism and Coleridge's early republicanism demonstrates Hartley's political perceptiveness. He clearly demonstrates how Coleridge could admit the material good produced by economic conditions, yet nonetheless decry their moral blindness. Condemnation of 'the system which considering men as things, instruments, machines, property does in effect make them so' accords with Coleridge's strong moral convictions, and serves as a succinct critique of the psychological effects of emergent capitalism. Such blind excesses threatened the moral foundation of society. Self-interest, following Adam Smith's precepts, provided the basis for the creation of wealth, but in and of itself was not balanced by 'clear principles'. This is not to say that Coleridge was a closet statist, and Hartley is at pains to describe how he viewed the limited role of the state in regulating social relations. Active amelioration was wrongheaded in its assumption that happiness was the legitimate end of human existence, but nevertheless he imagined a kind and wise paternalism that reflected the basic needs of all subjects, or as Hartley put it: 'comfort, competence, national free-agency, a kind and paternal treatment of the Many, which alone can render a duteous, filial loyalty possible—are the essential conditions of a healthy state either of individuals or classes'. Coleridge's conservatism, then, was not partisan and belligerent, but founded on deeply held moral views. Nor was it static—change was essential in that the state had the responsibility to remove social grievances that served as the preconditions for revolution thus making 'filial loyalty possible'. Lest he be misunderstood, Hartley reassured Henry by repeating the family mantra that Coleridge was, like himself, 'at no time in his life a Jacobin'. Nonetheless he insists that Coleridge never lost his youthful hatred of tyrants. He emphasizes the point by claiming that it was one of the few examples of 'hatred' in Coleridge's life. In fact, the vehemence of his antipathy to kings and prelates marked his father's views as more extreme than his own. According to Hartley, contempt for those who sought status through their relationship to political power and authority also played a part in Coleridge's estrangement from Wordsworth and Southey over what he took to be their 'political subservience'.

Hartley's perceptive reading of Southey's ultra-Toryism as psychologically consistent with the belligerent Jacobinism of his young adulthood forms a transition to the second part of the letter where his account of STC's politics gives way to a description of his own. The ultra-Toryism he decries as extremism is, of course, precisely the politics of his correspondent. If anything, Henry was to the right of Southey. In the contest for whose Coleridge better reflects the historical STC, he positions Henry as the author of an extreme version while claiming a moderate version for himself. In delineating his political views in the second half of the letter, he shows them to be founded on those of his father as he has just described them. He presents a moderate view of the duties of the state: 'to give security to person and property, to protect religion and morality from insult or oppression—the third, to promote the healthy circulation of property by a well-regulated taxation, and, as far as may be, to prevent individuals from growing rich by making or keeping others poor, to see that private wealth is not increased without a proportionate increase of public wealth'. The only hint of a radical Whig agenda comes in asserting that a 'single class' should never determine the law. In arguing against self-interest in establishing laws, he asserts what he calls his 'German liberalism'; the law should be produced by the exercise of 'practical reason'. Rallying the Kantian understanding to his cause allowed him to present it as the 'passionless exponent' of philosophical reflection. The 'ten pound qualification' restricting the franchise was presented as 'blundering' because it was arbitrary and irrational. Hartley's politics placed him in a centrist position between Henry, Gillman, Green, and the Ottery crowd on the one hand and, Poole, Cottle, and the old Bristol circle on the other. So on the evidence of this letter, the politics that Sara characterized as placing him in the 'minority' in the family were hardly the embarrassing radicalism that the Wordsworth circle feared would tarnish their respectability were he to promulgate them at Oriel.

Hartley's letter, then, presents an alternative Coleridge—still conservative, but as passionately committed to the moral necessity of social justice as ever. No longer confident in programmatic change via reform, he nonetheless attempted to imagine a transformed state where the relations among various class fractions were rational and based on consent, not coercion. The ideal role of the state was to regulate these relations by preventing abuse by the powerful, and, in so doing, prevent the preconditions of revolution. Coleridge's vision of the clerisy, a wise, disinterested elite, follows directly from Hartley's portrait.

The logic of the letter can, of course, be turned on its head by asserting that just as Henry heard his own views when he listened to Coleridge, so Hartley heard his. Sara called this phenomenon 'natural' even as she denied its effects. Hartley produces moderate Whig table talk to balance the ultra-Tory, and provides a broader political context. The crucial difference is Hartley did not compile notes from his discussions with his father with a view towards posthumous publication. The letter is a private document, unknown until the 1940s and little known since; whereas *Table Talk* was one of the most successful and widely known works attributed to STC in the nineteenth century,[15] and remains officially in the Coleridge canon, even though he wasn't the author.

*

If the book is not the work of STC, what is it? Coleridge's speech was doubtless its source, so can we conceive of the work as an example of multiple authorship? Henry, however, complicated this hypothesis by presenting himself as the editor, so over time STC became the nominal author by default. Contemporary perception of Henry's voice and ideas in the text faded little by little until the volume became accepted as Coleridge's work. There are many reasons to object to this historical forgetting. *Table Talk* is a distortion of Coleridge's views, and the distortion takes several forms. First, it misrepresents itself in the broadest terms as 'specimens' of Coleridge's table talk; second, examination of the notebook entries that served as the basis for the text shows subtle, but clear, evidence of deliberate distortions in the published text; and, most decisively, Henry actively censored the notebooks in an effort to make Coleridge's ideas more palatable to his intended audience. Concerns about respectability and fear of scandal, evident in their handling of De Quincey, were transformed from anxiety about STC's reputation into positive assertions of the most reactionary views of the Coleridge family; these views were then passed off as Coleridge's. The most glaring casualties in this process were Coleridge's religious views, in general, and his engagement with the Higher Criticism and Biblical philology in particular. Without that matter in the text, the religious views, as presented, are a travesty.

To begin, the title of the volume is a misnomer. Contemporary readers would have expected from the title, *Specimens of the Table Talk of Samuel Taylor Coleridge*, an account of Coleridge's famous Thursday evening conversations at the Grove, the Gillman house in Highgate. Not a single 'specimen' of that talk occurs in the volume. The overwhelming majority of the entries are based on notes taken by Henry of private conversations between the two of them in Coleridge's room at the Grove in Highgate. The notes were taken after the fact; Coleridge was never consulted on their accuracy, or even clearly informed of Henry's plan for posthumous publication. Woodring notes that only a handful of entries took place when anyone other than Henry was present, and these were occasional events,[16] not the carefully arranged Thursday evening sessions that established Coleridge's fame as a talker. Woodring is generous in characterizing the result: 'For the most part *Table Talk* contains what Coleridge said to his nephew, not all of what he said and little of it designed exclusively for Henry, but said directly to him'.[17] The question, then, is how much influence did these specific circumstances play in determining what Coleridge said? Sara's letter to Hartley raised the issue by admitting that Coleridge would present his most Tory views to a Tory. The fact that the conversations were in private, not the public performance of the Thursday after-dinner discourses, complicates the issue by making the likelihood of STC presenting ideas to please his young acolyte much greater. Unleavened by being uttered in the public forum of the Gillmans' table, Coleridge's opinions would naturally tend towards extreme statements, partly to please his nephew and partly because of the sense of being off the record. Henry closed the circuit by hearing his own views confirmed. So while Woodring asserts that 'little of it was designed exclusively for Henry', the problem remains that we cannot determine how much. On the troubling issue of Henry's account of Coleridge's views on the Reform Bill, contemporary opinion was in accord with Hartley. Coleridge's old friends like Poole were naturally aggrieved at the portrait Henry produced, but John Gibson Lockhart's review in the *Quarterly Review* offered a strikingly similar account: 'We think it right to record that, under the circumstances in which the Reform bill had placed the country, there was much more likelihood of good than evil results from extending still further the electoral suffrage. The great mischief, he always said, had been placing too much power in one particular class of the population ... '[18] As Woodring notes, in response to Henry's account, STC's friends were 'not more shocked than suspicious', assuming that they were reading Henry's views.[19] On this important issue, there was consensus among contemporary readers that the belligerent partisan voice attacking reform was not just 'designed exclusively for Henry', but actually was Henry's.

Most readers agreed that the voice itself was unlike Coleridge's conversation. The simple explanation for this is that Henry made no effort to record the conversation as such. The two notebooks that contain the majority of the manuscript material that was transformed into *Table Talk* contain not conversation or Coleridgean monologue, as Woodring observes, but 'Coleridge's topics, apparently at first without regard to the order of topics or to transitions between them'.[20] In the published work, Henry introduced the topics, and the aphoristic form. Henry deliberately chose the style, and revision of the notebook entries makes it clear that he chose his own sense of clarity over accurate portrayals of Coleridge's verbal style or even his diction.[21] The result could hardly be less like Coleridge's talk, and readers were quick to say so. Julius Hare was frank in his assessment of the book's account of Coleridge's conversations: 'their depth, their ever varying hues, their sparkling lights, their oceanic ebb and flow; of which his published Table-talk hardly gives the slightest conception'.[22] The disjointed entries failed to capture either the range of subject matter, sound of voice, or intellectual structure of their presumed author. Samuel Carter Hall put it bluntly: 'only a collection of scraps, chance-gathered'.[23] Nor was this simply a stylistic problem. De Quincey's famous description of Coleridge's conversational method in his first essay on Coleridge in *Tait's Edinburgh Magazine* made it clear that it *was* a method. Given his account, Henry's choice of style entirely missed the point of the discourse from which it was drawn. According to De Quincey, Coleridge's speech:

> swept at once, as if returning to his natural business, into a continuous train of eloquent dissertation, certainly the most novel, the most finely illustrated, and traversing the most spacious fields of thought, by transitions the most just and logical, that it was possible to conceive. What I mean by saying his transitions were 'just', is by way of contradistinction to that mode of conversation which courts variety by means of *verbal* connections. Coleridge, to many people, and often I have heard the complaint, seemed to wander; and he seemed then to wander the most, when in fact his resistance to the wandering instinct was greatest,—viz. when the compass, and huge circuit, by which his illustrations moved, traveled farthest into remote regions, before they began to revolve. Long before this coming-round commenced, most people had lost him, and naturally enough supposed that he had lost himself. They continued to admire the separate beauty of the thoughts, but did not see their relations to the dominant theme.[24]

In part, this account represents De Quincey's attempt to construct himself as Coleridge's only qualified auditor, as I observed in the previous chapter. However, in the context of *Table Talk*, the image of vast fields of erudition finally revolving into a complex whole renders Henry's method and result absurd; it atomized that whole into incoherent fragments. Those fragments rarely captured 'the separate beauty of the thoughts', and destroyed any sense of Coleridge's cognitive processes. The narrowness of Henry's view, both ideologically and, more broadly, intellectually, coupled with the artificiality of the closed-room private interviews guaranteed that faithful representations of Coleridge's conversation could not be reproduced in his book.

Henry's ideological and stylistic habits act as a screen obscuring Coleridge, who we nonetheless assume to be back there somewhere. The patterns of distortion can never be adequately accounted for, but an analysis of how Henry's numbered notebook entries changed as they were transformed into dated *Table Talk* entries gives some indication of the level of scepticism we need to bring to the text. Sara's January 1836 letter to Hartley defended her husband against the possible charge of distortion, that he had 'picked and culled' from his materials introducing a deliberate bias. She also assured Hartley that Henry was completely independent of 'the Ottery crowd' and not influenced by them in making editorial decisions. Neither of these claims is true. It would be convenient to blame Henry for deliberately misleading his wife, leading her to misspeak, but Henry wrote to her directly as he completed the manuscript detailing the role of the 'Ottery crowd', primarily in the person of his brother John, in censoring the religious views recorded in the notebooks. Henry reports that John advised him to suppress Coleridge's speculations on the literal truth of the Bible:

John has read about half of what I had drawn up. He was electrified by some parts—delighted & instructed by more—but wholly disapproves of a good deal, especially, as might be expected of all those parts in which sceptical remarks on the genuineness of the books in the Bible appear. In part I agree with him upon the propriety of omitting them from this little book. They or their fellows will, no doubt, appear ere long; but I at least shall incur no responsibility, & they will then appear in the great man's own language. The omission of those parts will make a hole in my materials—but that must not be regarded. John read the earlier part in which most of the obnoxious dicta occur; the latter part is more literary & less objectionable. I have very nearly drawn it all out.[25]

This correspondence largely confirms Hartley's worst fears—his father's opinions were carefully edited so as not to upset a specific audience, the most reactionary, and in his view, credulous elements of the Church. On this issue STC would clearly side with Hartley. Henry suppressed the material not because he doubted it, but because he feared a scandal and wanted to make sure that he 'incur no responsibility' for the ideas. He admitted that the censorship would 'make a hole in his materials'; an understatement given that Biblical philology and its accompanying theological arguments represented one of the consistent themes throughout his notes. Coleridge, probably since his college days at Cambridge, had been deeply engaged with Biblical philology and the German Higher Criticism. As a reader of the *Analytical Review*, he was intellectually at the centre of those debates in Britain. Alexander Geddes, the *Analytical's* religion reviewer, corresponded with Eichhorn and their competing theories of multiple authorship and chronology appeared in the journal.[26] Coleridge travelled to the University of Göttingen in 1798 to study theology with Eichhorn. He produced detailed marginalia in two copies of Eichhorn's 1791 *Commentarius in Apocalypsin Joanniss*.[27] Unsurprisingly, such subjects appeared in Coleridge's conversation many years later, and Henry dutifully recorded them. But what had appeared uncontroversial in 1822 or 1823 (the most likely date of the entries) carried a public risk in 1836. The Church was in a period of extreme controversy, buffeted by Low Church evangelicals on one side and the Oxford Movement on the other. Henry and Sara were friends of Dodsworth and dedicated readers of Newman, so he cannot be excused on the grounds of naivety. A fundamental Enlightenment discovery, the compositional structure of the Bible, became controversial and risked being denounced by Biblical literalists. Most surprising in the letter was his eventual assent with John's view that the entries presented 'obnoxious dicta', while comforting himself that the publication of the *Literary Remains* would bring STC's ideas to light, thus relieving him of blame for censorship while protecting him from public attack. This is not a flattering portrait—caving to opinions his father would have considered absurd, all to avoid alienating influential conservative Churchmen. Distortion took two forms: the direct removal of passages deemed offensive by John and later Edward or Derwent, who served as secondary censors once John's anxieties were voiced, and the subtle manipulation of Henry's entries to excise the possibility of controversy. He kept the original recorded phrases of the notebook entries, but placed them in conditional constructions so that the opinions were stated as public opinions about which Coleridge had no definitive personal view. Thus, the assertion: 'Xtianity might be believed without the first six chapters of Daniel',[28] became: 'Whatever may be thought of the genuineness or authority of any part of the book of Daniel; it makes no difference in my belief in Christianity'.[29] Simple acceptance of a philological proposition, the spuriousness of the beginning of the Book of Daniel, becomes a restatement of faith in light of such scepticism. This is a subtle distortion, but a distortion nonetheless— and one with a self-conscious purpose, distancing Coleridge from the non-literal interpretation of the Bible that he actually professed.

Passages in the notebook manuscript deemed dangerous 'obnoxious dicta' were physically cut out. The matter of the genuineness of the Book of Daniel was put beyond doubt in one of the excised scraps: 'The first six chapters of the book of Daniel cannot have been written by the author of the rest. They are full of Greek words. Now there could have been no Greek words in any thing written by Daniel, & there *are* no Greek words in the rest of the book'.[30] Selective removal of certain ideas was bad enough, but also lost was Coleridge's reasoning based on strong philological evidence. Doubtless more troubling for John, and for Derwent embarking on a career as a conservative Churchman, were the entries challenging the ideological basis and political dominance of the Athanasian Creed underlying Trinitarian Church doctrine. Those scraps reveal STC taking care to explain his objections and reasoning to Henry. Coleridge asserted that the Creed had no historical authority, 'emanated from no general council', and amounted to a tool for 'persecution'. His open contempt is striking: 'in the beginning & end [the Creed] is intolerant, & in the middle is heretical in a high degree. I mean in particular the flagrant omission, or implicit denial, of the essential article of the Filial subordination to the Godhead ... '[31] Henry later softened the passage by crossing out the word 'persecution', but that was not enough to save it from censure. In a later entry on the subject, STC described how he would finesse mandatory adherence to the Creed if he were to assume the pulpit. Reminding Henry that one of the articles of the Church of England stated that 'all Churches have erred, & that the Scriptures alone are infallible', Coleridge insisted that 'the doctrines of the Church of England may be erroneous, in so far as you are unable to reconcile them with the word of God'. In this theological context, his objection to the didactic repetition and exclusionary rhetoric of the Creed did not disqualify him as a member of the Church, even though the Creed was primarily used as a political tool for that very purpose. Clergy could take comfort from the inevitability of the conclusion of his syllogism: 'Accordingly, it is beyond a doubt that you may conscientiously reject in your own mind the Athanasian Creed, whether as heretical or uncharitable or both, & still remain a faithful Church minister'.[32] This advice worked well in the privacy implied by the phrase 'in your own mind', but what to do about the fact that as a Church minister you were required to profess the Creed? The advice on this point was extremely pragmatic: 'If you are amongst peaceful people, don't read the Athanasian Creed; if you suspect an informer, read it, because the Rubric, which is by Act of Parliament, orders it'.[33] So, dispense with the offensive ideological violence implicit in the use of the Creed if possible, but if you must profess it do so with the understanding that it is a legal, not religious, obligation. Coleridge clearly recognized the Creed for what it was, a repressive tool in the service of a nervous conformity. That the passage was excised from Henry's manuscript at the direct request of representatives of that narrow and, in Coleridge's view, credulous constituency makes this probably the most treacherous of Henry's exclusions. Coleridge explained how he would resolve this conflict between political and religious duty if he were a minister: 'I would explain the true doctrine of the Trinity, & either leave the contrast to be observed by the congregation, or I would point out with decency the imperfections of the Creed which I had been required by law to read in the morning'.[34] By excising these entries Henry made it impossible for the reader to 'observe' the 'contrast' between Coleridge's views of the 'true doctrine of the Trinity' and the political cant that stood as its public manifestation.

The inevitable inference to be drawn from this censorship is that Henry, John, Edward, and Derwent were concerned that open heretical views could harm Coleridge's posthumous reputation, and they were willing to distort or suppress those views so that the author be palatable and uncontroversial. Religious controversy had no place in the subsequent construction of the author, even though it was clearly central to Coleridge's intellectual life. Worried about the vehemence of those asserting the literal truth of the Bible, probably John among them, Henry simply avoided the subject. As a result *Table Talk* noted Coleridge's awareness of Biblical philology and theories of authorship, often so he could appear to assert that they made no difference to his faith, but removed his lifelong engagement with those theories.

Henry's perception of the possibility of scandal dictated his editing of *Table Talk*, and thus created a broader problem as he assumed the role of literary executor. A desire that Coleridge's reputation reflect his view of him as an orthodox Tory sage demanded the posthumous imposition of his own nervous relation to the ideological status quo—made nervous by his anxiety not to offend. That in *Table Talk*, the first instance of posthumous reconstruction, they (Henry, John, Edward, Derwent, the Gillmans, Green) produced a work where it appears that Coleridge was an unreflective adherent to the Athanasian Creed, a doctrine he found contemptible, did not bode well. Hartley represented a potentially useful dissenting voice, but his status of being in the 'minority' in the family meant that his politics had already been judged as scandalous, especially in the wake of the Oriel debacle.

The problems, then, of considering *Table Talk* the work of Samuel Taylor Coleridge are almost too numerous to list: the artificiality of Henry's private conversations representing themselves as Coleridge's public voice, the conscious or unconscious screen produced by having Henry as the sole auditor, the insertion of Henry's politics so clearly present in remarks on reform, Henry's lack of political sophistication especially when compared to Hartley's, and finally a willingness to censor the work in response to reactionary political and religious opinion, makes any such designation highly dubious. The matter would be less serious were it not for the sheer success of the volume, for even Henry knew that Coleridge's views would emerge with the publication of the *Literary Remains*. There would be little point censoring STC's actual writing, although nervousness could still play a role in deciding what to publish, in what order, under whose editorship, with what introductory matter, et cetera. The dissemination of *Table Talk* throughout the nineteenth century, ratified by the family editors and its subsequent inclusion in *The Collected Works of Samuel Taylor Coleridge*, made it a representative voice of Samuel Taylor Coleridge, and Henry Nelson Coleridge became a kind of inadvertent cuckoo, in that even though when it first appeared it was recognized as 'Henry's book', over time its complex multiple authorship became gradually obscured.

4
Coleridge the Plagiarist

As detailed above, Henry Nelson Coleridge and the other literary executors managed De Quincey's plagiarism charge in 1834 with a combination of partial acknowledgement of the charge and an attack on its source—the erratic De Quincey. They had found themselves in the unenviable position of having to defend Coleridge's reputation at a point where it was far from secure. Luckily, Henry had an immediate opportunity to address the crisis and acknowledge these 'debts' in his Introduction to the second edition of the *Table Talk*, and thus limit the damage. The acknowledgement, via the interpolation of Hare's essay, argued that while the passages were indeed Schelling's work, and they were unacknowledged as such, they were nonetheless produced either through an innocent scholarly practice (keeping ideas in informal notebooks) or excusable through the mitigation of Coleridge's footnote on the coincidence of his and Schelling's thought. And, Henry had the advantage of simply following De Quincey's reasoning, that despite the fact that *Biographia Literaria* included a '*verbatim* translation from Schelling' Coleridge was nonetheless 'as entirely original … as any one man that ever existed'.[1] Indeed, De Quincey's professed interest in the plagiarism originated, he said, in his deep admiration of Coleridge, and he felt compelled to publicize the 'borrowings' in order: 'to forestall … other discoverers, who would make a more unfriendly use of the discovery'.[2] In other words, De Quincey paradoxically intended to expose the plagiarisms in order protect Coleridge's reputation. Henry's failure to take De Quincey at his word in this matter and address the issue of plagiarism as a psychological and intellectual puzzle introduced a set of moral stakes where none were broached. De Quincey was not arguing that Coleridge was a bad man. This unfortunate moral frame was the creation of Henry and developed by Hare in his essay, referring to

De Quincey throughout as 'the Opium-eater' in a show of open contempt. The question has remained in this overheated atmosphere ever
since, and part of the intention of this chapter is to offer a reading that
resists moralizing as much as possible.

   De Quincey's exposure was not entirely altruistic, and he could therefore be attacked for not being a gentleman. Utterly lacking in substance,
and the product of a likely misreading by the executors, this line of
defence proved the most successful with the reading public—they could
ignore the charge as an unseemly posthumous attack on the author,
made more offensive by the culprit's friendship with the deceased.
Thus when De Quincey introduced the subject of plagiarism as part of
his biographical narrative, recounting a conversation with Tom Poole
on the subject in 1807 that had provided: 'the first hint of a singular
infirmity besetting Coleridge's mind',[3] he could be dismissed for his
manners. Nonetheless, De Quincey quickly established his authority in
the matter of this 'infirmity' and claimed a kind of ownership of the
information: 'Here was a trait of Coleridge's mind, to be first made
known to me by his best friend, and first published to the world by
me, the foremost of his admirers!'[4] Such evident self-dramatization
infuses De Quincey's subsequent account of the instances of plagiarism
throughout Coleridge's works. Only he is adequate to discover these,
and he employs understatement in making the point: 'I shall here point
out a few others of Coleridge's unacknowledged obligations, noticed
by myself in a very wide course of reading'.[5] De Quincey constructs
himself as the ultimate Coleridge reader (or perhaps the only qualified
Coleridge reader), and, in turn, establishes his own eccentric genius.
Exposing the borrowings from Schelling, for example, provides an
opportunity to summarize chapter twelve of *Biographia Literaria* in a
single sentence:

   In the 'Biographia Literaria' occurs a dissertation upon the reciprocal
   relations of the *Esse* and the *Cogitare*,—that is, of the *objective* and
   the *subjective*: and an attempt is made, by inverting the postulates
   from which the argument starts, to show how each might arise as a
   product, by an intelligible genesis, from the other.[6]

The purpose of this sentence is not the communication of the content
of chapter twelve; no one who hasn't already read the chapter is likely to
follow such a distillation. Neither is the purpose the accurate summary
of Coleridge's version of Schelling's now famous deduction. Rather,
the sentence demonstrates the precision of De Quincey's philosophical

mind. It is an intellectual tour de force, and claims complete mastery over both Coleridge and Schelling.

Sara Coleridge was able to diagnose De Quincey's self-dramatizations, and summarized her view with understandable disdain, connecting what she took to be the reasons for De Quincey's public 'fall' with the qualities displayed in the essay: 'De Quincey's fall has been effected by an irritable vanity as well as a proneness to self indulgence'.[7] This subtle reading would have served as a better foundation for their public response to De Quincey's claims, but, unfortunately Sara was peripheral to editorial strategies at that juncture, and a relatively simplistic, if initially success-ful, version of 'shoot the messenger' prevailed. None of this would have mattered had it proved successful in the long run, and the plagiarism charge been laid to rest. As we know this was not to be the case.

The more serious attack on Coleridge's reputation occurred six years later with the appearance of J. F. Ferrier's essay 'The Plagiarisms of S. T. Coleridge' in *Blackwood's Edinburgh Magazine*. Whereas De Quincey's attack assumed that acts of plagiarism were psychological aberrations, part of a pattern of brilliant inconsistency, Ferrier carefully delineated Coleridge's unacknowledged uses of Schelling in the most damning intellectual and moral terms—terms justified by Hare's rebuttal of De Quincey. Coleridge was a thief. Ferrier introduces his attack with the assurance that he does not intend to 'affix a stigma upon the memory, of Mr Coleridge'. *Blackwood's Magazine* had always, he reminds us, 'assigned' Coleridge's 'genius' an 'exalted rank'. He declares himself 'extremely unwilling to hold him guilty of any direct and intentional dishonesty',[8] a subtle piece of rhetoric holding open the *possibility* of Coleridge's guilt of some lesser offence, or of simple thoughtlessness. The language of culpability, even in a negative formulation, is telling, because Ferrier soon abandons his disingenuous pose, and reformulates the question as a trial with Coleridge's reputation in the dock. Ferrier offers very little in the way of possible mitigation, imagining that per-haps we can 'attribute to some strange intellectual hallucination a prac-tice, which in the case of any other man, we should have called by the stronger name of a gross misdemeanour'.[9] In short, the defence would be well advised to limit itself to the testimonials of character witnesses. He finally states his charge plainly:

> [Coleridge], at the age of forty-five, succeeded in founding by far the greater part of his metaphysical reputation—which was considerable—upon *verbatim* plagiarisms from works written and published by a German youth, when little more than twenty years of age![10]

The emphasis on age probably represents a roundabout celebration of Schelling's genius, rather than a slight on Coleridge. I'll return to Ferrier's philosophical devotion to Schelling later.

In many ways Ferrier's charges were nothing new. He had located some other questionable passages from Schelling and other German authors in Coleridge's work, but the case still rested on the unacknowledged appropriation of Schelling's incomplete deduction of the imagination, drawn from the *System of Transcendental Idealism* and other works, in chapter twelve of *Biographia Literaria*. Ferrier accused De Quincey of confusing the issue by misidentifying the specific work, but De Quincey's charge could hardly have been put more plainly—stating that '[chapter twelve] was from the first word to the last, a *verbatim* translation'.[11] The great difference in Ferrier's essay is the effect that information has on the reader. It is one thing to say Coleridge translated Schelling's work and presented it as his own, especially with the generous proviso that the whole of the passage might ultimately be subsumed in Coleridge's more capacious philosophical system, but it is quite a different thing to have twenty-one passages scrupulously presented in a detailed demonstration of the actual offence. Hare's angry rebuttal in the *British Magazine* (January 1835) and later incorporated into *Table Talk,* in which he suggested that Coleridge had borrowed maybe 'half-a-dozen pages' from Schelling, comes in for immediate ridicule, Ferrier asserting that 'there are nearer twenty'.[12] Hare's strategy of simply dissembling was untenable after Ferrier 'proceed(ed) to particularize Coleridge's plagiarisms, in the order in which they occur'.[13] Hare had spent most of his review attacking De Quincey's treachery and betrayal of Coleridge's trust. To this, Ferrier stated the obvious: even if De Quincey's offence was as bad as Hare suggested (and as a representative of *Blackwood's* this was not something Ferrier was willing to simply concede), that did not serve as an 'exculpation of Coleridge, or [have] any thing whatever to do with the merits of the case'.[14]

The most devastating feature of Ferrier's attack is not the presentation of the physical evidence, but his questioning of the defendant. Coleridge, of course, had published his defence along with the offending passages. Ferrier gives 'the *whole* of his defence', and then systematically interrogates each of its claims to see if they bear scrutiny. In acknowledging Schelling as the philosopher responsible for 'the most important victories of this revolution in philosophy',[15] Coleridge makes his general indebtedness clear, but muddies the waters with a qualification:

> Whether the work is the offspring of a man's own spirit, and the product of original thinking, will be discovered by those who are

its sole legitimate judges, by better tests than the mere reference of dates. For readers in general, let whatever be found in this or any future work of mine that resembles or coincides with the doctrines of my German predecessor, though contemporary, be wholly attributed to *him*; provided that the absence of distinct references to his books, ... be not charged to me as an ungenerous concealment or intentional plagiarism.[16]

I have deliberately omitted Coleridge's list of reasons why we should do this (faulty memory, inability to locate the citations, uncertainty of precedence). Ferrier is perfectly right to read these reasons as subterfuges. Taking Coleridge at his word then, we should 'attribute' chapter twelve to Schelling, and he puts the onus on readers to make this discovery and the correct attribution. In order that we may do so, he alerts us to its presence and designates 'legitimate judges', qualified readers, to adjudicate the matter. The effect of the passage then is to acknowledge the offence, and name its terms, 'ungenerous concealment' of Schelling's contribution and 'deliberate plagiarism'. Asserting that a 'general acknowledgement' of indebtedness is sufficient in such a complex matter can only be laughable in light of chapter twelve. A systematic rearrangement of Schelling's ideas cannot be an oversight, so cannot fall into the category of accidental missed references that the footnote describes. There are three key points in Ferrier's cross-examination. First, to Coleridge's warning to the reader that: 'an identity of thought, or even similarity of phrase, will not at all times be a certain proof that the passage has been borrowed from Schelling',[17] Ferrier makes the obvious objection that: 'an identity of thought and similarity of phrase, occurring in the case of two authors, must be held as very *strong* proof that one of them has borrowed from the other'.[18] He ignores Coleridge's ambiguous qualifier, 'will not at all times be a certain proof', which leaves open the possibility that sometimes 'identity of thought and similarity of phrase' are proof of 'borrowing', and instead makes a more direct objection, pointing out that the question is not one of 'similarity' so much as 'sameness'.[19] The second, and more serious, point examines the 'sameness' of the passages and concludes that Coleridge contributed nothing to the discussion. Coleridge's assertion that there was a 'genial coincidence'[20] between his thought and the ideas he subsequently discovered in Schelling is found, on the evidence, to be untenable. Ferrier argues that there is nothing in Coleridge's published works to indicate that he was working in a similar metaphysical vein either before or after his use of Schelling in *Biographia Literaria*. Ferrier could not have known that

Coleridge had completed the ten theses at the heart of chapter twelve in a notebook some ten years earlier, and even if he had known would likely have interpreted the fact as further evidence of subterfuge—Coleridge's meticulous analysis and use of Schelling, and his commitment to the ideas at stake, do not suggest casual engagement. In any case, Ferrier assumes the worst. He does grudgingly allow 'a few extremely insignificant variations and interpolations',[21] but argues that Coleridge's offence is 'worse than plagiarism'[22] because the preemptive defence can only be taken as an attempt to mislead the reader. So, the third point, and the one that clearly enrages Ferrier, is that Coleridge deliberately misled his readers via a kind of rhetorical homeopathy wherein a partial disclosure attempts to prevent full-blown discovery. In Ferrier's view:

> *So long* as these plagiarisms are undetected, this manner of wording the protest [Coleridge's defensive footnote] will ensure to the author (as it did to Coleridge for the whole of his life) the credit of being original, and *when* they are detected, (if that ever happens,) it will give him the benefit of his protestation as a defence: in other words, if they are *not* detected, Schelling's passages remain Coleridge's, and if they *are* detected the latter calculates upon getting out of the scrape by pleading that he had, in a manner, admitted them.[23]

The 'manner' of admitting them was the real issue for Ferrier. If Coleridge intends to mislead, and the example of Hare suggests that he succeeded, then he has *self-consciously* taken Schelling's work and passed it off as his own. As we will see in a moment, 'self-consciousness' is of primary importance in Ferrier's moral philosophy, as it is in Coleridge's. Intentional deception struck at the core of both philosophical systems, especially if we remember that in Thesis VII Coleridge asserted that the subject couldn't be a substance (Spinoza's mistake), but rather must be an act and: 'it follows therefore that intelligence or self-consciousness is impossible, except by and in a will'.[24]

At the end of the essay, Ferrier offers a theory to explain the most famous of what he characterized as 'extremely insignificant variations and interpolations'—the sudden abandonment of Schelling's deduction at the end of chapter twelve with the interpolated, self-penned, letter from a friend. Ferrier concludes that Coleridge's stated project of deducing the imagination from this complex material cannot succeed because Schelling only produces 'glimpses and indications' of 'some stupendous theory on the subject of the imagination',[25] and Coleridge was inadequate to the task of completing the work, thus 'leaving his readers in the lurch'.[26] This theory has some appeal. For Ferrier, it provides a plausible account of what otherwise might appear to be an inexplicable rhetorical device. However, this seems too easy, because what Ferrier leaves out is the 'insignificant variation' of Coleridge's distinction between the fancy and the primary and secondary imaginations in chapter thirteen. The roots of this omission may lie in his philosophy. As I mentioned above, Ferrier was an enthusiastic reader of Schelling, and engaged in a complex effort to adapt Idealist philosophy to Scottish philosophical controversies. His chosen philosophical focus at the time of the Coleridge essay was the philosophy of consciousness, and he derived most of his aesthetic views from Schelling. In the year before the essay, he wrote in *Blackwood's* that 'metre and rhyme owe their value in poetry to the fact that they are expressions of the poet's will',[27] a very Scottish turn on Schelling's aesthetics. Arthur Thomson, Ferrier's biographer, summarizes these aesthetics as based on 'the free play of the will on the limited, externally determined order of ideas'[28]—in other words, Coleridge's 'fancy'. To Coleridgeans, then, what appears to Ferrier to be an 'insignificant variation', the shift to chapter thirteen following the interpolated letter, actually rescues Coleridge's poetics from being limited to the manipulation of known things, thus opening the possibility of a constitutive theory of the creative imagination. To understand fully the implications of the plagiarism charge, both for Coleridge's philosophical system and posthumous reputation, and for nineteenth-century Scottish philosophy, it is crucial to compare Coleridge and Ferrier—their shared philosophical goals and methodological differences, but first I turn to Ferrier and his Edinburgh philosophical milieu.

Who, then, was James Frederick Ferrier that he felt compelled to defend Schelling in this way? He was much more than simply a sometimes *Blackwood's* contributor. Ferrier was without question one of the most important Scottish philosophers of the nineteenth century. He was also the nephew and son-in-law of John Wilson, the legendary Christopher North, editor and leading contributor of *Blackwood's* and holder of the ornamental chair in Moral Philosophy at the University of Edinburgh. Three things happened in quick succession in 1838 that transformed Ferrier's life and created the immediate context for the Coleridge essay. First, William Blackwell died, leaving his inexperienced son Robert in charge of *Blackwood's*; second, Wilson's wife died, leaving him in a deep depression from which he never recovered; and third, Ferrier married Maggy, Wilson's daughter. The need for an income to support his new family and the utter lack of direction at *Blackwood's* quickly made Ferrier a key contributor and the de facto editor. When he employed the editorial 'we' in the Coleridge essay, he really was speaking as *Blackwood's*. He was uniquely qualified to challenge Coleridge, as he represented not only the voice of Edinburgh intellectual culture, but as the protégé of Sir William Hamilton, the Scottish philosophical tradition. Indeed, Ferrier was the obvious candidate for both Wilson's ornamental chair in Moral Philosophy, and Hamilton's in Metaphysics. In the end, conservative churchmen on the Edinburgh council froze him out of both positions; their decisions were so outrageous that the second marked the end of the tradition of the burghers of the city making the appointments. The snubbing of Ferrier spurred the University to declare intellectual autonomy as a matter of self-defence. I mention this story because it speaks to one of the perennial problems in understanding Ferrier's motives for the Coleridge article. His strong engagement in Scottish intellectual and academic life must be understood in relation to the German philosophy both men were championing in order to gauge the apparent vehemence of his attack.

The lack of an apparent motive for the attack was one of the most upsetting aspects of the affair for the Coleridge family. Hartley wrote to Henry Nelson in July 1840 putting the matter in stark terms and indicating the emotional strain of the charges:

Did you see an article in the January number of Blackwoods 'On the Plagiarisms of S.T.C.?' It not only reiterates the charges of De Quincey (without however any hypocritical pretense of friendship or reluctance) but asserts that the metaphysical portion of the Biographia Literaria is with the exception of a few insignificant interpolations and variations seldom for the better translated verbatim from Schelling and that the partial acknowledgements are calculated if not intended to mislead the reader as to the extent of obligation. It denies that S.T.C. had one idea of the transcendental philosophy which he did [owe?] to the German, and supports his charges with a formidable array of references ... Now there are probably not fifty copies of Schelling in the three kingdoms, not many more individuals who would or could refer to them ... But the question is—is it true or is it not? Even if I possessed the books asserted to have been rifled I doubt whether I should be capable of an efficient reply. Yet something should be done before the Biographia is reprinted. The article was written as I am informed by James Frazer, [*sic*] a son in law of Professor Wilson, whom I formerly knew. As he is neither Liberal nor Dissenter nor ever received advice or admonition from [STC], I can conceive no motive of personal dislike which could induce him to fill nearly a sheet of Maga with matter which to 99 out of 100 of her readers must be fact.[29]

Unlike De Quincey, Ferrier, mistakenly re-named Frazer, could not be dismissed because of any animus towards Coleridge. The result, for Hartley, was emotional distress based on the joint terrors of uncertainty ('is it true?') and inadequacy. The lack of a qualified readership of Schelling's works made the matter worse. One of De Quincey's personal motives for his Coleridge articles was a desire to claim himself as the only qualified reader of Coleridge, and his discovery of the plagiarisms confirmed that fact in his mind. That no one in the interval between De Quincey's and Ferrier's accounts bothered, or felt qualified, to test the charges confirmed Hartley's point. I'll return to the problem of qualified readers below when I take up Ferrier's hypothesis about the disingenuousness of Coleridge's Schelling footnote. The question of motive has persisted. In their Editors' Introduction to the *Collected Coleridge* edition, Bate and Engell refer to 'Ferrier's vindictive, more detailed attack',[30] an odd claim given his total lack of animus. Their use of 'vindictive' probably follows from their reliance on Thomas McFarland's analysis of the plagiarism issue in his influential *Coleridge and the Pantheist Tradition*.[31] They make their reliance clear: 'If the history of the discussion had not been authoritatively presented by Thomas McFarland, it would be appropriate to devote several paragraphs to it here ... '[32] They then simply list the De Quincey, Ferrier, and Hamilton[33] charges without addressing the questions they raise. McFarland's account of Coleridge's habits of composition, profound synthesis of the German materials, etc. remains influential for good reason—intellectual rigor and psychological subtlety. However, when it comes to Ferrier's motives, he concocts a Scottish philosophical conspiracy against Coleridge in particular and English philosophy in general that in the end makes no sense, and contributes to the tradition of misreading Ferrier's intent. That is not to say that it isn't true that the Scots had long held the state of learning at the Oxbridge Colleges in contempt. Adam Smith's assessment from *The Wealth of Nations* is typical of the Scottish view of the English Colleges as moribund and backward institutions, 'sanctuaries in which exploded systems and obsolete prejudices found shelter and protection after they had been hunted out of every other corner of the world'.[34] That said, McFarland's assertion that this prejudice signified a unitary Scottish philosophical view represents a serious over-simplification. In claiming that William Hamilton's subsequent attack on Coleridge for plagiarizing

Maas[35] was a simple continuation of Ferrier's efforts to 'claim German abstract thought'[36] for the Scottish tradition, and that these attacks were somehow related to Carlyle's efforts to assume Coleridge's mantle as the pre-eminent Kantian in Britain, McFarland distorts mid-century Scottish philosophy. Leaving aside the fact that nationalism didn't actually work that way, Carlyle the Scotsman was a London intellectual and De Quincey the Englishman was an Edinburgh intellectual, and neither were philosophers, the proposition that the Scots simply embraced German Idealism does not bear scrutiny. The relationship between Ferrier and Hamilton, his mentor, had cooled over Ferrier's interest in Schelling and the philosophy of consciousness. Hamilton saw the subject as a threat to the tradition of 'Common Sense' derived from Thomas Reid and his inheritors, himself foremost among them. When the reactionary burghers of Edinburgh blocked his election to Hamilton's University chair, for which he was clearly the most qualified candidate, they asserted that Ferrier's Idealist views were treacherous to the memory of his teacher and a danger to Scottish moral life; so much for a Scottish philosophical conspiracy as motive. To finally get at Ferrier's motives, it is thus essential to compare the development of his philosophical principles with Coleridge's parallel development.

Coleridge famously set himself the task of justifying his religious belief 'on a rational basis', a process that led to his unique appropriation of German Idealism and which occupied him until his death (he dictated clarifications to Green in his final days). The process began with the annexation of Kant's theory of mind in the service of his religious goals. The a priori Ideas of the Kantian Reason, immutable, from God, offered Coleridge a solid intellectual foundation on which to build his argument, despite the fact that, as the editors of the Norton Critical Edition succinctly state: 'there is a crucial difference between their conceptions of reason; for Kant reason *cannot* yield insight into metaphysical issues such as the existence of God, because it only regulates experiences; for C[oleridge] it *must* do, because it originates in God'.[37] His theistic imposition on Kantian structures could only hold if Schelling and others could be adapted into a theory of self-consciousness that established it as the seat of all knowledge *and* implicitly tied to total consciousness—God. Coleridge thus further developed his Kantian model by associating the 'fancy' with the cognitive processes of the Understanding, and positing the 'imagination' as radically creative, prior to cognition, autonomous and pointing towards the Reason. Religious scruple insisted on the further distinction of the primary and secondary imaginations, distinct 'in degree', 'not kind', preserving their divine origin while guarding against religious blasphemy and philosophical absurdity. The primacy of the mind and mental processes in Coleridge's philosophy ensured a place for religious belief within rational enquiry, or as he formulated it in *The Friend*: 'We name God the supreme Reason; ... Whatever is conscious *Self*-knowledge is Reason'.[38] Thus when the Preface to *Aids to Reflection* exhorted readers: 'If you are not a *thinking* man, to what purpose are you a man at all? ... or to what end was man alone, of all animals, indued by the Creator with the faculty of *self-consciousness*',[39] the passage called not only for thoughtfulness but for the recognition of the divine implicit in self-consciousness. Apperception, the mind conceiving of itself conceiving, for Coleridge the recognition of the primacy of the Reason coloured by his theistic interpolation, and with it the existence of God, became essential to this rationalized faith. Chapter twelve of *Biographia*, the systematic subsuming of objective knowledge into subjective knowledge via Schelling's incomplete deduction of the Imagination, served this philosophical goal. If the creative Imagination could be posited as the central mental faculty, apperception would gain ultimate significance as the foundation and means by which we perceive the divine.

This project, often characterized as eccentric, nonetheless bears strong resemblances to controversies in Scottish philosophy provoked by Ferrier, especially in the years immediately prior to and following Coleridge's death. Ferrier's attack on Coleridge's plagiarism of Schelling's deduction in *Blackwood's* in 1840 can be read as an expression of that Scottish controversy. This reading helps address the vexing question of Ferrier's motives for his attack. The question of establishing Ferrier's motives, as I've noted, began with the family's bewilderment; they were at a complete loss. Since then, distracted by the desire to defend Coleridge, critics have spent insufficient time investigating Ferrier's philosophical project, and how the Coleridge article plays a role in it. Coleridgeans have denied the charge (beginning with Julius Hare at the family's behest), contextualized it (De Quincey's description of it as a 'psychological curiosity'), made it evidence of Coleridge's unique approach to the universality of ideas, or blamed it on poor memory (a strategy first suggested by Hartley to Henry Nelson Coleridge in a letter, repeated by Hare and then Sara Coleridge, rehearsed by McFarland, left unquestioned by Bate and Engel), but we have not really examined the specific philosophical context of Ferrier's attack. The Scots had finessed the problem of 'belief' for generations through the dominance of the 'Scottish Common Sense School'. In brief, they retained the rigour of Humean method but avoided its most extreme, and to their minds, dangerous, sceptical tendencies. They held that questions that were apparent to the 'common sense' of ordinary people (the independent existence of physical objects, for example) did not need to be deduced, and further argued that questions of 'belief' could be exempted from rational method on the same grounds—self-evident 'common sense'. 'Belief' could be grouped with the other mental objects that we simply assume. Hamilton's student Ferrier shattered this consensus when he stated the obvious: a belief/knowledge distinction was arbitrary and there was no justifiable reason to exempt questions of belief from methodological rigor. Ferrier then spent his career paralleling Coleridge in employing Schelling, developing a theory of apperception, et cetera. in attempting to rescue 'belief' from philosophical absurdity. Ferrier's philosophy engaged his Enlightenment predecessors, and he and Coleridge worked towards similar goals. Reconsideration of Ferrier's famous attack on Coleridge's plagiarisms of Schelling from the perspective of those shared goals reveals his philosophical motives in their real complexity, and opens up a related issue of Ferrier's readings of Coleridge's motives.

Beginning in January 1838, Ferrier began publishing an article in *Blackwood's* called 'An Introduction to the Philosophy of Consciousness', which ran to seven installments ending in 1839. In this article, which Thomson polemically calls 'the most important philosophical article ever published in a British journal',[40] Ferrier began a sustained critique of the status quo in Scottish philosophy. In the first part of his treatise, Ferrier summarized the 'Common Sense' response to Hume, and its limitations:

At the time of Hume three facts were admitted in the prevailing doctrine of perception, and understood to stand exactly upon the same level with regard to their certainty. First, the object *i.e.* the external world perceived. Second, the image, impression, representation, or whatever else it may be called, of this. Third, the subject *i.e.* the mind of the man perceiving. Hume embraced the second of these as a fact immediately given; but displaced the other two as mediate and hypothetical. Reid, on the other hand, rejected the second as mediate and hypothetical, and maintained the first and third to be facts immediately given. So that between the two philosophers the whole three were at once admitted as facts, and rejected as hypotheses. Which is right and which is wrong cannot be decided here. Probably Hume is not so much in the wrong, nor Reid so much in the right, as they are generally imagined to be; for it is certain that common sense repudiates the conclusion of the latter, just as much as it does that of the former.[41]

In other words, claims of 'common sense' for the existence of the objects of the external world and the consciousness of the subject were ultimately arbitrary: 'Common sense, therefore, is not more enlisted on the side of Reid, than on the side of Hume; and the truth is, the question remains as much open to question as ever'.[42] Ferrier's 'An Introduction to the Philosophy of Consciousness' thus attempted a necessary (to his mind) intervention into a false consensus, and he enlisted German Idealism, especially Schelling, in pursuit of what he termed *the question*.

His mentor Hamilton answered back in 1838 with an article attacking idealism, denying that 'Berkeley's kind of idealism was compatible with common sense'.[43] Hamilton was still the major figure in the 'Scottish School of Common Sense', so the article must be read as a direct challenge to Ferrier's approach. In 1842, in a five-part *Blackwood's* article, Ferrier answered back in turn with 'Berkeley and Idealism', a complex theory of perception that forcefully argued that: 'what lies beyond the limits of knowledge, also lies beyond the limits of belief. The only possible objects of knowledge and belief are the objects that are immediately present to us in sense and the minds that perceive them'.[44] In deference to Hamilton, Ferrier used the 1842 essay by Samuel Bailey attacking Berkeley's 'Theory of Vision'[45] as the occasion for his critique of persistent mistakes in the reception of Berkeley, and his rehabilitation of Berkeley's idealist conception of objects. Ferrier's emphasis on the relationship of sensual objects and perceiving subjects is of such importance that in the formal working out of his philosophy in 1854, he posited as the founding proposition, the only one not requiring logical demonstration, that: 'Along with whatever any intelligence knows, it must, as the ground or condition of its knowledge, have some cognizance of *itself*'.[46]

'The Plagiarisms of S. T. Coleridge' appeared precisely in the middle of this debate, and must be considered in this context. Schelling played an important role in the development of Ferrier's idealist position, and he was hard at work integrating German idealist philosophy into an ongoing Scottish philosophical debate. He, like De Quincey, and Coleridge before him, and Sara Coleridge after him, had a proprietary interest in Schelling, and mastery, although for different reasons, was as important to him as it was for them. His irritation with Coleridge's misappropriations is understandable if you consider that Ferrier would have viewed the *Biographia* as an inaccurate obfuscation of crucial philosophical ideas. Ferrier's emphasis on 'self-consciousness' as the crucial ground both of knowledge and human freedom, led him to judge most harshly Coleridge's apparently deliberate effort to mislead the reader.

Seen through the lens of Ferrier's philosophical assumptions, Coleridge's preemptive assertion of a 'genial coincidence' reads, psychologically, like a confession—a desperate attempt to retain a vestige of freedom through self-conscious deliberation on the inevitable discovery of his offence. While this lens doesn't provide an answer for the puzzle of why Coleridge appropriated Schelling and then disclaimed it in almost the same moment, it opens up a possible reading of Coleridge's defence as an abyssal moment of self-recognition, which I'll return to.

However, there is one aspect of Ferrier's critique that was somewhat disingenuous. His use of the phrase 'verbatim translation' to describe Coleridge's 'borrowings' gave the impression (despite his thorough footnotes) that the incomplete deduction was simply lifted directly from *The System of Transcendental Idealism* as a single piece. This, of course, is not the case. While every word is Schelling's, and we need to simply admit the substance of the plagiarism charge, they were taken from a wide variety of Schelling's works, and the arrangement of the various parts was entirely Coleridge's. For example, the centrality of self-consciousness, the 'I Am', the assumption that begins 'Thesis VI', has its source in Schelling's *Vom Ich*, but equally in Fichte's *Grundlage*, a work central to both Coleridge's and Schelling's thought.[47] Furthermore, when Coleridge makes his theological turn at the end of the 'Scholium', 'sum quia in deo sum' (I am because God is) he is following Schelling with the important difference that it is a position Schelling discarded as philosophically untenable, or as Bate and Engel summarize: 'Schelling states that theoretical philosophy cannot, given its own criteria, successfully assert that God is the ground of our *knowledge,* nor can it identify God with the *Ich*; God is an object determined by the *Ich*, an object whose *existence* cannot be proved ontologically'.[48] Overall the ten theses draw primarily from Schelling's *System des transscendentalen Idealismus*[49] interspersed with pieces from Kant and Fichte *and* Coleridge for the first five theses, then rely on the *Vom Ich* for 'Thesis VI'. The next two depend entirely on Schelling's *Abhandlungen zur Erläuterung des Idealismus,*[50] the clearest case of 'verbatim translation'. The recapitulations and extensions of the final two theses again range over all Schelling's works as well as Kant and Fichte. For as Ferrier said, the theory of the imagination existed, if at all, as 'shadowy intimations'. Coleridge could not rely on Schelling to create the deduction, and, despite Ferrier's conviction, it makes more sense to see Coleridge as self-consciously aware that that was the case. Indeed, he clearly understood that for his ultimate goal of subsuming 'theoretical philosophy' as the intellectual foundation for his religious faith, Schelling offered no 'swim bladders' at all. If we

read the chapter as a performance of some hybrid genre, improvisational plagiarism perhaps, then we get a more accurate, or at least more
interesting, picture of Coleridge's reliance on Schelling's 'swim bladders'. Coleridge reassembled Schelling, an activity of the 'fancy', that
he might at least posit the imagination. In turn that manoeuvre might
allow him to connect his belief in God as pure consciousness to the
'theoretical philosophy' that otherwise excluded it. This reading may
account for Ferrier's utter indifference to Colerige's theory of the imagination from chapter thirteen. Not derived directly from Schelling, it did
not merit his attention because of its complete lack of methodological
rigour. If the incomplete deduction served as a long improvisation from
given elements, then the 'letter from a friend', and the brief discussion
of Wordsworth's reliance on the 'fancy' continued a rhetorical performance culminating in positing the existence of the 'primary imagination' sited in a quasi-Kantian Reason, and the 'secondary imagination'
made present to the mind via self-consciousness—in short, the ultimate
philosophical and religious goals of both philosophers. That Coleridge
staged his discovery as a grand rhetorical performance disqualified it in
Ferrier's mind, and thus with *The Institutes of Metaphysic* he attempted
a rigorous logical deduction of the imagination based on first assuming
apperception, the necessary assumption he shared with Coleridge, and
in the end their only methodological point of contact.

This returns us to the damning footnote and Ferrier's astute reading that:
'should they [the plagiarisms] *not*, be detected, Schelling's passages remain
Coleridge's, and if they *are* detected the latter calculates upon getting out
of the scrape by pleading that he had, in a manner, admitted them'.[51] This
is a perceptive reading and suggests a psychological insight that contributed greatly to the morally overwrought tone of Norman Fruman's assertion of Coleridge's bad faith in *Coleridge: The Damaged Archangel*. As part
of my effort to dismantle this moral frame that has, in my view, inhibited
discussion of the case, I want to offer a different psychological reading
of the footnote, one in which I hope a familiar Coleridge emerges. The
footnote should not be read as an imposture and evasion, but as a confession. The qualification at the end of the footnote puts the onus on future
readers to adjudicate the matters of attribution, originality, and precedence. Coleridge recognized these questions inevitably 'will be discovered
by those who are its sole legitimate judges',[52] his future readers.

Asserting that a 'general acknowledgement' of indebtedness is sufficient in such a complex matter can only be laughable in light of chapter
twelve. A systematic rearrangement of Schelling's ideas cannot be an
oversight, so cannot fall into the category of accidental missed references

that the footnote describes. His notebook entries, rather than suggesting a confusion of sources occasioned by an eccentric method, suggest a systematic working out of philosophical ideas from various sources immediately at hand. That the end result is Coleridge does not remove the fact that the parts are plagiarized in the published account. One reason to read the footnote as a confession is *because* of its call to leave judgement of the matter for future readers. In the complete note, he provides the offence, the subject matter, and the author. Ferrier's hypothesis that Coleridge successfully usurped authorship because of the continued absence of qualified readers contains a glaring fallacy—himself. He was a qualified reader. Rather than hoping that widespread understanding of Schelling's ideas would never occur, Coleridge recognized the absolute historical inevitability of such readers, and designated them as the 'legitimate judges' of the question. This chapter continues that historical process. Remember that De Quincey considered himself to be the only qualified reader of Coleridge, and sought to support his view by first bringing the plagiarisms to light. Reflecting on his own motives for the exposure when he published a collection of his works in 1854, De Quincey addressed the inevitability of other qualified readers directly:

> Well I knew that, from the direction in which English philosophic studies were now traveling, sooner or later these appropriations of Coleridge must be detected; and I felt that it would break the force of discovery, as an unmitigated sort of police detection, if first of all it had been announced by one who, in the same breath, was professing an unshaken faith in Coleridge's philosophic power.[53]

The footnote hastens his exposure by admitting the offence and guiding us to its origin. Psychologically, this reading emphasizes quintessentially Coleridgean subjects—guilt and irreparability. As early as October 1797 in a letter to John Thelwall, Coleridge had lamented his incapacity as he sought to reconcile his rationality and faith: 'I can contemplate nothing but parts, and parts are all little! My mind feels as if it ached to behold something *great*, something *one* and *indivisible*—'.[54] The portrait of his analytical faculty at odds with his spiritual goals strikes a poignant note that resonates throughout his efforts to marshal the 'parts' of German philosophy in an effort to 'behold' 'something *one* and *indivisible*'. The deduction does not—cannot—exist. He creates instead the possibility of a rigorously determined relation between self-consciousness and the pure consciousness of the divine which is at once its substance and source. Alas that relation can only be posited.

This central infirmity, the lack that is always expressed as part of a dam-aged interiority, haunts much of Coleridge's work; the wish that Hartley receive the spiritual solace he cannot achieve structures the logic of 'Frost at Midnight' and seems apposite in this context. Partial amelioration of his condition remains paradoxically possible as the very irreparabil-ity of his incapacity constitutes an endless series of possible moments where his wishes for others leave open the realization of oneness with the divine, even if not for himself. For Coleridge, this abyss is none-theless the space of faith. In a brilliant reading, Peter Larkin works through a similar constituted moment in 'Rime of the Ancient Mariner'. Rereading the Mariner's repetition compulsion in light of postmodern theology, Larkin describes a possible strategy: 'The Mariner's own bur-dened prophecy calls for relief at the horizon of an other-constituted community [the wedding feast], less a corrective norm than as a sup-plementary space within which his words might unravel differently, might find continuation rather than blockage'.[55] Larkin's summary of the problem *as* possibility could be applied to the future function of the footnote in Coleridge's imagining, and to his vain pursuit of the necessary deduction in chapter twelve. Commenting on 'the originary ontological violence functioning like a transcendental condition for the possibility of knowledge' central to the Mariner repetition, Larkin states: 'This [ontological violence as possibility] opens the possibility that the Mariner's act not only provokes an abyss (which at the level of the narrative it certainly does) but that it also encounters a transcendent horizon (which as the sheer desire for relief from narrative repetition it may well do)'.[56] There can be no defence from the charge of plagiarism, and as is the case with his Ancient Mariner, no expiation can complete the deduction, repair the breach, and foreclose the necessity of telling. All Coleridge can do with his footnote/confession is open a horizon in which qualified readers emerge as his 'sole legitimate judges'.

Ferrier confessed to a friend in later years that he regretted two things about the affair: first, that he had not presented the passages in adja-cent columns to put the question beyond all doubt, and, second, and surprisingly, that after all was said and done perhaps Coleridge's offence 'should be attributed to forgetfulness rather than wilful plagiarism'.[57] These two regrets do not add up. 'Wilful plagiarism' was entirely his point. Perhaps he recognized that the tone of his essay constituted bad manners, but more likely, despite remaining convinced of his charges, he was moved by Sara's spirited defence of her father's fragile reputation in her astonishingly rigorous, and many ways still definitive, 1847 edi-tion of *Biographia Literaria*, the subject of the next chapter.

5
Her Father's 'Remains': Editing and Filial Love

In January 1843 Henry Nelson Coleridge finally succumbed to a degenerative nerve disease. He had been paralysed and bedridden from May 1842 to the end.[1] His premature death had forced the roles of editor and literary executor onto Sara. She went through the motions of deferring to the other executors and the men in the immediate family circle by offering the job of rebutting Ferrier in an Afterword for the new edition of *Biographia Literaria* to Green, and speculating with Hartley about whether he might take up the task of writing a biographical sketch of their father, something for which they had felt the need since De Quincey's essays. Posthumous hagiographies, first Heraud's, and more recently Gillman's biography, had proven embarrassing, at least for Sara, and she longed to set a comprehensive portrait of her father before the public, that he might escape the caricatures of the partisans as much as the perceived enemies. Her view of Gillman's account, although she was careful to appear enthusiastic in public, was withering: 'A surer way to blur the bright face of his newly bought fame and credit through my father's name [Gillman] could hardly have hit upon than to bring out this absurd hodge podge of stale and vapid ingredients, just to shew how long an unwise man may live with a wise one without catching any of his wisdom'.[2]

Green at first responded enthusiastically to the idea of providing the necessary expertise in German philosophy to put the question of intellectual debt to rest once and for all. He had after all served as Coleridge's amanuensis and companion as he developed these ideas into the unfinished *Opus Maximum*.[3] Sara, however, did not wait for Green's contribution. As she worked her way through the daunting German material her confidence grew and she began her Introduction by addressing the plagiarism charges directly. At that point Green's proposed Appendix became redundant and he bowed out of the process early in the new year, saving face by noting:

> I lose no time in writing this line to say that I am quite of the opinion that no time should be lost in putting forth the new edition of Biographia. I feel what you say with respect to the share, which we proposed that I should take, and I fear that in carrying out the plan, the account of S.T.C.'s philosophy, which it was intended to give, would be either meagre and obscure, or would be far too long and cumbersome for an appendix. There might not be the same objection perhaps to a brief comparison with Schelling's philosophy. I will try my hand at it at all events as far as my time and ability permit, and should it be valueless or not ready at the period of publication—why, it need cause no delay in bringing out the new edition.[4]

Green was ill equipped for the task, despite his general familiarity with the German philosophers involved. There is no evidence that he had the intellectual scope to evaluate the key questions of attribution or obligation. Sara alone had the intellectual gifts and determination necessary to undertake such a project. As she put it to Hartley in a letter absolving him of any responsibility for the new edition: '—it would have been a pity for you to set aside your own original compositions, & taken against the grain—to the study of Kant & Fichte & Schelling & Maasz, just for the sake of editing my father's B.L. There is no more thankless labour than that of an editor. I do not want <u>thanks</u> for my little labours—because I like these literary examinations for their own sake. Still I am glad that my task is drawing to a close'.[5] Sara acknowledged her achievement despite referring to it as her 'little labours'. Hartley knew better, and she set his mind at ease in the matter by assuring him that she gained much from her 'literary examinations for their own sake'—a claim that is powerfully confirmed by the edition itself and her emergence in it as an important intellectual voice.

Hartley was in no position emotionally or psychologically to comply with her request for a biographical sketch of their father, let alone to take on editing *Biographia Literaria*. The sense of paralysis he felt upon reading Ferrier had remained, and he was no nearer to making himself a 'qualified reader'. So, on the surface it appears as if Sara inherited the position. However, in truth, her role in the production of the posthumous works had been extensive from the outset. Even the seemingly modest role of dutiful wife helping to copyedit Henry's four-volume *Literary Remains* shows her to be a rigorous editor, unafraid to query decisions or challenge word choices in introductory material. Mudge makes the case unequivocally for the centrality of Sara to the project: 'Although instrumental in the planning and publication of both works [*Literary Remains* and *Table Talk*], Sara received no public acknowledgement: both were officially edited by Henry, and he felt no compunction about neglecting to mention his wife's labors, either on the title page or in the preface, where he graciously thanks a number of friends'.[6] Her correspondence with Henry reveals a complex partnership, which he acknowledged in private, as Mudge makes clear by citing a representative letter from Henry from the period: 'All your remarks & alterations on my poor proofs are just—do what you like with them, & I am thankful. You are much superior to me in fineness of feeling & discrimination, I willingly acknowledge'.[7] These were not the publishers' proofs in want of superficial corrections, but rather Henry's disorganized transcriptions of Coleridge's notes. It seems clear that Sara provided much of the shape for what became four published volumes. Mudge's assertion about her role in *Table Talk*, however, is somewhat overstated; Henry was working from his own brief notes and the final text was roughly chronological.[8] A typical set of interventions can be seen in her letters to Henry about a more complex project, the new edition of *The Friend*. The philosophical complexities of the work meant that she had to be especially vigilant in proofing Henry's copy:

> My dear this proof [of *The Friend*] puzzles me. There is a sentence which is unintelligible to me as it now stands: do you still possess or can you refer to the MS. from which Harding [the printer?] transcribed! Not knowing your mind I think it the safer side to write today with my queries—and if my suppositions are right, in the smaller instances and you can propose no alternative of the sentence I am about to transcribe you need not answer before your usual time. Also mention the <u>name and address</u> of the printer. 'However this may be, the understanding or regulative faculty is manifestly distinct from life and sensation; its function being to take up the passive affections into distinct <u>thought of the sense</u>, <u>both</u> according to its essential forms.' 'Thought <u>of the sense</u>' I do not clearly understand, but <u>both</u> makes nonsense. If I do not hear from you I shall alter <u>both</u> into <u>but</u>, and leave the rest as it is.[9]

She finishes the letter by saying that she will correct some other obvious punctuation errors that damage the logic of Coleridge's arguments. Given carte blanche to do as she wishes with any copy Henry produces, she is not averse to plain speech, in this case leaving Henry the uncomfortable alternatives that he has passed on a transcription error, made a transcription error, or does not sufficiently follow the argument to know the difference.

Through these labours, as her tone attests, Sara grew more confident in her understanding of her father's views. In truth she was the best suited of the family for the task of editing the works and always had been; she and Henry seem to have reached this conclusion in private and the division of labour increasingly reflected this conclusion. Wifely deference made Henry the nominal editor, but the impetus was often from her, and as she gained confidence she took on the new edition of *Aids to Reflection*, significant because as Pickering was at pains to remind them, it and the poems, were the only volumes to make a profit. *Aids* acted as a watershed in another way, as it demanded that she become familiar with Kant's aesthetics, a reading project she relished. Sara had made the determination early on that she needed to make a systematic study of her father and his sources. As she wrote to Henry in September 1834 in a letter discussing the formation of public opinion, particularly after a visit from Robert Lovell in which he expounded on the issues of the day: 'I mean to read my father's works regularly through'.[10] Her motivation was complex. She wanted to understand her father's views so that they might be better expounded, convinced of their potential efficacy in contemporary intellectual and social debates. When she received the final version of *Literary Remains* while convalescing in Ilchester,[11] she wrote Henry with her famous assertion about Coleridge's cultural influence:

> They [all her father's works] will be more sold at last than at first; like alum, these metaphysical productions melt slowly into the medium of the public mind; but when time has been given for the operation they impregnate more strongly than a less dense & solid substance, which dissolves sooner, has power to do: why? Because the closely compacted particles are more numerous & have more energy in themselves. By the public mind I here mean of persons capable of entertaining metaphysical discussions. The same cause that makes alum long in melting makes it impregnate more powerfully when it does dissolve.[12]

This brilliant analogy captures both the difficulty of the task of comprehending Coleridge and the transformative potential of making oneself equal to that task. The transformed 'public mind' must, as an article of faith, improve the social sphere. By circumscribing the 'public mind' so that it includes only 'persons capable of entertaining metaphysical discussions', those on whom the alum might work, she also reproduced her father's concept of the clerisy, and imagined this intellectual elite as an actual social possibility. This position and its social aims dictated many of her subsequent editorial decisions, as we will see, and established her view of Coleridge's audience and the corollary goals for future dissemination of the works.

The public deference at the heart of her relationship with Henry was nothing new for Sara. She had had to negotiate her talent through the social constraints of her sex from the outset. When a teenager, she had responded to Robert Southey's interest in South American Indians by translating Martin Dobrizhoffer's book on Paraguay, *Historia de Abiponibus*, from the Latin. The project had been offered to Derwent as a means of offsetting university costs, but he soon lost interest, and Sara, enlisted as his helper, completed the translation. Derwent received much of the credit from Sara, not because of his contribution to the work, but because of his determination to help her with her Latin studies—formal instruction being closed to her by social convention. However, once John Murray published *An Account of the Abiphones, an Equestrian People of Paraguay* in 1822, Sara became a published translator at the age of nineteen.[13] The translation proved especially useful for Southey in preparing his book, *Tale of Paraguay*, and some reviewers believed he was the author of the anonymous translation as well. Sara's prodigious gifts for languages and attention to detail and her sheer diligence made her an ideal translator. Her second translation, *The Right Joyous and Pleasant History of the Facts, Tests, and Prowess of the Chevalier Bayard, the good Knight without Fear and without Reproach*, translated from the Medieval French, appeared in 1825. Despite this success, Southey considered Sara's literary output a useful amusement for her, a harbinger of his notorious advice to Charlotte Brontë: 'literature is not the business of a woman's life'.[14] Her next project, 'Memoirs of Jean de Troye' never really got underway as Southey rebelled against her 'professionalization' and insisted that she conform to type and produce translations purely as diversions for a young unmarried woman. Once she became engaged to Henry, her literary ambitions (if she dared to harbour them) were deemed inappropriate. Her literary career went into abeyance until the births of Herbert and Edith provided the occasion for works to amuse children, culminating with her fairytale, *Phantasmion*, published in 1837. Not until STC died, and Henry took on the role of literary executor, did Sara find herself in a position to once again take up serious intellectual pursuits and more fully develop her talent, once again beginning as the deferential helper as she had with Derwent in her girlhood.

It is difficult to overestimate the impact of *Aids to Reflection* on Sara's intellectual development. It was the key text as she convalesced in Ilchester. Moved by its aphoristic power and solace, she imagined its efficacy in the wider community of 'persons capable of entertaining metaphysical discussions'—the ideal of the clerisy. After all she was an example of its power and potential as it played a key role in healing her, refining her religious sensibility and establishing strong philosophical principles from which to build a comprehensive social vision. It placed her amongst the clerisy, and confirmed, in her own mind, the rightness of this, her father's key social formulation. Demanding reflection above all else, aphorisms served as the slow-acting alum that caused fundamental change in the reader; their power to 'impregnate', as she characterized it to Henry in her letter from Ilchester, offered fundamental individual change—real moral improvement as opposed to a change in superficial opinion. Coming before her at a moment of psychological and physical crisis (depression, probably opium delirium and withdrawal), *Aids to Reflection* provided stability through its rigorous demands on her attention—again the foundational model for meaningful social change in Coleridge's late thought.

In its composition history *Aids to Reflection* is an unusual work, even by Coleridgean standards. Born of a period of profound despair in the spring of 1814 when Coleridge was forced to confront his opium addiction by his Bristol friends, the depth of his addiction and despair was expressed in a series of excruciating letters to Joseph Cottle during April of that year. Coleridge was finally compelled to come clean with his old friend and detail the 'state of [his] bodily & mental sufferings' at the hands of his opium addiction, then at its height. He had borrowed money from Cottle on false pretences and used the money to procure the drug. Cottle responded with equal parts anger and concern couched in religious language, and counselled prayer. Coleridge succinctly described his condition: 'the anguish of my spirit has been indescribable, the sense of my danger *staring*, but the conscience of my GUILT worse, far far worse than all!'[15] The relationship of bodily and mental suffering is emphasized, and the intractable problem of determining which is the source shown to be the site of self-loathing and indescribable guilt. Cottle's exhortations to prayer as the surest means to escape the vicious cycle of addiction—physical pain, relief, dependence, guilt, abstinence, physical pain—were met with a terrifying letter declaring Coleridge's personal spiritual doubt, and profound sense of unworthiness:

> Oh dear Friend!—I have too much to be forgiven to feel any difficulty in forgiving the cruelest enemy that ever trampled on me: & *you* I have only to *thank*.—You have no conception of the dreadful Hell of my mind & conscience & body. You bid me, pray. O I do pray inwardly to be able to *pray*; but indeed to pray, to pray with the faith to which Blessing is promised, this is the reward of Faith, this the Gift of God to the Elect. O if to feel how infinitely worthless I am, how poor a wretch, with just free will enough to be deserving of wrath, & of my own contempt, & of none to merit a moment's peace, can make a part of a Christian creed; so far I am a Christian—[16]

It would be a mistake to read this as simple self-pity. Conscience and will are the only means to the rational faith crucial to Coleridge's philosophical system. To be unable to pray, or to be in a potentially permanent remove from direct prayer (praying to pray), opens an abyss, the 'infinitely worthless', from which there can be no sublime recuperation—moral terror without end.[17]

This is the immediate context in which Coleridge discovered the work of Robert Leighton. Writing the day following the devastating letter above, Coleridge asked Cottle if he was familiar with Leighton's writing, and deployed the author's ideas to further expound on his crisis of prayer, and the rational necessity of belief which offered comfort despite his feelings of incapacity and unworthiness:

> Christians expect no outward or sensible Miracles from Prayer—its effects and fruitions are spiritual, and accompanied (to use the words of that true *Divine*, Archbishop Leighton) 'not by Reasons and Arguments; but by an inexpressible Kind of Evidence, which they only know who have it.'—To this I would add that even those who (like me, I *fear*) have not attained it may yet *presume* it—1. because Reason itself, or rather mere human Nature in any dispassionate moment, feels the *necessity* of Religion; 2. but if this not be true, there is no Religion, no *Religation* or Binding over again, nothing added to Reason—& therefore Socinianism is not only not Christianity, it is not even *Religion*—it doth not *religate*, doth not bind anew—[18]

Coleridge's assertion that 'Reason ... feels the *necessity* of Religion' rescued him from total reliance on religious feeling, the lack of which produced his current suffering, while also correcting Cottle's reductive Socinian rationalism. Mystery is essential to faith, and given that reasoning our way to religious knowledge remains, by definition, impossible, not to say absurd, the truly religious must give themselves over to their faith, allow themselves to be 'religated', in Coleridge's brilliant etymological formulation, or they risk rationalizing Religion out of existence and cutting themselves off from their own spiritual existence. The letter also established what would become the compositional method and logic of *Aids to Reflection*. The fragment from Leighton functions as an aphorism connecting Faith and Reason, seeing in the latter 'an inexpressible Kind of Evidence, which they only know who have it'. Faith and prayer become rational responses to lived spiritual experience. This aphoristic nugget becomes the aid to reflection that enables, and legitimizes, Coleridge's corollary that 'Reason ... feels the *necessity* of Religion', which in itself becomes the occasion of further reflection. Meditation on Leighton produced religious solace via reason in a moment where solace appeared unavailable. The act of meditating on a text produced a complex religious commentary, produced new aphorisms to occasion future mediation, and so on. Furthermore, the letter also had a didactic purpose—something crucial to *Aids to Reflection*—in its engagement with Coleridge's old friend Cottle's Socinian beliefs. The long letter that followed challenged Cottle and justified Coleridge's interest in the Trinity as necessary to the creation of religious feeling. In such meditations, Coleridge located the potential ground for realizing his goal of justifying his faith on a rational basis, in this instance via his Kantian reflection on Leighton's aphorisms. Beginning from Leighton's postulate that the Trinity is 'a doctrine of faith, not demonstration', Coleridge attempted to demonstrate that the doctrine of the Holy Spirit could nonetheless be made consistent with rational discourse on the philosophy of mind. Arguing for the 'subordinate nature of mere *matter*', Coleridge deduced that that 'which gives direction to the organic parts of nature, is wholly *mind*'.[19] Once consciousness is accepted as the basis for all knowledge, the hypothesis that all mind is part of a single regulating mind, at once the gift of and presence of God, then the Doctrine of the Holy Spirit becomes a legitimate means to understanding the unifying activity of divine consciousness. Once demystified, the Holy Spirit becomes the name for the agency of self-consciousness as it seeks that which it can never achieve—unity of mind. Furthermore, this feeling of 'the *necessity* of Religion', as he described the experience in the previous letter, must itself be rational despite the impossibility of it reaching a conclusion. Coleridge rationalized the processes of faith. The only danger that remained was a charge of heresy given the obvious conclusion of this piece of reasoning: 'To suppose that ONE Independent Power, or Governing mind, exists in the whole universe, is absolute Polytheism'. The deduction was inevitable: 'if there be but ONE directing MIND, that Mind is GOD!',[20] so accordingly Coleridge Christianized his account by asserting Scriptural authority for the whole of his argument. The letter, then, demonstrated a crucial piece of reasoning in Coleridge's developing philosophical and theological positions—the emphasis on self-consciousness and rational determination in establishing the foundation of faith, the key hypothesis that he deployed Schelling, Fichte, Kant, et al. to elaborate in *Biographia Literaria*. In this early iteration, he attempted to provide intellectual respectability for the Doctrine of the Holy Spirit as 'ONE directing MIND', while creating spiritual solace for himself as he struggled to imagine his relation to this vast intellectual force in the midst of a profound crisis of doubt, symptomatically expressed as an inability to pray.

That Leighton fell into Coleridge's hands amidst the chaos of April 1814 was an astonishing gift. Reaching the bottom of perhaps the worst period of opium addiction of his life, Coleridge's erratic behaviour sorely strained his oldest Bristol friendships with Cottle and Josiah Wade, and made him a moral reprobate in the eyes of the Southey and Wordsworth circles. Out of money, unable to borrow further funds from Cottle, delivering lectures to earn a meagre living, terrified of going mad should he go into withdrawal, Coleridge felt an incredible sense of debt to the calm certainty and beauty of Leighton's prose. His annotations of the copy of *The Expository Works and Other Remains of Archbishop Leighton* lent to him by William Elwyn[21] understandably take the form of affective responses, although some theological analysis begins to emerge. A typical entry, and one apropos the pattern I am tracing, follows one of Leighton's expositions on the agency of the soul:

> [Faith] causes the Soul to find all that is spoken of him in the Word, and his Beauty there represented, to be abundantly true, makes it really taste of his Sweetness, and by that possesses the heart more strongly with his Love, persuading it of the Truth of those Things, not by Reasons, and Arguments; but by an inexpressible Kind of Evidence, that they only know that have it.

Coleridge responded strongly to the sense of appetite and sensual relish in Leighton's language, longed to be possessed, and heard in the phrase

'Kind of Evidence' the possibility of a rational recognition of the power of faith:

> Either this is true or Religion is not *Religion* i.e. *adds* nothing to Human Reason, non religat. Grant it, grant it me O Lord.[22]

The turn on 'grant it' captured the drive to establish a profound link between faith and reason, the first sense of the phrase denoting 'grant' the argument to be so, while the repetition, 'grant to me' (my emphasis), emphasized the crisis from which he needed relief. The pleading 'O Lord' signals emotional intensity, especially given his struggle to find efficacy in prayer during this period. Leighton's aphorisms provided moments of reflection, the possibility of spiritual recognition, and thus their immediacy and power was emotionally sustaining and potentially salvatory.

In 1819 James Gillman acquired the four-volume edition of *The Genuine Works of R. Leighton, D. D. Archbishop of Glasgow.*[23] Coleridge read and annotated the volumes, and thus began the process that would end in *Aids to Reflection*. The book emerged as a didactic work on how one might philosophically and emotionally reconnect to Christian spirituality via reflection on the inspired words of others. Coleridge saw in Leighton's inspired words an echo of the words of the Son and, behind those, of the Father. An annotation in the 1819 edition makes the point clear:

> If even through the words a powerful and perspicuous author—(as in the next to inspired Commentary of Archbishop Leighton,—for whom God be praised!)—I identify myself with the excellent writer, and his thoughts become my thoughts: what must not the blessing be to be thus identified first with the Filial word, and then with the Father in and through Him?[24]

This is an extraordinary version of authorship and influence in which Coleridge created a commentary on the 'next to inspired' words of Leighton, thus creating a potential verbal connection, by backward extension, to the originary source of all such words in the divine. As annotations became commentary became aphorisms of their own, the composition process of *Aids to Reflection* provided Coleridge with the means to escape his pervasive sense of alienation from the divine and allowed him to offer readers the opportunity to reflect on his next to 'next to inspired' commentary. Faith in the efficacy of such a process, attenuated as it was, underwrote Coleridge's goals for disseminating the work, and therefore must be considered in any debate about authorship, originality and/or the legitimate use of ideas. As we will see, these views become necessary to understanding Sara's defence against the plagiarism charges in her Introduction to *Biographia Literaria*.

Leighton's aphorisms, and those of Hooker, Jeremy Taylor, and others as the work evolved, provided occasions for self-reflection and allowed Coleridge to investigate how rationality might move us towards recognition of Christian principles, despite its inability to describe them. The works of Robert Leighton, a seventeenth-century Scottish divine, first provided these occasions for Coleridge, but they received a decidedly Kantian cast as they were re-formed in Coleridge's mind, and regenerated as either commentary or new aphorisms. Leighton had inspired him to propose a new edition of his selected works with an extensive commentary by Coleridge. John Murray encouraged the project in 1820, sending Coleridge another edition of *The Genuine Works*, which he quickly annotated. Murray changed his mind and rescinded the offer the following year, whereupon Taylor and Hessey stepped in as publishers. In the meantime, the project had evolved from an edition of Leighton with notes by Coleridge to an edition of aphorisms by Leighton and Coleridge with extensive commentary by Coleridge to a version dominated by the Coleridge materials and organized around his central arguments about the understanding and the reason (his complex adaptation of Kant) and the need for precise language to enable self-reflection.[25] The Kantian aspects of the work, so crucial to its extraordinary influence, became increasingly central to the project, and the final section of the work, 'On That Which Is Indeed Spiritual Religion',[26] was dominated by Coleridge's Kantian exposition of the possibility of conceiving of faith as a rational process. The detailed reworking of Kant's distinction between understanding and reason (a difference of 'kind' as he continually emphasized) received a religious cast. In a tightly argued sixteen-page section, 'On the Difference In Kind of Reason and the Understanding',[27] he made his Kantian interpretation of Leighton clear by aligning them in their conception of the understanding: 'then it follows of necessity [from the assumption that the generalizing function of the understanding constructs names for the "notices received from the senses"], that the understanding is truly and accurately defined in the words of Leighton and Kant, a faculty judging according to sense'.[28] The understanding was tied to the sensuous body, while the innate reason provided the promise of some supersensible origin from which we might derive our faith. Coleridge closed the section with a long footnote demonstrating the potential of Kantian analysis for Biblical exegesis, implicitly at stake in his conceptions of aphorism and commentary. Establishing the reason as the 'higher gift', distinct from the understanding, he asserted that confusions of faith and unbelief followed from the failure to make this distinction, with the inevitable result that purely sensual 'notices' interfered with our ability to reflect on the potential of the mind itself. He reminded the reader of his fifth introductory aphorism to the volume: 'the noblest object of reflection is the mind itself', and the primacy of mind and reflection were stated as absolute: 'No object, of whatever value our senses may represent it, but becomes foreign to us as soon as it is altogether unconnected with our intellectual, moral, and spiritual life. To be ours, it must be referred to the mind, either as motive, or consequence, or symptom'.[29] Once readers comprehended this crucial distinction, error would recede and the 'lamentable effects and subcauses, *false doctrine, blindness of heart, and contempt of the word*' (his italics)[30] would be overcome. This list of maladies echoed his spiritual condition in 1814 when he first read Leighton, and his philosophical working through thus proved salvatory. He concluded by pivoting off St Paul's phrase, '*they did not like to retain God in their knowledge*' (his italics), as an expression of the blindness inherent in unsystematic thinking. Faith, via Kantian rigour, made possible the recovery of that originary 'light':

> yet because the darkness [those who had lost faith] could not comprehend the light, they refused to bear witness to it and worshipped, instead, the shaping mist, which the light had drawn upward from the ground (that is, from the mere animal nature and instinct), and which that light alone had made visible, that is, by superinducing on the animal instinct the principle of self-consciousness.[31]

The promise was clear—clarify the mind by self-reflection on its structure and nature, and clarify our relation to the 'light'.

It was this promise that arrived for Sara Coleridge at the crucial moment of her physical, psychological, and emotional crisis at Ilchester in October 1836. The crisis, partly induced by a loss of control in her opium use, creates a striking parallel between Sara's discovery of *Aids to Reflection* and her father's of Leighton in April 1814. The efficacy of *Aids to Reflection*, its entire raison d'être, was stunningly affirmed by its effect on Sara. While it is difficult to know the extent of her contribution to the 1839 edition (she was not mentioned in the acknowledgements), there is plenty of evidence to assume that it was significant. The 1831 edition had been a disaster. Coleridge's ill health and Henry's inexperience as an editor combined to create a botched volume. None of Coleridge's revisions or notes were included, the carefully noted attributions of sources differentiating Coleridge from Leighton from Jeremy Taylor, et cetera were omitted and/or obscured, Coleridge's deliberate use of capitalization was lost, and the 'Synoptical Summary' intended as an addition to the 'Introductory Aphorisms' was misplaced and added as an appendix at the last moment.[32] In the absence of a formal acknowledgement of Sara's contribution in the 1839 edition it appears the work was entirely Henry's, yet her involvement was extensive in all the volumes published in this period. Her work on *The Friend*, for example, showed her to be particularly concerned with accuracy and reliance on Coleridge's holographs—the very weaknesses of the 1831 edition. Mudge simply asserts that she was 'preparing a new edition of *Aids to Reflection*' during her ill-fated trip to Ottery St Mary and convalescence in Ilchester, which may be somewhat overstated.[33] Nonetheless, her contribution must be noted as it began her career as a Coleridge editor,[34] and served as a crucial event in her spiritual and intellectual life. It also continued the posthumous process of her coming to know her father through his mind. Their unintentional estrangement could finally be undone via her filial devotion to his ideas, and sympathetic response to his frailties. Another piece of circumstantial evidence of her involvement in the process is Pickering's decision to send her James Marsh's American edition of *Aids to Reflection* with the view of bringing her up to date with American ideas about the work.[35]

The significance of Marsh's edition to American intellectual history can hardly be overstated. *Aids to Reflection* became the ur-text of American Transcendentalism, and his Introduction to the volume introduced Coleridge's religiously skewed Kantian idealism to various American intellectual communities. While the book appealed to Bronson Alcott and Emerson in their individual searches for a philosophically rigorous metaphysics, Marsh himself was hardly a Transcendentalist. He was drawn to Coleridge's critique of Unitarianism, then dominant at Harvard College, and the potential of the distinction between the understanding and the reason for formulating a philosophical position free of Calvinist extremism on the one hand, and the bifurcated identity of Jonathan Edwards's Calvinist faith attached to Lockean empiricism on the other. As president of the University of Vermont, he believed the task of education should be to provide the means for young men to think for themselves. In pursuing this goal, *Aids to Reflection* was the perfect text. The ideas contained in the text were significant in and of themselves, especially the neo-Kantian solution to the crises of dualism inherent in positions of faith, the escape from philosophical absurdity. However, the true significance of the work was not to be found in *what* to think, but rather in *how* to think.[36] Coleridge's method of composition, unusual as it was, accorded with his strong belief in the nature and efficacy of ideas. Disagreements among various intellectual communities about the value, or even meaning, of *Aids to Reflection*, reflected not a fault, but its complete success as a transformative document. In his 'Editor's Introduction' to the *Collected Coleridge* edition, John Beer quotes a speech by John Dewey praising the role of Marsh, demonstrating the trajectory of Coleridgean thought in American letters initiated by *Aids*, but more importantly reflecting on its effect on the formation of the self-conscious individual mind: '[Marsh] wished to use scholarship and philosophy to awaken his fellowmen to a sense of the possibilities that were theirs by right as men, and to quicken them to realize these possibilities in themselves.'[37] The effect was anti-doctrinal in the extreme as it enabled reflection and the capacity for readers to develop their minds 'by right'. For Dewey, the inheritor of Coleridgean idealism, his debt was clear: 'this [*Aids to Reflection*] was our spiritual emancipation in Vermont. Coleridge's ideas of the spirit came to us as a real relief, because we could be both liberal and pious; and this *Aids to Reflection* book, especially Marsh's edition, was my first Bible'.[38] The book's currency was its ability to instill emotional solace, psychological grounding, spiritual comfort, and intellectual self-confidence in an increasingly sceptical age.

These were the gifts Sara Coleridge received at Ilchester. Depressed, emotionally paralysed, apparently helpless in the face of her opium addiction, her father's voice arrived as a crucial intervention. Pickering's gift of Marsh's 'Preliminary Essay' must have redoubled the confidence she gained from the work itself. She could see herself as the next reader to be sustained and rescued by Coleridge's rigorous argument and religious certainty. Just as Coleridge himself had been sustained by reading Leighton in Bristol in the spring of 1814, Sara could recover from her depression, in part via adoption of her father's rigorous method. Marsh summarized this value, and focused on the decisive adaptation of Kant:

> By reflection upon the subjective grounds of knowledge and faith in the human mind itself, and by an analysis of its faculties, he [Coleridge] develops the distinguishing characteristics and necessary relations of the natural and the spiritual in our modes of being and knowing, and the all-important fact, that although the former does not comprehend the latter, yet neither does it preclude its existence.

He proves that 'the scheme of Christianity, though not discoverable by reason, is yet in accordance with it—that link follows link by necessary consequence—that religion passes out of the ken of reason only where the eye of reason has reached its own horizon—and that faith is then but its continuation.' Instead of adopting, like the popular metaphysicians of the day, a system of philosophy at war with religion, and which tends inevitably to undermine our belief in the reality of any thing spiritual in the only proper sense of that word, and then coldly and unambiguously referring us for the support of our faith to the authority of Revelation, he boldly asserts the reality of something distinctively spiritual in man, and the futility of those modes of philosophizing, in which this is not recognized, or which are incompatible with it.[39]

Coleridge's system asserted that the metaphysical status quo amounted to a logical fallacy concerning the presumed separation of the spiritual and the philosophical, and he thus prevented faith from being tossed into the realm of the irrational, and believers from descending into a state of absurd inner contradiction.

The 1839 edition, then, addressed the problems and mistakes of the disastrous 1831 edition. The question of authorship was clarified, as it had been in 1825, with attributions in capitals at the head of each aphorism, the missing sections were restored, Coleridge's corrections and additions were incorporated. The two most important additions were the 'Synoptical Summary', the most concise rendition of the foundational Kantian distinction between reason and understanding, added as an Appendix, and Marsh's 'Preliminary Essay' serving as Introduction. Henry's new 'Advertisement' somewhat risibly introduced Marsh:

The Editor had intended to offer to the reader a few words by way of introduction to some of the leading points of philosophy contained in the volume. But he has been delighted to find the work already done to his hand, in a manner superior to anything he could have hoped to accomplish himself, by an affectionate disciple of Coleridge on the other side of the Atlantic.[40]

'Could have hoped' is an understatement; unfamiliar with Kant in any serious sense, Henry was completely unqualified to provide 'a few' or any words on the philosophical sources of the volume.

Sara's vision of the work, and developing relationship with her father, was cemented with her 1842 edition. Henry remained the nominal editor on the title page, but Sara determined the shape and even purpose of the volume. 'Purpose' is no exaggeration as it was the moral efficacy of *Aids* that distinguished it from other works. Dedicated to social intervention by instructing those intellectually serious and religious members of society, especially the young men at the Oxbridge Colleges, or Marsh's students at the University of Vermont, or the young Emerson, the work set out to create a social vanguard, later termed the 'clerisy', based on the solid moral foundation provided by his Kantian emphasis on self-reflection and the exercise of the moral will. Despite being a glorious anomaly (Coleridge did not imagine women as part of this moral intelligentsia, although neither did he exclude them), Sara became a central figure in her father's project. More complex than filial devotion to a legacy (a preservationist impulse), Sara sought to extend her father's ideas and influence into contemporary religious and philosophical controversies and debates. Just as her father's adaptation of understanding into a necessary trajectory, a faith in the rational basis for faith, Sara took *Aids to Reflection* and projected it into the future as a living work focused not on doctrine but on method. She divided the work into two volumes, the first containing the text, and the second three appendices. 'Appendix A' once again contained the 'Synoptical Summary', but 'Appendix B' was a new essay by Green elaborating the question 'What is Instinct?'[41] Coleridge had argued that instinct was a mode of the understanding lacking reflection, a digression that allowed him to elucidate the understanding/reason distinction by showing how apperception provides the only ground for mediating between them. As an anatomist and demonstrator at Guy's Hospital, the subject fascinated Green, and either Sara or Henry, or both, kindly provided him with a forum to rehearse views he had developed following Coleridge's digression. However, Sara's essay 'On Rationalism' ('Appendix C') dominated the second volume. Over two hundred pages in length, her central argument challenged the foundational thinking of the Oxford Movement. Long an interested reader of Newman, she eagerly extended her father's defence of rationalism as the basis for faith into the charged debates of the day. From a Coleridgean perspective, as articulated in *Aids*, Newman's emphasis on the irrational was a simple blunder—a logical fallacy based on the false inference that because one could not reason one's way to God, rationality could not move one towards God. This was, of course, the central notion attacked by Coleridge, and precisely the source of the text's power to inspire religious intellectuals on both sides of the Atlantic.

Newman and Pusey had both read *Aids* as young men and were impressed by its intellectual rigour, despite having no time for its doctrinal liberties. After all, despite Coleridge asserting his Trinitarian faith, the idea that apperception was a divine gift and represented the mediating power of the Holy Spirit was hardly conventional theology. Necessary for Coleridge in his pursuit of a 'rational basis' for his belief, seductive for young intellectuals seeking to bolster strong religious views, it was, nonetheless, from most perspectives unorthodox if not heretical. The text's real influence was not with the members of the Oxford Movement, but rather with the young Cambridge intellectuals who formed the Cambridge Apostles Club, including Coleridge's erst-while champion against De Quincey, Julius Hare. The most important member of the group, so far as theological significance is concerned, was F. D. Maurice.[42] He, Hare, and John Sterling were the leaders of what became known as 'the Broad Church Movement'. Taking *Aids to Reflection* as their foundational text, they developed a socially lib-eral theology focused on duty to others as the ultimate product of self-reflection. Once the scope and potential of self-consciousness was established, the individual had no alternative but to make such experi-ence available to others, and Christian charity became a central tenet of serious religious thought. Maurice's socialism developed directly out of Coleridge's ideas about the will, self-reflection, and moral action.

Sara corresponded with Maurice, and her essay 'On Rationalism' accorded with his belief in the necessary social role of principled intel-lectuals, and in the role of rationality in determining those principles. They drew very different political conclusions from a shared philosophi-cal method, but those differences did not cancel each other out, nor did they call into question the method that produced them—Coleridge's emphasis on the psychological processes that produced thought and action ensured that his applied Kantianism worked as a generative source. Differences were inevitable, perhaps even irresolvable, in a structure where ultimate knowledge was a religious impossibility, an absurdity, save by belief in the necessary trajectory of human rationality towards such an impossible goal. Tolerance was a function of method, and for Maurice a 'broad church' seemed the only means to avoid hubris and error—a view Sara clearly endorsed. The first section of her essay, 'On Reason and the Ministrative Agency of the Understanding', began with that most Coleridgean of processes, desynonymization. Beginning with the source of the problem, she cited her father in response to Jeremy Taylor's imprecise formulation of 'reason illuminated':[43] 'The making of reason a faculty, instead of a light, and using the term as a mere synonyme of the understanding, and the consequent ignorance of the true nature of ideas, and that none are the objects of faith, are

the grounds of all Jeremy Taylor's important errors'.[44] By limiting ideas
to the sensual understanding, they become wholly human products
and incapable of leading to God and are thus excluded in matters of
faith. Sara addresses this 'error' by meticulously rehearsing the Socinian
Anti-Trinitarian position concerning the essential limitations of all
doctrines as necessarily imperfect expressions of our ideas of the divine.
To assert otherwise is to be guilty of rationalism: 'The grossest form
of it [rationalism] is stated to be that which sets up the natural understanding as the standard and measure of divine truth;—which rejects as
incredible all that is not comprehensible'.[45] Such arch-rationalism was
in reality a parody, and Sara was careful to explain that the Socinians
did not in fact hold such a limited view, one that inevitably led to an
absurdity of non-belief based on denying the existence of anything
they were 'incapable of comprehending'.[46] The Socinians developed a
distinction between 'incomprehensible' and 'unintelligible', conceding
the essential unknowablity of God while holding on to the idea that
this central mystery did not render God unintelligible. Otherwise religion descended into irrationalism and superstition. Sara's objection to
Socinian doctrine, and her father's as his religious thought developed,
was its extension of ultimate incomprehensibility into all questions of
knowledge. She quoted from W. E. Channing in a footnote: 'We do not
pretend to know the *whole* nature and properties of God, but still we can
form some *clear ideas* of him, and can reason from these ideas as justly
as from any other. The truth is that we cannot be said to comprehend
any being whatever, not the simplest plant or animal'.[47] By including
the world of natural phenomena in the question, Socinians limited the
scope of human understanding, and placed all questions on the same
footing as *the* question. For Sara, and Coleridge, this led them into a crisis: 'Socinians are assailed with the fact of the reciprocal action of matter
and spirit, which is a seeming contradiction, because it is an evident
truth that "the law of causality holds only between homogenous things,
that is, things having some common property, and cannot extend from
one world to another"'.[48] Quoting from her father's earlier summary
of the Socinian position from chapter eight of *Biographia Literaria*, Sara
drew on his intellectual authority and demonstrated her mastery of his
theological reasoning. The doctrine of the Trinity violated the foundational structure of reason by absurdly confusing 'matter and spirit',
thus Socinians rejected it as the ground of superstition. By providing a
detailed account of the Socinian position, Sara demonstrated the full
scope of the divide between the incipient scepticism of their underlying logic, and the simplistic assertions of faith at the expense of human

rationality that characterized conventional Trinitarian positions. In short, then, she recreated the divide her father had sought to negotiate beginning with his growing dissatisfaction with Unitarianism at the end of the 1790s and carried forward in earnest in *The Friend* following his return from Malta. The critical commonplace that 'Coleridge converted to Trinitarianism' masks an extremely complex intellectual journey. He did not suddenly profess adherence to Trinitarian doctrine—he held the Athanasian Creed in contempt, he did not suddenly believe in miracles or the Virgin birth—but instead focused on developing intellectual tools for understanding the divinity of Christ. The rigorous method employed in the pursuit of understanding Trinitarian faith on a rational basis gave his writing the intellectual authority so attractive to writers as disparate as Marsh, Emerson, Maurice, Hare, Sterling, Dewey—and Sara. The ultimate purpose of her essay was to vindicate rationalism from the limited pejorative sense of it dominating religious discussions at the time. She took the utmost care to avoid rhetorically diminishing the theological views she critiqued by providing accurate accounts of their most sophisticated exponents, a principle she made clear in a footnote on Gladstone's attack on 'rationalism' in 'Church Principles considered in their Results': '[she chose] an author of note: that the unscriptural view which it [anti-rational rhetoric] seems to set up is that to which a certain theory of Sacraments has conducted a most thoughtful and gifted writer; that I have not encountered a chimæra, or commented on the random sayings of superficial men, who have no character for profundity or logical acumen, nor stand conspicuous in a nation's eye among the teachers of their school'.[49] In other words, in order to have a real effect in a debate of such importance, she had to as rigorously as possible represent those views she opposed. Such rigour allowed her to use her father's ideas to intervene in the debate, and more importantly for her, perhaps, to imagine her father's intervention. Sara's detailed understanding of the theological debates from the Unitarian controversies of the 1790s to the Oxford Movement provided her with the means to know her father for the first time in her life. She had spent almost none of her life in the same house with him, and working through his ideas and their sources allowed her to recreate his complex mind, not as a set of principles, but as a fluid, evolving consciousness—fallible, shifting, vulnerable, brilliant. The most ambitious and necessary piece of this complex mind for her edition of *Aids to Reflection* and her essay 'On Rationalism' was its masterly transformation of Kant's philosophy. Her own mastery of the source material became clear over the course of her essay. In arguing that when we see a rose, it does not become a rose until our minds deploy our understanding to establish its 'definite form', as opposed to its remaining a simple sensation, Sara presented Kant as the main authority in her analysis. Her footnote instructed the reader to: 'See Kant's *Kritik der reinen Vernunft*, pp. 59–60–61'. In support she gave the relevant passage in 'Free Translation',[50] and concluded with a concise summary:

> According to Kant the form of the intuition belongs to sense, inasmuch as every object we behold is contained in space and time, which he considers merely subjective, though real, mere modes of the passive and receptive mind, with which all that we passively receive is invested. But that objects present themselves to us in any definite form, as wholes, having each its own unity, depends upon the understanding and the imagination, that is the transcendental imagination, not that which reproduces past experience, compounds new things out of old, and thus dreams awake; but that which orders and shapes it, supplying form to the materials of sensation, and thus furnishing the original imagery of the mind.[51]

In providing the Kantian basis for her father's famous distinction between imagination and fancy, Sara announced herself ready to take on her most extreme act of filial love: producing a scholarly edition of *Biographia Literaria* in light of Ferrier's plagiarism charges.

6
Biographia Literaria, Sara Coleridge, and Self-Creation

Ferrier's charges demanded a serious philosophical response. In 1843 Sara threw herself into a systematic study of Schelling, and her subsequent defence in the Introduction to her edition of *Biographia Literaria* takes on Ferrier on all points. She could not afford to repeat Hare's mistake and show herself unprepared or misinformed; she had to know as much about post-Kantian German philosophy as Ferrier. The strong Kantian foundation of preparing her edition of *Aids to Reflection*, and synthesizing Kant and her father's religious adaptations of Kant for her essay 'On Rationalism', gave her a firm footing and she established her philosophical bona fides from the outset. It is to Sara Coleridge's great credit that she resisted the appeal of Hare's 'shoot the messenger' strategy, and took on the labour that is Schelling's philosophy so that she might adequately answer Ferrier's charges by claiming mastery of the ideas necessary to judge this complex set of philosophic relationship, outside the morass of moral recrimination. That is not to say she did not attack Ferrier personally; she was sharp throughout as she expressed surprise that the author often lapsed into moral judgement despite declaring his intention not to do so. This was a fair criticism as Ferrier said throughout that he did not believe that Coleridge intended to defraud Schelling, yet his essay's rhetoric made this charge implicit as he called Coleridge to the bar, charged him, and found him guilty. Sara offered a brilliant psychological account of the likely effect of such equivocation on the reader. In asserting in the end that he gave Coleridge the benefit of the doubt, Ferrier undermined his supposed good faith by couching his acquittal in a negative formulation: 'That Coleridge was tempted into this course [plagiarizing Schelling] by vanity, by the paltry desire of applause, or any direct intention to defraud others of their due, we do not believe; this never was believed and never will be believed.'[1]

Sara objected that this declaration came too late as Ferrier had used 'language respecting him [Coleridge] which the merest vanity and dishonesty alone could deserve'.[2] His late declaration of his faith in Coleridge's probity merely served as self-protection against charges of bad manners; the damage had already been done, and by restating the charges only to disclaim them he created doubt in the reader's mind.

That Sara's main goal in her Introduction was to challenge Ferrier is evident from its organization. The first subheading is *Mr. Coleridge's obligations to Schelling, and the unfair view of the subject presented in Blackwood's Magazine*,[3] and the first forty pages are dedicated to the task of reviewing the charges and evaluating their import. The other sections, on Coleridge's religious opinions and the 'misconceptions and misrepresentations'[4] of them, and on his sometimes hostile relationship with periodicals were equally extensive, but the stakes for his reputation dictated that the plagiarism charge be addressed first. She begins by creating two distinct lines of argument. First, she will settle the matter once and for all with her new edition: 'Whether or no my Father's obligations to the great German Philosopher *are* virtually unacknowledged to the extent and with the unfairness which the writer of the article [Ferrier] labours to prove, the reader of the present edition will be able to judge for himself; the facts of the case will be before him'.[5] She is certain that the detailed critical apparatus and notes that accompany the philosophical sections of *Biographia Literaria* will allow readers to make their own judgements by clearly identifying *all* of her father's borrowings for the first time. In other words, despite Ferrier's learnedness, the 'facts' will be made available for the first time. Her second line of argument seems, at first, contradictory. She will leave the matter to history, and does not intend to defend her father directly: 'the protest here entered is a duty to his memory from myself rather than a work necessary to his vindication, and the remarks that follow are made less with a view to influence the opinions of others than to record my own'.[6] Rhetorically, this is a clever gambit, considering her father's guilt; he inserted unacknowledged passages from Schelling throughout chapter twelve. But, more importantly, it announces her motive as filial love—a daughter's 'duty'. This is more than rhetoric. Sara's preparation of her edition simultaneously became the means by which she came to know and sympathize with her father. She does not so much as solicit the reader's sympathy as register her own. Furthermore, her statement makes the focus of the Introduction fundamentally psychological as she struggles to understand the mental and physical frailties of her father, investigates Ferrier's motives, speculates about Ferrier's effect on readers, and comes to understand something of herself as she discovers her father.

Given that Coleridge cannot be defended per se, she begins by objecting to the tone of Ferrier's charges. The question of guilt hinges not only on the factual, a lost cause as she well knows, but also on 'intention':

> Now it will be remarked, by way of preliminary, that no man can properly be said to *defraud* another, nor ought to be so spoken of, who has not a fraudulent *intention*: but it never yet has been proved, after all the pains that have been taken to this effect, that Mr. Coleridge *intended* to deprive Schelling of any part of the honour that rightfully belongs to him, or that he has, by Mr. Coleridge's means, been actually deprived of it, even for an hour.[7]

Admitting the offence, while disputing its nature, is the only course open, and Sara exploits it in the only way she can—by creating a psychological portrait of her father's 'habits'. She presents a puzzle requiring hypotheses:

> it is doubtless to be regretted by every friend of the accused, that he should have adopted so important a portion of the words and thoughts of Schelling without himself making those *distinct* and *accurate* references, which he might have known would be required as surely as he succeeded in his attempt to recommend the metaphysical doctrines contained in them to the attention of students in this country.[8]

The utter inevitability of the future discovery of his offence by those students troubles her. My hypothesis, as detailed in chapter 4, reads the inadequate footnote as a confession and invitation to future judgement by 'qualified readers', like those future students, like Sara. Sara operates on a similar premise, yet invests more energy in imagining mitigating circumstances. She also follows De Quincey's line, despite her initial response to his *Tait's* article, by inviting the reader to consider Coleridge's psychological frailties as they consider his genius. The primary reason she gives for his neglecting his scholarly responsibility to identify his sources, for example, is that he was lazy. She couches it in gentler terms: 'the neglect for which he is now so severely arraigned, would have caused him trouble of a kind to him particularly irksome',[9] but her headnote to her text on the relevant pages makes the matter clear enough: '*Mr. C.'s Literary Habits indicative of Bodily Languor and an incautious mind'*.[10] Furthermore, she argues that his method of composition exacerbated this tendency. She points out that he often wrote from his notebooks, and that references were thus not readily available. Ferrier of course could not have known of this, but Sara has the advantage of having the notebook, and so can assert with confidence that: 'the passages from Schelling, which he wove into his work, were not transcribed *for the occasion*, but merely transferred from his note-book into the text'.[11] While the claim that Coleridge couldn't be bothered to reread Schelling in order to identify each passage of the notebook version of the 'Theses' for chapter twelve is unflattering, it nonetheless rings true. Her choice of 'wove' to describe the practice is disingenuous as he simply inserted the passages en masse. Sara is on even less firm ground in her proposed corollaries that: 'some of them, in all likelihood, [were] not even [transcribed] from his note-book immediately, but from recollection of its contents. It is most probable that he mistook some of these translated passages for his own'.[12] That Coleridge could remember verbatim his translated passages from the notebook seems unlikely enough, despite her assertion to the contrary, but that he would then not remember that the notebook entries were Schelling is implausible to say the least.

Sara makes matters worse by inserting a section from Hare's disastrous, and completely discredited by Ferrier, defence in which he claims that he also sometimes forgets what was written by himself and what was translated from Kant. Hare's poor memory, lamentable as it is, is unlike Coleridge's, which was nearly photographic—a point Sara has already made. This is not her only slip in an otherwise compelling account of her father's intellectual habits and modes of composition. She deliberately conflates the issue of Coleridge's attributions to Schelling in chapter nine, the accuracy of which Ferrier challenges, with the complete lack of attribution in chapter twelve—the real issue in the plagiarism charge. She also attempts to vindicate him by arguing that Ferrier's charge is 'perverse' in that it suggests that:

> he [Coleridge] should *gain credit* for the transcendentalism contained in his book, while at the same time no comparison betwixt his writings and those of the original transcendentalist would for years, if ever, be made. It was the fact that for years his obligations to Schelling were not discovered; but it is ridiculous to suppose that he *calculated* on this, with the amount of those obligations distinctly present in his mind, for this could only have happened through the failure of the attempt he was making to interest his countrymen in the transcendental system.[13]

This seems fair enough, but it simply repeats the original puzzle. The historical inevitability of 'qualified readers' meant the 'truth would out', to borrow Ferrier's phrase. The interesting underlying reasoning in this part of Sara's defence has to do with the whole nature of human knowledge and its production. She had previously quoted her father's famous passage on the subject: 'he "regarded Truth as a divine ventriloquist, not caring from whose mouth the sounds are supposed to proceed, if only the words are audible and intelligible"'.[14] In other words, claiming credit for Schelling's ideas was anathema to Coleridge's understanding of how ideas formed. Ferrier made a mistake in assuming that Coleridge's claims that his ideas had been long running in the same channels as Ferrier's were disingenuous—this historical process was fundamental to Coleridge's views and philosophical method. For example, his use of Kant and Schelling to reconfigure the religious idea of the Holy Spirit into the divine agency enabling self-reflection, was intended as an historical advance on the superstitious primitive notions of the subject mindlessly passed on by contemporary doctrine.[15] Sara makes the point by reminding readers that Kant's idealism arose from Berkeley's, and thus knowledge comes into being. Doubtless this was one of the great lessons of editing *Aids to Reflection*. Coleridge did not seek to reproduce the ideas of Robert Leighton, but rather to show how they contained the seeds of powerful ideas that historically must pass via Kant through him and into the public sphere at large, where, as Sara so powerfully demonstrated in her edition, they might influence and spur thinking in others—American transcendentalists, the Broad Church Movement, Sara, perhaps even Ferrier. In short, he disclaimed the whole idea of intellectual property as naïve egotism. The difference, of course, between the use of the ideas of many thinkers in relation to one another as demonstrated in *Aids to Reflection* and *Biographia Literaria* is that in the former the source of the ideas is scrupulously noted. Sara undermined this line of reasoning by arguing that Coleridge could not have '*enjoyed the credit*' of Schelling's ideas because German philosophy was so unpopular when he was writing that he 'had no enjoyment and no credit'.[16] While it is true that it was a critical commonplace that Coleridge was harmed by his interest in German philosophy, both publicly and creatively, and that this attitude persists, she undermined her historical view by reducing his influence to the time of his original composition. Her essay 'On Rationalism' projected Coleridge's ideas into future religious and philosophical controversies, and the logic of her defence demands that her father saw such a projection as both apt and inevitable. This posthumous deployment of her father's religious views, in particular, returns to the fore in her subsequent section on his religious opinions.

In describing her father's unique gifts and complex method of synthesizing ideas, Sara began a detailed cognitive account of his literary activity in general, and the composition of *Biographia Literaria* in particular. She recognizes that Coleridge often presented his ideas in defiance against the view that he was 'neglecting to employ or ... misemploying his natural gifts',[17] a view she knew at first hand from the everyday attitudes of the Southey and Wordsworth circles in which she grew up. The underlying reason given for this misapplication of his gifts was assumed to be psychological: 'that he suffered his powers to lie dormant, or to spend them in fruitless activity'.[18] In response, Sara offers a compelling psychological account of her father's career:

> They [friends and critics] were struck by his marked intellectual gifts, but took no note of his intellectual impediments,—were not aware that there was a want of proportion in the faculties of his mind, which would always have prevented him from many or good books; for, even had he possessed the ordinary amount of skill in the arranging and methodizing of thought with a view to publication and in reference to the capacities of a volume, this would have been inadequate to the needs of one whose genius was ever impelling him to trace things down to their deepest source, and to follow them out in their remotest ramifications. His powers, compounded and balanced as they were, enabled him to do that which he did, and possibly that alone.[19]

This is an extraordinary passage. By 'good books', she clearly means well-made books, and by that standard *Biographia Literaria* may be a work of genius, but it is not a 'good book' as it vacillates between personal anecdote, religion, philosophy, and Wordsworth's poetry—it isn't really a book at all. Coleridge simply could not make conventional books, not because he lacked discipline or patience, but because that was all he could do. His work was the direct expression of his particular genius. The lack of agency in Sara's psychological account is striking as we witness Coleridge 'impelled' to follow each idea to its furthest possible point, its 'deepest source', its 'remotest ramification'. This accords with De Quincey's account of the brilliance of Coleridge's conversation, and the phenomenon of his audience often losing their way as he pursued the inevitable end to any train of thought he put in motion. Sara's account differs from De Quincey's in that he describes what he takes to be the quintessence of intellectual rigour, whereas she is describing a kind of compulsion—a psychological condition from which Coleridge could not escape. In Sara's argument, authors can write only the books that their cognitive makeup allows.

Beginning with a play on the 'body' of his work, Sara turns to the underlying physiological symptoms that underwrote Coleridge's psychological malaise. 'He loved to go forward, expanding and ennobling the soul of his teaching, and hated the trouble of turning back to look after its body'.[20] This witty claim captures the relentlessness of pursuing a line of thought so characteristic of Coleridge's mind, and also subtly references his habit of not bothering about such niceties as attribution and footnotes. Her psychological precision is evident as she describes how Coleridge's pursuit of ever more complex abstractions functioned as a palliative, connecting him to his soul while allowing him a momentary escape from his suffering body. The discussion of the physiological body ceases to be figural, and she offers a concise diagnosis:

> The nerveless languor, which after early youth, became almost the habit of his body and *bodily mind*, which to a great degree paralysed his powers both of rest and action, precluding by a torpid irritability their happy vicissitude,—rendered all exercises difficult to him except of thought and imagination flowing outward freely and in self-made channels; for these brought with them their own warm atmosphere to thaw the chains of frost that bound his spirit.[21]

Again the palliative aspect of thinking and composition is at the forefront. The 'chains of frost that bound his spirit' include both his chronic physical pain and his opium addiction—indeed they could hardly be separated, and which was cause and which effect had been lost long ago. The perceptiveness of this reading is striking, and it explains the intensity of the debt he felt to Robert Leighton's works when they released him from his 'bodily mind' at the nadir of his addiction in 1814. After establishing the general symptomology, Sara turns her discussion to the specific case of *Biographia Literaria*. The goal, or perhaps drive, of creating the experience of 'thought and imagination flowing outward freely' created the intense improvisational form of the work. Its very disorder is a mark of the force of engagement, and Coleridge's deranged body accounts for its deranged form:

> The *Biographia Literaria* he composed at the period of his life when his health was the most deranged, and his mind most subjected to

the influence of bodily disorder. It bears the marks of this throughout, for it is even less methodical in its arrangement than any of his
other works. Up to a certain point the author pursues his plan of
writing a literary life, but, in no long time his 'slack hand' abandons
its grasp of the subject, and the book is filled out to a certain size,
with such miscellaneous contents of his desk as seem least remote
from it.[22]

She overstates the case; the composition is not random, but disordered
is an apt description. His languor is seen as the source of the problem
as he flags in his task, loses his place, begins again in a different vain,
et cetera. Her psychological reading of the form of the work allows her
to address one of Ferrier's more damaging charges—that Coleridge did
not complete his deduction of the imagination because Schelling did
not complete his. Sara sees this as a naïve and cynical theory in light of
the circumstances of composition she describes. Her hypothesis for the
perennial mystery of breaking off the argument with the interpolated
'letter from a friend' makes much more sense than Ferrier's if we take
this intense experiential view: 'he broke down in the prosecution of his
whole scheme, the regular history of his literary life and opinions, and
this not for want of help in one particular line [Schelling's nonexistent
theory of the imagination], but because his energies for regular composition in any line were deserting him'.[23] In other words, the deduction
broke down because Coleridge broke down.[24]

   This is an incredibly frank admission, barely coding the opium addiction, and readily discussing Coleridge's physical suffering and resulting
psychological frailties. The motive, besides the rhetorical strategy of
explaining what cannot be defended, stems from intense sympathy—
not only as a daughter for her father, but as another sufferer. As I
argued earlier, Sara's discovery of *Aids to Reflection* during her breakdown and long convalescence in Ilchester in 1836 echoed her father's
discovery of Leighton's works in 1814—both sufferers received temporary respite as their minds moved into new channels and they experienced the exhilaration of 'thought and imagination flowing outward
freely'. The mind could lift itself out of the morass of bodily suffering
and the 'bodily mind'. Sara's personal insight offers a profound reading
of the stakes in her father's attempt to spiritualize the subject via his
assembly of Schelling's ideas in chapter twelve. If divine agency can
be established as the ultimate source and basis of self-reflection, then
suffering might be temporary—and the transcendental moment always
potentially at hand.

Sara had worked some of this out at the psychological level much earlier. As Bradford Mudge observes in a note to her unpublished essay on 'Nervousness', Sara had 'suffered from "nervous derangement" since early in 1832'.[25] Her opium addiction, likely a consequence of her series of difficult pregnancies, rendered her prone to bodily suffering, depression, and harsh self-judgement. Her essay, constructed as a dialogue between the 'Invalid' and the 'Good Genius', clearly prefigures her detailed account of her father's mind 'deranged' by 'bodily disorder'. An early exchange between the two figures sets out the central difficulties of 'nervousness' as an ailment:

> Invalid. Nervous derangement manifests itself by so many different symptoms that the sufferers themselves are puzzled what to make of it, and others, looking at it from different points of view make wrong judgements on the case. Those who perceive only how it affects the mind are apt to forget that it also weakens the body; those who perceive it as a bodily disease wonder that it should produce any alteration in a well regulated mind.
> Good Genius. Mania is also a disease in which the mind is affected through the body; but in the sort of nervousness we are discussing Reason, Free Will, & consequently responsibility remain, while what may be called the more sensuous part of the mind, feeling emotion, partakes of the morbid conditions of the body: to consider, to determine, to act are still within our power, but whether we shall be gladsome or gloomy, buoyant with hope or trembling with apprehensiveness, all this depends on the state of the corporeal part.[26]

The absolute relationship between the body and the mind, so obvious to the sufferer, is constantly misunderstood or misrecognized by 'others' who, lacking experience, do not feel the 'bodily languor' dragging on the mind, nor the listlessness and loss of affect that are the hallmarks of depression. The paradox, that despite the fact that, unlike Mania, the reason remains unimpaired, the sufferer still feels powerless, becomes a kind of terror. The reason allows for self-judgement, and the sufferer witnesses his or her own suffering. Despite retaining the ability 'to consider, to determine, to act', their state is ultimately determined by 'the corporeal part'—the treacherous body.[27] The naïve judgement of 'others' makes the condition worse by reinforcing the harsh self-judgement the reason facilitates. The 'Invalid' complains: '[h]ow often we are called upon, when wretchedly disabled, to derive comfort from this source or from that: "to draw honey in a sieve!" It is not material for comfort but the capacity for comfort that is wanting. And how often are we told that cheerfulness & hopefulness are a *duty*.'[28] Southey's behaviour toward Coleridge in 1814 is a singular example of this phenomenon— Coleridge did not require medical help; he merely needed to exercise his moral will. Sara slightly misquotes her father's poem, 'Work Without Hope', to illustrate the frustration at the heart of being able to reflect on one's powerlessness. Over a decade later, in an eloquent passage in her Introduction describing her father's symptoms during the composition of *Biographia Literaria*, 'the apathy and sadness induced by his physical condition reabsorbed his mind', she gives the longer passage from the poem:

> With lips unbrightened, wreathless brow, I stroll;
> And would you learn the spells that drowse the soul!
> *Work without hope draws nectar in a sieve,*
> *And hope, without an object, cannot live.*[29]

The repetition is striking, both for the precision of the psychological diagnosis in each case, but also for the recognition of the ways in which Sara discovered herself as she discovered her father. Seeing herself in his 'nervous derangement', feeling herself constantly at risk for a re-descent into depression, she understood the stakes of securing moral salvation at the heart of Coleridge's adaptations of Schelling in chapter twelve. If self-reflection and the unimpaired will were at once a source of moral terror, they were nonetheless the source of hope—a moral religious foundation made possible by recognizing the activity of the Holy Spirit in the act of apperception.

It is to be lamented that Sara did not spend more time addressing the differences in the ultimate goals of Schelling and her father. The most fascinating feature of the plagiarism is that every word is Schelling, but rearranged to serve a purpose he would not have recognized or considered possible. Sara finally offers a defence of this mode of composition, but only in a long footnote attacking Jeffrey and his 'disciples' some one hundred and ten pages following her section on plagiarism. She concludes her earlier argument by admitting the charge while decrying Ferrier's lack of fairness and manners: 'It will already have been seen, that no attempt is here made to *justify* my Father's literary omissions and inaccuracies, or to deny that they proceeded from anything defective in his frame of mind; I would only maintain that this fault has not been fairly reported or becomingly commented upon.'[30] In other words, the charges are accurate, but Ferrier's various conjectures about

Coleridge's motives are inept, unsubtle, rude—and clearly superseded by her detailed psychological account. She vindicates her father by recovering his suffering humanity—through sympathy and recognition of their shared 'nervous' disposition. Her eloquent defence of the compositional practice that produced the offence thus required an interval lest it confuse the intention of the first section. Nonetheless, it is a compelling account and needs to be quoted in full. Responding to the unfair partisan treatment of Coleridge in the *Edinburgh Review* and the *Penny Cyclopædia*, Sara revisits the plagiarism issue in the context of a less formidable adversary than Ferrier, by describing her father's method of composition as a legitimate and intellectually rigorous form:

> An author is to be judged, in respect of original power, by the total result of his productions. Is the *whole* a new thing, or is there *in* the whole a something new interfused? Can you find the like elsewhere? By this test my Father's writings must be tried, and perhaps they will be found to stand it better than those of many an author, who has carefully abstained from any formal or avoidable borrowing. That his are 'the works of one who requires something from another whereon to hang whatever he may himself have to say,' is just such a specious objection as the former. But it should be considered that every writer, in moral and religious disquisition, starts in fact from previous thought, whether he expressly produces it or not. In the *Aids to Reflection* and the *Remains* my Father has given his thoughts in the form of comments on the passages in the works of other men; and this he did, not from want of originality of mind, but from physical languor,—the want of continuous energy,—together with the exhaustive intensity, with which he entered into that particular portion of a subject to which his attention was directed. I do not believe, however, that the value of what he has left behind is so much impaired by its immethodical form as people at first sight imagine. The method and general plan of a literary work are often quite arbitrary, and sometimes, for the sake of preserving regularity of structure in the architecture of a book, a writer is obliged to say a great deal which is but introductory to that of his own which he has to impart.[31]

This is a finely reasoned account of De Quincey's perception of Coleridge as a singular genius. Unwilling to sacrifice depth of understanding for the superficiality of formal regularity (the well-made book), Coleridge pursued ideas relentlessly whenever his mental energy allowed him to.

With the Schelling at hand in his notebook, its incorporation directly into his argument, in the new form his notebook rearrangements had created, was an absolute inevitability—the means by which he composed. Furthermore, the logic of the passage suggests that chapter twelve, as a part, serves a *'whole'* that *was* 'new'. At the very least, 'a something new' was 'interfused' in the overarching line Coleridge pursued. So in the end, Sara cannot acquit her father of the charges against him, but she can understand how his offences occurred and delimit their seriousness by understanding them in the context of his intellectual habits, physical limitations, and compositional method. To dismiss *Biographia Literaria* as unoriginal is to risk losing the power of the entire corpus, and in that larger test, 'the total result of his productions', she has complete confidence. Her edition of *Aids to Reflection* demonstrated the power and influence of his ideas, and the means by which they were disseminated via the transformed consciousnesses of qualified readers, like herself.

The section of the Introduction in defence of Coleridge's religious views amounts to a second part of her essay 'On Rationalism', and its attacks on Newman and Pusey, and Tractarianism more broadly, are much more pointed. At over one hundred pages, *Mr. Coleridge's Religious Opinions; their formation; misconception and misrepresentations on the subject* presents a substantial treatise on Coleridge's political commitments and strives to defend his views while extending them into contemporary religious debate. The two 'opinions' she focuses on are his defence of Luther and adaptation of Kant. The Luther section quickly turns into an aggressive analysis of Newman's critique of Luther's views on the doctrine of Justification, and opens the way for her critique of Newman's anti-rationalism. Kant, considered an atheist writer and thus suspect by the devout, is more broadly defended by arguing that such views are credulous and philosophically 'primitive'. First, though, she lays the general groundwork by arguing that knowledge, including religious knowledge, is historical—a direct challenge to the Tractarian reliance on orthodoxy and Scriptural precedent. She also answers the charge that her father, and the Romantics more generally, sought to replace religion with a secular faith based on imagination and nature, that literature: 'is thus more liable to become a permanent substitute for religion with the higher sort of characters'.[32] She directly challenges the assumed incompatibility of religion and literature, and argues the converse: 'yet surely, by exercising the habits of abstraction and reflection, it better disciplines the mind for that life which consists in seeking the things that are above while we are yet in the flesh, than worldly business or pleasure'.[33] Once freed from artificial constraint, religious orthodoxy being the most notable, the mind, through 'leisure and contemplation', can escape 'particular bias' as it admits 'a diversified experience, and the power of beholding the diversity it contains'.[34] The alternative to this meditative openness is the confines of 'party' prejudice, the blinkered logic of ideological certainty at the heart of Doctrinal faith. Coleridge's philosophical project deliberately undermines ideological closure by opening new possibilities for understanding faith via self-reflection, apperception. Such a view smacks of the rationalism the Tractarians decried, and which Sara defended so powerfully in her essay. The argument needs to be restaged as part of her defence of her father, and she chose very specific theological points as the sites of contestation in arguing for the necessity of an 'enquiring spirit', as opposed to mindless Doctrinal submission.

To pursue her point she uses her father's history as an example. His critics assumed that he had been theologically damaged by his early adherence to Unitarian Socinianism, but she argues the opposite. Coleridge's openness to theological views had allowed him to explore and discover the internal deficiencies of the Unitarian position—that it was 'a mind like his, full of activity and resistancy' that allowed him to make the important theological contributions that Sara sought to secure and further in her various editions. The word 'resistancy' tells the tale; the alternative is submission to orthodoxy, blindness, willful stupidity. She is quick to attack the view that *Aids to Reflection* serves 'as a half-way house to Anglo-catholic orthodoxy' as 'radically wrong'.[35] Any partial appropriation of her father's theology had to be resisted as a distortion, and, in a prescient insight into the inevitable drift of the logic propelling the Oxford Movement, she observed its likely outcome: 'Anglo-catholic doctrine [becomes itself] a half-way house to what they consider the true Catholicism,—namely the Church of Rome'.[36] If all matters of faith must be derived from patristic precedent, then there is no other possible outcome. She objects to absolute reliance on Scriptural authority as a reductio ad absurdum, in which only the Apostles have any authority because only they had Christ's actual charge for the church. The abuse of claims of authority based on a presumption of an uninterrupted line from this originary source were at the root of the Reformation, and Sara assumes that efforts to reclaim such authority are based on social anxiety bordering on hysteria. To illustrate her view, she attacks Pusey's reliance on claims of Scriptural authority; he asserted that whatever he touched on was Scriptural, making nonsense of his own position. The only thing that allowed Pusey to succeed was his eloquence in which his claims were polished like gleaming 'brass'.[37] This view makes Pusey dangerous to the public mind as he influences the credulous, and abuses his authority, returning religion to superstition. She puts the problem of over-reliance on doctrine concisely:

> The doctrine may not be directly injurious to morality, since it allows actual faith to be a necessary instrument in all moral renovation; but the indirect practical consequences of insisting upon shadows as if they were realities, and requiring men to accept as religious verity of prime importance a senseless dogma, the offspring of false metaphysics, must be adverse to the interests of religion. Such dogmatism has a bad effect on the habits of thought by weakening the love and perception of the truth, and it is also injurious by producing disunion and mutual distrust among Christians.[38]

Laying the production of unnecessary sectarian strife at their feet, Sara briefly gets ahead of herself in showing her opponents' doctrine to be the antithesis of the Kantian rigour she presents as a tonic in the second part of her argument:

> The great aim and undertaking of modern mental philosophy [the work of Kant, Schelling, Fichte, Coleridge, herself] is to clarify the inward eye, rather than to enlarge its sphere of vision, except so far as the one involves the other—to shew what spiritual things are *not*, and thus to remove the obstructions which prevent men from seeing as mortals may see, what they are.[39]

Against her father's great religious project, the Oxford Movement produces an appeal to superstition, an appeal she must oppose through Coleridgean method.

Pusey is too easy a target, so eventually she turns to Newman in a detailed critique of a very specific piece of doctrine, his attack on Luther's position on Justification. Sara begins with a more general claim that the Tractarians hold on to a 'primitive' understanding of the 'Spirit' by closing their minds to their own inner capacities. She offers baptism as an obvious example. The power of the sacrament can be recovered through a modern understanding of the words, '*presence of the Holy Spirit to our Spirit*',[40] at the heart of the ceremony. She explains:

> When the doctrine is unfolded and presented to the masters and doctors of it, they fly off to the notion of an inward *potential* righteousness.

But this mere *capability* of being saved and sanctified, we have from our birth, nor can it be increased, because it is essentially, *extra gradum*,—not a thing of degrees. Our capability of being spiritualized by divine grace is unlimited.[41]

Rather than leave the matter cloaked in mystery and confusion, her father sought to explain how the sacrament related to the understanding of our spiritual potential. He 'looked upon baptism as a formal and public reception into a state of spiritual opportunities ... , a consignment of grace to the soul'. Reflecting on spiritual potentiality supports faith by making its reality available to the mind. The alternative is willful confusion and a cult of irrationalism:

> The objection to the Antiquarian doctrine is not that it implies a mystery, not that it implies the reception of a spiritual opportunity independently of the will of the receiver, but that, as it is commonly stated, it contradicts the laws of the human understanding, and either affirms what cannot be true,—what brings confusion into our moral or spiritual ideas,—or else converts the doctrine into ineffectual vapour—'a potentiality in a potentiality or a chalking of chalk to make white white'.

Having shown that reflection on the agency of the soul presents no danger to faith, she exposes the superstitious fearfulness at the core of doctrinal blindness. In support, she uses her own figure of the 'chalking of chalk' taken from the essay 'On Rationalism' to which she refers her readers for her full argument. To characterize this as self-confident is an understatement—Sara has evolved a formidable theological position from the seeds of her father's work. As with her engagement with *Aids to Reflection*, this growth provides evidence for the efficacy of 'the modern mental philosophy', and the power of dissemination as ideas transform the consciousness of the receiver and make new ideas possible—again emphasizing the historical nature of knowledge, including in this case our knowledge of the 'Spirit'. She parodies the near hysteria implicit in superstitiously bracketing reason:

> 'We must not *rationalize* [they declare]—must not reason *à priori* on these matters, but receive faithfully what the voice of God has declared.' ... Alas! that men should thus separate the voice of God from reason and moral sense, which God has given us as an inward Holy of Holies, wherein He may appear to us ... [42]

Her opponents labour under a false distinction, trapped in a confining circularity—they cannot conceive of 'reason and moral sense' being from God because they fear to conceive at all.

The choice of the doctrine of Justification, and Newman's professed dispute with Luther on the subject from *Tracts for the Times*, makes sense, focusing as it does on Newman's claim that Luther is in error for believing that we can be justified by our good works—arguing instead that justification proceeds from God alone. Sara shows how historically both writers strategically emphasized certain sacraments, in Newman's case to bolster 'whatever can be brought forward relative to priestly power and authority'. In choosing Justification, he is no different from Luther who also preached with an 'emphasis on particular parts [of the Gospel] to suit the exigencies of the day'.[43] This is a mischievous claim, as it takes what Newman presumes to be immutable and places it within the realm of historical contingency. In the final analysis, Sara reveals the purported disagreement, as stated by Newman, to be purely semantic, 'a verbal dispute'. In a witheringly succinct formulation, she puts Newman's basic reading error in a nutshell:

> Now Mr. Newman declares that faith is 'the only instrument or connecting bond between the soul and Christ.' What signifies it, *as against Luther*, to say, that according to St. James, we are justified *in* good works? Luther only denied that we are justified *by* them.[44]

That 'good works' are an outward sign of 'the connecting bond between the soul and Christ', not the means by which such a 'bond' is formed, is revealed to be a simple blunder on Newman's part. Presuming that Newman is not a theological blunderer begs a more dangerous question: is he a pious fraud creating a bogus controversy in order to bolster his authority? Or as Sara puts it, is he producing: 'doctrine developed for the temporal advantage of the clergy',[45] in the service of maintaining power over a credulous flock made afraid of their own capacity for moral judgement? The obvious question at this stage in her argument is: what does any of this have to do with *Biographia Literaria*; has she lost the plot and started once again to pursue her line from 'On Rationalism'? The easy answer is yes, and this is further testament to her theological bona fides, but the relevance for the Introduction becomes clear once she shifts her discussion to a defence of Kantian philosophy.

The charge of atheism against Kant is the first obstacle to overcome in her defence of her and her father's reliance on German philosophy in constructing their theological positions. Her approach is ingenious; she does not deny that Kant had no theological ambitions for his philosophy and was not particularly religious. Instead she shows how Kantian thought can serve as a necessary part of a philosophical method, a set of tools, which the religious can use to purify their views. She gives her argument a particularly nationalist cast in describing the English use of German thought: 'Everything that the Germans teach requires to be substantiated by the English mind, to be enlivened and spiritualized'.[46] The objection that German thought consisted of cold abstraction, the feared rationalism, is removed by showing it to be but the point of departure within an extant spiritual practice. Sara emphasizes the critical tools Kant provides: 'They [German philosophical procedures] are analyses ... shatterers into pieces. But this process is a necessary preliminary to the construction of what is sound—a necessary work *toward* pure religion'.[47] Turning to her father, she explains how he shows that philosophy must play a part in developing religious thought, lest we remain in a state of 'primitive' superstition concerning things as fundamental as the nature of the Holy Spirit. She defends his choice of philosophical method:

> The difference between the critical and the mechanical philosophy is this, that the latter is incongruous and inconsonant with Christianity; while the former (as far as it goes,) is capable of flowing along with it in one channel and even blending with it in one stream, as I contend that it does in the Christian philosophy of my Father.[48]

Even though the subject of this section is presumably a defence of the use of Kant, by speaking more broadly about the 'critical philosophy', Sara demonstrates how Schelling is subsumed into Coleridge's 'Christian philosophy'. The plagiarism charge is no longer the subject, but this piece of analysis offers a broader context in which to consider and weigh it.

Sara claims Kant was able to show the way forward in religion, despite having no interest in it. This wonderfully counterintuitive argument makes sense when we consider the force of ideological conformity that surrounds us. Kant, by historical chance, escapes this force. He 'was not religiously educated. Had he been brought up a Churchman he could never have divested himself of dogmatic divinity; he could never have given the *a priori* map of the human mind as independently as he has given it'.[49] This insight also serves as a concise critique of ideology and ideological formation. Despite her native conservatism, her analysis is reminiscent of Louis Althusser's famous conception of 'interpolated subjects' born into the strict confines of ideological apparatuses, especially the church. Sara operates within a double gesture. Self-consciously aware of the iconoclastic nature of her arguments and her father's philosophy, she nonetheless seeks to make that philosophy normative, convinced that it participates in revealed truth. Belief in historical progress in matters of religion underpins her arguments, and provides the confidence, and occasional belligerence, of her treatise—for at this point it is difficult to see how this section serves as a simple Introduction to *Biographia Literaria*.

To place the *Biographia* in a broader Coleridgean context makes sense as part of the plagiarism defence, and she recreates part of the foundation for a much larger system by paraphrasing her father's religious adaptation and accommodation of Kant:

> Reason cannot oblige us to receive, said Kant, more than reason can prove. But what mere Speculative Reason cannot oblige us to receive, the Moral and Spiritual within us may. This is the doctrine of the *Aids to Reflection*; I believe that my Father, in his latter years, added something to it, on the subject of Ideas, which will appear, I trust hereafter.[50]

Her conclusion here seems reminiscent of one of her father's famously unfulfilled promissory notes, the famous promise of a future 'theory of the imagination', from the end of chapter twelve, that so agitates Ferrier. Sara was at pains to challenge Ferrier's assumption of bad faith by insisting that 'he [her father] still cherished the intention of continuing the subject', and that he had in fact produced work on it in his joint projects with Green toward the end of his life. Extraordinary as it may seem, Sara has been partially vindicated, and this material has appeared finally with the publication of the *Collected Coleridge* edition of *Opus Maximum* in 2002. The re-evaluation, which Sara assumes and defers to future readers, is now underway[51]—providing more evidence for her historical view of the efficacy of ideas.

Returning to a focus on chapter twelve, without expressly referring to it, she defends the primacy of inner subjective knowledge, with Newman again serving as the obvious target: 'The only office of external testimony with respect to the spiritual substance of faith, in my father's view, was that of exciting and evolving the ideas, which are the sole sufficient evidence of it—at once the ground which supports it and the matter of which it is formed'.[52] Coleridge's arguments for the primacy of subjectivity and self-consciousness serve this religious purpose, making spiritual life possible. Any systems relying on external knowledge, whether arch-rationalism's reliance on things or Tractarian anti-rationalism's reliance on the external evidences of God, become logical absurdities without a self-conscious will to perceive them. This concise formulation combines her 'father's religious opinions' and the contested Schelling passages from chapter twelve, and thus knits together the two sections of her Introduction. They act reciprocally, the Schelling supporting the religious opinions, and the broader religious opinions mitigating the plagiarism offence.

Sara ends the religious section with a rhetorical flourish, defending her father against 'irrationalists' in a rousing conditional construction placing the onus clearly on them:

> I would fain learn of those, who look upon my Father's scheme of faith as something less satisfactory to a religious mind than that which they have embraced, if they can point out an important moral truth, any great spiritual idea, any soul-sustaining belief, any doctrine unquestionably necessary or highly helpful to the support and safety of the Christian faith, which was rejected or unrecognized by him. Can they shew that his 'rationalizing,' as some designate the efforts he made to free the minds of Christians from schemes of doctrine, which seemed to him 'absolutely irrational,' and therefore derogatory to God and injurious to man, excluded him from participating in any practical results, that can be deemed favourable to a pure, deep, earnest Christianity. If they are unable to do this ... [53]

Her contempt barely concealed, she exudes absolute confidence that Coleridge's critics must fail this test. The resounding inference is that they should therefore remain still; they are welcome to their credulous superstitions, but should not presume to judge someone who spent his life attempting to make 'moral truth' an active principle available to the self-reflective minds of Christians. Suspecting that in their desperation, now that she has exposed the fundamental flaws in their doctrine, they would revert to personal attack, Sara points out that characterizing Coleridge as idle, 'as having spent a life of inaction', is as absurd as it is 'an injustice both to him and to the products of his mind'.[54] The ultimate test of the value Coleridge's thought is 'a careful survey of his writings', a survey she makes available as his editor, and an intellectual feat that few can claim. By the end of the Introduction she has created herself as the ultimate Coleridge reader, as evidenced by her facility at deploying his ideas.

Sara's impeccable intellectual credentials, on show throughout, clearly superior to Ferrier's or even De Quincey's, allow her to fulfil her father's intellectual duty while fulfilling her filial duty. Her notes for chapter twelve of *Biographia Literaria* put questions of attribution beyond doubt, and complete her father's scholarly obligations on his behalf. In addition, the question of plagiarism has been erased as Schelling's contributions become completely clear. The sheer labour of identifying each passage by reading the original German and mentally translating, while keeping the detail of chapter twelve in mind, must stand as one of the great feats of mental gymnastics. Not only does she identify passages, she translates those most central to her father's argument so that Schelling's contribution becomes completely clear. In clearing her father's debt, she produces stunningly accurate English renditions of the originals—a fact made clear in the Bate and Engell edition for the *Collected Coleridge* where they simply reproduce her translations of major passages.[55] In short, she produced what are still the standard versions for the purposes of editing *Biographia Literaria*, and she remains the Germanist of record for subsequent scholars.

*

Sara ends her Introduction with a preemptive response to the obvious objection to her as an editor and judge of her father's work—her love for him was 'sure to corrupt' her 'testimony'.[56] The italicized head-notes for the final three pages summarize her response: *'Reports of Lovers and Friends the best Materials for Biography Blindness of Love denied'.*[57] She points out the obvious, that biography can only proceed 'from friends, from enemies, or from indifferent persons', and that the indifferent have no 'testimony' to give while enemies will give theirs 'gratuitously'. Logically then, she becomes the ideal editor and biographer: 'what better grounds for the judging of a man's character, upon the whole, can the world have, than the impression it has made on those who have come the nearest to him, and known him the longest and the best? I, for my part, have not striven to conceal my partialities, or to separate my love for my Father from my moral and intellectual sympathy for his mode of thought'.[58] That she has only 'come nearest to him' recently through her enormous intellectual labour, sympathy, and psychological insight goes unstated, yet must serve as part of the drive that brings the edition into being. She serves as the harbinger for her readers, the influence on her thought, the promise for theirs.

   J. F. Ferrier, through an act of negative creation, initiated the serious editing of Coleridge. The intellectual rigour demanded for a sufficient response to his detailed charges began the historical task of editing

Coleridge (recently completed with *The Collected Coleridge*), and was born out of the shifting terrain of intellectual property and plagiarism, Sara's love, her desire to rescue her father's reputation, and her filial obligation to unapologetically assert and project his influence into the broader public sphere. Out of the complex web of Sara Coleridge's motives was born the first major scholarly edition—the very model of rigorous editing.

7
Posterity and Writing 'for the Day'

Following the success of *Aids to Reflection* and *Biographia Literaria*, Sara Coleridge's drive to construct her father's posthumous reputation continued in two veins: she organized and reorganized the corpus, inventing editions, arguing for his historical significance; and she continued to defend him from the swirl of charges that threatened his reputation. Having seen off charges of heresy by placing him in the vanguard of emerging theological developments, and plagiarism by admitting the charges within the context of a frank psychological and emotional portrait, she confronted the older charge—Jacobinism. This unenviable task became inevitable once she decided to publish a three-volume collection of Coleridge's journalism in what became *Essays On His Own Times Forming a Second Series of the Friend*.[1] Her task was made especially difficult by her desire to reduce her father's long career to a perfectly coherent system of belief she termed the 'consistency of the author's opinions'. One of Sara Coleridge's main goals in the construction of *Essays On His Own Times* was the creation of an ideologically closed text out of heterogeneous source materials. Sara Coleridge's version of her father's 'opinion' attempted to evade the messy emotional chaos of his life, surprising given the frankness of her Introduction to *Biographia Literaria*, by presenting a set of consistent political principles underwriting his apparently shifting views. This goal necessitates Section II of her 'Introduction', 'Consistency of the Author's career of Opinion', and provides the logic for the sections that follow. She seeks a means to stave off potential damage to Coleridge's decidedly Tory Victorian reputation as a man of letters and a key figure in the intellectual development of Anglicanism—the creation of her contributions to her editions of *Aids to Reflection* and *Biographia*. Having extended her father's intellectual formulations into contemporary theological debates, she did not want to risk sullying them with old aspersions on his political judgement. In essence, she attempts to employ an extremely pious biographical sketch that describes her father's journalism as a key component of his literary remains. Yet, she must include among those remains material that most observers (without the benefit of her guidance in the 'Introduction') would take to be impious in the extreme. If she can successfully shape his 'career' in her edition, then she can reasonably assume that his reputation (so carefully constructed during his lifetime, and defended and even extended by her) will be secure.

By 1850, Coleridge's 1790s radicalism had ceased to be the focus of attacks on him, replaced by accounts of his moral failings. For example, in September 1850, the year Sara Coleridge published her edition of *Essays On His Own Times*, he came under attack in *The Times*. In reviewing *The Autobiography of Leigh Hunt*, an anonymous reviewer used the occasion to launch a highly moralistic attack on Coleridge's character. Unlike the venom of *The Anti-Jacobin* or Hazlitt's tone of disappointment and regret, this attack did not focus on perceived political shortcomings, but rather on Coleridge's failings as a husband and parent:

> Coleridge, with all the grandeur of his mind, condescended to humiliations from which many a day labourer would have shrunk; and, grievous as the effects of his conduct were upon his own fortunes, they are still worse upon the lives of his successors, who see no shame in what their master gloried in. No man might have passed through life more creditably than Coleridge. He had a wife and children to support, the means of earning money at command, yet he would not work, and he suffered his family to receive the protection and earnings of a brother writer whose heart was as sound as his moral sense was perfect.[2]

This slander suggests that there may have been something morally suspect in Coleridge's intellectual and poetic genius, and the passage's emphasis on bodily vice, sensual 'humiliations', suggests a degraded intellect. The reviewer repeats the rhetoric of a diseased sensibility betraying the reason, and dragging it into a sensual torpor. The use of the word 'creditably', sets up restrictive economic terms for considering the value of his philosophical work. In fact, the life of the mind and its productions, the foundations of present-day valuations of Coleridge, are denied value by the assertion that 'he would not work'. In this quintessentially Victorian critique it is no longer Coleridge's political ideas that represent a public danger, but rather his moral turpitude and lazy sensuality. The review's high moral tone of condemnation also affects the value of the family's ongoing posthumous production of Coleridge's literary and philosophical corpus, his remains. We are told to be suspicious of 'successors' blind to their 'master's' moral culpability. The suggestion is that the children have been morally disabled by the father's dissipation. Southey's moral character, and presumably his exemplary Tory political views, are extolled as a means to denigrate his 'brother poet', and the terms employed to make the distinction between the two men emphasize the equilibrium in Southey between head and heart, the realms of feeling and intellect, that Coleridge lacked: 'a brother writer whose heart was as sound as his moral sense was perfect'. This posthumous judgement of Southey, after a long career as poet laureate and Tory sage, reflects his and his descendents' success in effacing the memory of 'the author of *Wat Tyler*'. The attack on Coleridge's reputation was considered serious enough by the family to merit an immediate response from Derwent Coleridge in the form of a letter to the editor of *The Times*. Derwent's defence focused particularly on the vitiated definitions of work and value implicit in the review. He countered the accusation of sloth by challenging the reviewer's definition of productive work:

> In the words of his nephew and son-in-law, 'he did the day's work of a giant.' True, it was of a kind calculated to enrich the world with wisdom than himself with money; but if his children are far more than content that it should have been so, who else need complain?[3]

The letter's rhetorical strategy turned the reviewer's assumed moral categories on their heads, and exposed his definition of work as shallow and vulgar in its reduction of all value to commerce. The legitimacy of Coleridge's intellectual project was at stake, and while Derwent Coleridge defensively asserted that, 'the time will come when he [his father] will be better known', he simultaneously asserted his faith in the eventual place his father would have in the history of English letters. It was this 'work of a giant' that Henry had attempted to describe in *Table Talk*, and that resulted, through Sara's meticulous work, in the posthumous creation of that giant, the sage of Highgate.

It was this dubious, if commonplace, view of Coleridge as dissipated and ineffectual, based as it was on malicious gossip and half-truth, which Sara Coleridge sought to remedy. It should be remembered that Victorian reviewers lacked access to the MS of *Opus Maximum*—the definitive evidence that the charge of idleness was misplaced. The status of that work was unclear to the family editors as well, and I will take up that point in the next chapter. For Sara, 'consistency' was not just an intellectual value, the vindication of past political and religious views, but a moral value, the assertion of the overall contribution made by her father's intellectual 'work', and its vindication *as* work. Far from being lazy, the construction of a coherent set of literary remains would reveal Coleridge as the most splendidly industrious of men. The prototypical Victorian value of 'industry' thus formed part of the immediate context for her ongoing construction of the literary remains.

Collecting his journalism provided an opportunity to present Coleridge's day-to-day labours to the public as evidence of his moral worthiness. If the work were received as a mishmash of occasional pieces, then that goal would be lost. Sara had to create an overarching coherence for the whole of the career, which she characterized as 'consistency of the author's opinions'. Otherwise, the ambitious subtitle, *Forming a Second Series of the Friend*, seemed absurd—an inept comparison of one of Coleridge's most concentrated pieces of writing to a compendium of heterogeneous material. That the risks were more than offset by the potential benefits for Coleridge's posthumous reputation was made clear by Sara herself from the outset, as she accepted the risk of reminding the public of the charge of Jacobinism after it had faded from view. Vindicating her father's politics was a considerably more complicated task than establishing his centrality in contemporary theological debates:

> I cannot doubt that this collection, irregular as it is, will both cor-roborate former defences of his political honesty [Coleridge's self-generated 'Once a Jacobin' debate], and establish his claim to the praise of patriotism and zeal on behalf of his fellow-countrymen, especially that portion of them, to whom more especially the Gospel was to be preached, whom every beneficial scheme of politics more especially concerns, namely the Poor.—I think it will serve also as a vindication of him from contemporary charges affecting his private life and conduct, as that of indolence and practical apathy.[4]

The focus on 'the Poor' framed her collection as having significant social interest, but lest the reader misunderstand and take the work to be a simple chronological arrangement of occasional pieces, her short Preface preempted the notion that, as journalism, the volume was 'unworthy' of republication. Her father, she argued, was never a popu-lar journalist for the very reason that he could not limit himself to the issues *'of the day'*:[5] 'With my Father the *subject* on which he wrote was engrossing and pursued for its own sake, the occasion and immediate object of publication being in some degree lost sight of'.[6] The phrase 'in some degree' is necessarily slippery; it would be absurd to assert that Coleridge 'lost sight' of Pitt's war policy while writing *The Watchman*. Sara's editorial principle of selecting those pieces worthy of posterity competed directly with the value of an edition based on reconstructions of the moments of history they record. Indeed, the only history at stake in the book was personal and intended for a small, but influential audience—the clerisy: 'those who are now, or those who hereafter may be, concerned in my Father's personal history, both his literal descendants and all who are *as children to him* in affectionate reverence for his mind'.[7] By combining his biological and intellectual children, and projecting into future generations ('those who hereafter may be'), Sara situated her edition within the same historical idea of dissemination that allowed her to plausibly critique Newman as an extension of her father. Just as Maurice, Hare, or even Emerson drew sustenance from Coleridge's rationalized faith, future readers of his journalism might deduce foundational principles to govern their political beliefs and action. That this process assumed an effacement of the history 'of the day' in the service of derived principles is implicit in the edition's logic, and necessitated Sara's construction of political 'consistency'.

Sara presents a three-part strategy for reading her father for 'consistency'. Each part depends on the notion that each individual has a 'precious essence' that remains consistent over time—a notion bolstered by her father's complex appropriation of Kantian reason so carefully reconstructed in her Introduction to *Biographia Literaria*. The 'essence' is not quite stable in the first case (called 'his own system of belief'): 'But even because it is thus *part of himself*, it needs must grow and alter with growth, and will surely exhibit, in its earlier stages, the immaturity of his being'.[8] This is to say that he is not consistent, and subject to youthful folly (his contempt for Pitt, or opposition to the first Ministerial war with France become examples of his 'immaturity'), and, yet, simultaneously he is consistent at the abstract level of the foundation of the system; it is a single system subject to superficial alteration over time. In support of this notion she makes the distinction that Coleridge's opinions differed only in detail and, 'that the cast of [her] father's opinions was ever of one kind—ever reflected his personal character and individuality'. Again, this idea depends on the claim that each individual has an inner 'essence' that is the only true measure of consistency:

the vast majority of reasoners seek to set forth that which is comfortable with the divine will and reflects the light of the Supreme Reason, differing only as to the medium of outward condition and circumstance, in which the precious essence is exhibited.[9]

Transposed onto the social realm, her assertion of the Kantian foundation of her father's faith becomes the very definition of ideology: historical specificity ('outward condition and circumstance') is transcended by an abstract level of ideality where the skilful reader can find comfort in the presence of consistency; coherence is guaranteed by the explanatory force of the divine will as expressed through individual 'essence'. The final sentence of the section repeats this claim in the language of religious exegesis, arguing that: 'The spirit of his teaching was ever the same amid all the variations and corrections of the letter'.[10] Taken on its own terms, this claim is unassailable other than to point out that the religious interpretative practice alluded to may more properly be viewed as eisegetical—dependent on the insertion of meaning into the text rather than its extraction, or what Žižek would call 'ideological quilting'.[11] Reminiscent of Coleridge's emphasis on method in the pursuit of both philosophical and theological questions, Sara creates an idealizing reading strategy for her edition—she will extract 'consistent' evidence of her father's underlying principles and use that exegesis as the basis for making her selections. In practice, this strategy is less intellectually ambitious; she simply forgets to include pertinent facts. Her long paragraph on the 'consistency' of his religious beliefs goes to great pains to argue that Coleridge was consistently anti-Romanist (something that was not at issue), and uses that as a screen when describing his early opposition to 'the evils of a rich hierarchy'. The reader can only assume that this is the earliest example of his anti-Romanist feeling, rather than what it is, a reference to his contempt for the Anglican establishment; Coleridge's withering Unitarian critique of Trinitarian superstition does not appear, replaced by deliberate obfuscation.

Sara Coleridge's defence of her father's opinions, then, constructs itself in such a way that any 'circumstance' can be made to conform to an ideologically closed system; it 'quilts' events into a 'consistent' pattern. Historical fact, removed from the richness of its complex original context, can be absorbed as evidence of a greater power (abstract, perhaps divine) at work. Deploying the famous distinction between degree and kind, Coleridge's 'consistency' becomes evidence that his political beliefs were always of 'one kind'. With this stable foundational principle in place, she can question her father's stated views, cautiously, by presenting views more acceptable for her Victorian readers. For example, on the subject of the first Ministerial war with France, in her section on

'The Author's Course of Political Opinion',[12] she leaves the question of merits of her father's views open by posing them in a question:

> Who can say whether England did not lose more by the poverty and discontent produced by the war, before it appeared clearly necessary to the public at large, than was gained by that of preparedness and that proficiency in warfare, which an early entrance into the great European contest ensured?[13]

This is a subtle piece of fence-sitting, leaving open the possibility of her father being right to oppose the war, while carefully siding with the political establishment's conclusions that the 'great European contest' was 'clearly necessary', even if some of Britain's subjects had been slow to recognize this. Coleridge would not have shared her doubts. His opposition to the first war was steadfast, and his shift in supporting the war policies of the early nineteenth century (his purported political apostasy) was defended and explained as the result of the profound changes in the structure and behaviour of the French state. But, on the subject of the necessity of opposing Pitt in the 1790s, as a patriot, he never wavered.[14]

Sara Coleridge's conclusions about the 'necessity' of the 'great European contest' may not have been entirely the product of her desire to harmonize her father's political views with those of the political status quo. More immediate pressures certainly played a role in her desire for moderation. The Chartist demonstrations in April 1848 had a profound influence on her. In a letter to Aubrey de Vere of 14 April, she recounted recent political disturbances and her feelings about them. She had received 'an awful account of the Chartist preparations for insurrection and violence',[15] and had become concerned about the security of her own neighbourhood, fashionable Regent's Park. Hysteria was such that 'gentlemen of the neighbourhood' called to inform her of 'the arrangements for the defence of the Park' and to 'offer protection'. Rumours circulated of possible army rebellions if the Chartist resistance 'proved very formidable', of the army's hatred of the Duke of Wellington, of the uncertain sympathies of the 'middle or shop-keeping class', et cetera. In a strong echo of the political rhetoric of the 1790s, she described the source of the danger in such a way as to betray her class anxiety:

> having no *principle* to guide them [the middle class] one way or the other, and not being given to theories and abstractions, or to go beyond the present hour, they might throw themselves into the arms

of the mob, as did the shopkeepers and National Guard, who are so much composed of that class, in Paris.[16]

She is referring to the events immediately preceding the creation of the Second Republic in Paris in the aftermath of the 1848 revolution, but the anxieties about French political precedent sound remarkably like those of sixty years earlier, with the exception of the interesting inversion of the value attributed to 'theories and abstractions'. Whereas conservative opinion in the 1790s, following Burke, characterized 'theories' as a species of madness, intellectual excess that had overwhelmed the French, 1848 conservative opinion feared that a lack of abstract principles could lead to a descent into irrationalism and violence. Presumably this shift could be seen as the evidence of the influence of Coleridge's rationalism on emerging political elites among the Oxbridge educated gentry, Sara's hoped-for clerisy. The absence of any ideological check on public feeling became the great danger, rather than the demagoguery ideological 'principles' made possible. Victorian anxiety over excessive politics and the fear of violence politically inverted the emotionalism of 1790s sensibility, championed as the heart of Englishness by the conservatism of Burke, and decried by radicals as damaging the capacity to exercise reason. This fear of the mob, she claimed, was one she shared with her father, and was listed among his 'consistent' political views in her Introduction:

> though like all other leaders of reflection, he was equally an opponent of the *mob*, whether consisting of the uneducated many in the humbler ranks of society, or the herd of mediocre and undisciplined intellects in the higher, who seek to tyrannize over their betters by the mere shew of hands.[17]

This anti-democratic slur has little to do with Coleridge's political positions of the 1790s, of which it is an obvious distortion, but much to do with her own political anxieties. As the Chartist crisis deepened, she finally acceded to her son's wishes and collected the family 'plate' and fled to the safety of Eton and Windsor. The purported danger posed by the Chartists was absurdly overstated, as was their irrationalism (after all they were the ones promoting the rational reform of British institutions as a means to avoid class violence). Writing to Aubrey de Vere, she celebrated the 'happy event' of the failure of the Chartist demonstration with a brief encomium to the Duke of Wellington:

> The arrangements of the Duke for the preservation of the metropolis were worthy of the hero of Waterloo, and how merciful thus to

preclude, by the formidable and complete nature of the preparations, any attempt on the part of the misguided Chartists.[18]

The use of the words 'preservation' and 'merciful' reinforced the sense of religious deliverance and cast the Iron Duke as a messianic light against the potential darkness of 'pure anarchy alternating with despotism'. While she acknowledged the possibility that the Chartists' 'demands were in themselves reasonable', Sara Coleridge relied on conventional conservative argument to deny their ultimate legitimacy. She could present herself as concerned with the amelioration of human suffering, and still oppose constitutional efforts to effect the necessary social changes:

> It does not seem at all clear to me that there would be the slightest use in giving votes to more and poorer men, without bettering their condition or improving their education before-hand.[19]

This is a convenient, and circular, piece of paternalistic reasoning— 'poorer men' cannot be given the political means to improve their condition until their condition has been improved. The letter ends by betraying the good faith she said existed between her and the 'reasonable' demands of the reform movement. Her earlier equanimity collapses into reactionary slander:

> A great proportion of them are sufferers by their own fault, ... who become Chartists in pure ignorance, with a blind hope of bettering their state by changing the present order of things.[20]

To accuse the most disadvantaged members of society of selfishness and/or laziness was a stock conservative response, then as now, and, as an unreasoned reaction, pointed to the ingrained nature of Sara Coleridge's conservatism. An additional irony in her opinions, of course, lies in their repetition of the very charges brought against her father in this period, laziness and intellectual blindness.

This is not to say that the situation was not dangerous in the run-up to the planned demonstration. While it is tempting to play this scene as farce, the fashionable gentry engulfed in comical hysteria, the public build-up to the demonstration suggests that the danger of civil unrest was very real. Whether the source of the danger was the Chartist agitation or the Ministry is another question. Accounts of the events in *The Times* show that a general sense of panic overtook the country as the date approached of planned simultaneous Chartists demonstrations throughout the country. It was the organizational strength of the movement, not its demands, that alarmed authorities. According to *The Times*, the Chartists planned to assemble in Kensington common in a crowd of as many as 200,000 and then cross the bridge picking up more followers as they went. *The Times* gloated that on the day the original crowd was 'not more than seven thousand' and only grew to just 20,000 (and probably only half of those were active participants) before dispersing. The editor took a triumphal tone and praised the members of the massive counter-demonstration, described in this extraordinary assertion: '150,000 special constables spontaneously enrolled *against* the movement'.[21] 'Spontaneously enrolled' conjures an image of an endless queue of men receiving a shilling in one hand and a truncheon in the other. That image proves accurate as the story goes on to describe the members of the Ministerial mob as 'picked and trustworthy men who could procure vouchers to their respectability, who took an oath to defend the QUEEN'S peace and were ready to wield a truncheon in its defence'. Wielding a truncheon for peace seems counterintuitive, and the reduced number of demonstrators hardly comes as a surprise in these circumstances. The most extraordinary thing about the counter-demonstration was its utter recklessness. Unable to rely on the army, the Ministry armed the mob. Had a confrontation ensued, no one was in control of the 'special constables'. This account puts a rather different light on Sara's evocation of her father's lifelong fear of the mob, and the point is not facetious—Coleridge had plenty of experience with king and country mobs in the 1790s.

It is telling, then, in the light both of the construction of her father's posthumous reputation as an Anglican Tory, and her personal desire to ground her own Tory politics in her father's, that the subject most absent from *The Watchman* material, as a direct result of her editing, was the war. Opposition to the war dominated the journal from its inception; it was the occasion of its coming into being, the reason Coleridge felt compelled to be heard despite the considerable risks involved (charges of treason had been levelled against those who had said much less). Furthermore, the most salient feature of the journal was its heterogeneous structure. Number 1 began with a detailed overview of the war debate from December 1792 up until the week of publication, culled from the Parliamentary record. This was juxtaposed with a summary of recent French peace overtures, and Coleridge's assertions of the reasonableness of the French terms. In short, the journal began by constructing the political context in which it appeared in stunning detail.

This context was followed by the only poem in the issue, 'To a Young Lady', subtitled, 'With a Poem on the French Revolution'. The poem acted as an individual appeal to feeling, based on the potted history of the war debate that preceded it, as a means to convert the 'young lady' to the revolutionary cause. This was the original context of the first of the two selections Sara Coleridge made from Number 1, Coleridge's review of Edmund Burke's 'Letter to a Noble Lord'. Coleridge's review is a model of political wit. He judiciously praises Burke's record of eloquence, 'Mr. Burke always appeared to me to have displayed great vigour of intellect, and an almost prophetic keenness of penetration', and then switches out of the past tense to register his present disappointment in the subject of his review:

> With such notions of the matter and manner of Mr. Burke's former publication, I ought not to be suspected of party prejudice, when I declare the woeful inferiority of the present work—Alas! we fear that this Sun of Genius is well nigh extinguished.[22]

The review goes on to ridicule Burke and his unseemly connections (financial and otherwise) with the Pitt Ministry, and thus represents, in the context of the rest of the first issue, Coleridge's willingness to enter the fray on both aesthetic and political grounds. Crucial to Coleridge's attack was the strategic admission of Burke's eloquence, and Coleridge defined 'true eloquence' as the ability 'to argue *by* metaphors'.[23] The strategic use of aesthetic figures disarms the reader, and moves them to the author's point of view through the use of pathos. This rhetorical trait, essential to Burke's political success, and praised here by Coleridge, was a common target of radicals. Paine famously described Burke's use of excessive description and figuration in *Reflections on the Revolution in France* as 'Mr. Burke's horrid pictures', and Godwin considered the hysterical emotional tone of Burke's treatise a prime example of the way excessive sensibility disabled the capacity to reason clearly. As Marilyn Butler has noted, Burke's 'Letter to a Noble Lord', as polemic, was 'even more powerful than the *Reflections*'. The chill it spread through radical circles was profound. Butler rhetorically asks: 'after this [the publication of the "Letter" and its impact], who would freely own to being a radical philosopher?'[24] That Coleridge would choose to attack that particular document in his first issue indicates the level of his political commitment and his willingness to carry the fight to his political enemies. While it might be tempting to consider Coleridge's initial praise of Burke's rhetorical eloquence as merely strategic, such a conclusion ignores Coleridge's use of similar appeals to feeling later in the same number of *The Watchman*.

When Sara Coleridge selected this review and, thus, removed it from its specific historical moment, she directed readers towards an aesthetic appreciation of its wit and away from its political implications. After all, how could the reader of 1850 be expected to be familiar with the war debate of the week of 1 March 1796? Similarly, the other selection she made from Number 1, 'Copy of a Handbill', becomes an example of her father's abilities as a satirist. It consists of a parody of a public handbill offering a reward to any one who can decipher Pitt's last speech in the House:

> and whereas the entire, effectual, and certain meaning of the whole of the said sentences, phrases, denials, promises, retractions, persuasions, explanations, hints, insinuations, and intimations, has escaped and fled, so that what remains is to plain understanding incomprehensible, and to many good men is matter of painful contemplation: now this is to promise, to any person who shall restore the said lost meaning, or shall illustrate, simplify, and explain, the said meaning, the sum of FIVE THOUSAND POUNDS, to be paid on the first day of *April* next, at the office of John Bull, Esq. PAY-ALL and FIGHT-ALL to the several High contracting powers engaged in the present *just* and *necessary* War![25]

This is uproariously funny, but what we lose in our laughter, and what was lost in Sara Coleridge's selection of it for her edition is both the raw emotion of the sarcasm in the phrase, '*just* and *necessary* War', a phrase first used by George III and repeated by Pitt in the House, and the risk run by its author in challenging Pitt.

In order to attempt to restore this 'lost meaning', to follow Coleridge's own theme, we need to consider how the original readers of the 'Copy of a Handbill' would have heard the satire's tone. As noted earlier, *The Watchman* was an extremely heterogeneous document. The Handbill ridiculing Pitt was followed by a report on the 'Proceedings of the House of Commons' for Monday, 22 February that detailed the profligacy of the Pitt government in forcing through a Credit Bill to allow them to continue the War policy. But, more telling, the two sections that preceded the Handbill were titled 'Foreign Intelligence', and 'Domestic Intelligence' (these two sections appeared in all the Numbers of the journal). In particular, under 'Domestic Intelligence', Coleridge included an item from Salisbury on the fate of 'the remnant of the

88th regiment' that had recently arrived in that city. Two years earlier, he reported, they had 'embarked for the Continent', 1,100 strong. After 'the severe winter of 1794–95' they had been reduced to 250 men, and subsequently embarked for the West Indies wherein they were attacked and 'reduced to about 100 men'. Coleridge concluded this sad history by ominously noting that they were to march to Portsmouth, 'probably to be drafted into some other corps'. This report left little doubt about the author's attitude to this '*just* and *necessary* War', juxtaposed as it was with Southey's lines from 'Joan of Arc':

> Of unrecorded name
> Died the mean man, yet did he leave behind,
> One who did never say her daily prayers
> Of him forgetful; who every tale
> Of the distant war lending an eager ear,
> Grew pale and trembled. At her cottage door
> The wretched one shall sit, and with dim eye
> Gaze o'er the plain, where, on his parting steps,
> Her last look hung.[26]

The pathos of considering the widows of each of the lost members of the 88th regiment was overwhelming in its effect, and this direct appeal to the sensibilities of his audience repeated the Burkean 'eloquence' so decried by republican rationalists. In relation to this unqualified condemnation of the War, Sara Coleridge's equivocation in her summary of her father's 'course of political opinion', that 'Who can say' if the War was just, comes close to obscenity. It functions as a betrayal of her father's 'opinions' and their justification, and, paradoxically, a betrayal in which he himself was complicit.[27] The deliberate muddying of his views as defence from the charge of Jacobinism, and the characterization of his political career in the 1790s as a naïve adolescent folly, as detailed in chapter 1 above, gave license to Sara Coleridge to continue the project of political reinvention, posthumously.

Given the heterogeneous structure of *The Watchman*, the very process of selecting from it destroys its historical specificity, and with it the reasons for its coming into being; it is impossible (in Coleridge's words) to 'restore said lost meaning'. Coupled with Coleridge's own practice of decontextualizing previous works in order to re-deploy them in a new political context (the history of his use of the 1795 Bristol lecture, or of the re-publication of the 'Frost at Midnight', 'Fears in Solitude', 'France: An Ode' pamphlet,[28] for example), this systematic displacement of the complex heterodoxy of the historical moment in favour of the ideological certainty of 'consistency' is representative of a tendency to regulate meaning, and must be understood as one of the driving goals in posthumously constructing Coleridge's politics in a socially acceptable form. Such a goal sacrifices the sheer variety of the rhetorical tropes and strategies of the political game as it was played, its use of pathos in creating political sympathy for example, in the service of the posthumous process of 'quilting' the ideological fiction of Coleridge's 'consistency'. In creating the 'precious essence' of the authorial subject, Sara Coleridge erases the historical moments in which that subject lived. By 1850 the 'shame', as the *Times* reviewer put it, of the chaotic Romantic body, excessive, sensual, degraded by feeling, had to be hidden from the view of polite society. In the field of politics Sara demurred from the candour that formed such a striking feature in her account of the chaotic composition of *Biographia Literaria*.

*

From her letters it is clear that in her efforts to represent what she assumed to be her father's Tory politics, Sara inadvertently reproduced Henry's reactionary bigotry, and succumbed to the paranoid fantasies of her Regent's Park neighbours. Her flight to Windsor can be understood as a moment of political hysteria, but the contradiction at the heart of her strange ambivalence to the Chartists (their demands were justified, but could not be met without creating anarchy) suggests a deeper problem. Sara's brilliant reconstruction of her father's ideas in the realms of theology and philosophy could not be translated to the political sphere. No matter whether Coleridge's views were produced by a rigorous method derived from an underlying faith in neo-Kantian Reason, discovered through self-consciousness and deployed by the will, historical circumstance impinged on his actions nonetheless, and historical contingency stubbornly resisted idealization. This problem manifested itself in her Introduction in the form of the otherwise unaccountable decision to dedicate almost forty pages to the mid-century political crisis raging in Ireland during the time she was writing. Structurally, this section paralleled the critique of Newman and Pusey in the Introduction to *Biographia Literaria*, and 'On Rationalism' from her edition of *Aids to Reflection*—an example of the extension of her father's principles into the present. In practice, the section quickly became a parody of that pattern. Coleridge's expressed views on Ireland were few, and hardly made a ripple in the three volumes of journalism that followed. Only the first of her six short sections on Ireland dealt with '[h]is sentiments respecting Ireland',[29] and even there the 'sentiments' cited were not his, but ones Sara assured the reader he shared. In particular, she interposed the views of James Mackintosh as identical to her father's. Her choice produced an uncanny effect; Mackintosh's public denunciation of his youthful 'Gallicism' stood in for Coleridge's professed shift to Toryism, a shift that could not be so easily mapped in the essays that followed, at least not without again raising the spectre of youthful Jacobinism. Despite the subject being the historical misrule of Ireland, Sara included the Mackintosh comparison to suggest a coincidence in authorial character as much as in their views of the relationship of the governor and the governed:

> My Father's opinions on the representative proportions of blame betwixt Britain the Great and the Little agreed with those of Sir James Mackintosh, no harebrained Irish agitator, or high-flown Hibernian literateur, but a calm Scottish philosopher in the calmest and wisest stage of his career, a statesman and a judge enured to business, whose benevolence was free alike from vulgar humanitarian fanaticism and from the selfishness of the declaiming demagogue, the wild oats of his early Gallicism transmuted, or retained only to form a brisker ingredient in the wheaten bread of his well-weighed philanthropy.[30]

This is a clever transposition; Coleridge, according to the rhetoric of the Introduction, never really had 'wild oats' during the Revolution debates given the solidity of his underlying 'consistency', but even if he had they would function, as did Mackintosh's, to enrich his intellectual maturity. Furthermore, 'declaiming demagogue' was an obvious, if unfair, charge to level against Coleridge during his Bristol political career, and Sara vindicated her father from that charge as well as the charge of 'vulgar humanitarian fanaticism' when she vindicated Mackintosh. In the end she did not really offer Mackintosh's views, only his reformed character.

The other speaker who stood in for Coleridge in her account was Aubrey de Vere. Irish intellectual and poet, de Vere was also Sara's constant correspondent and confidant. Her agitated letters during the 1848 Chartist demonstrations were written to him, and Mudge speculates that given the least encouragement he would have actively courted her. Ten years older than de Vere, Sara may have felt herself past the age for marriage. She may also have been enjoying the intellectual and personal independence of life without Henry. The cautious intimacy of their letters provided her with close friendship without the risk of relinquishing her independence. She admired de Vere's poetry and they engaged in detailed correspondence on religious questions, philosophy, and contemporary politics.[31] Her discussion of the history and contemporary crises of Ireland were mainly derived from de Vere's volume, *English Misrule and Irish Misdeeds.*[32]

She recapitulated de Vere's central arguments, citing them directly in a footnote in the section on her father's views. His analysis was subtle, and clearly beyond anything her father had considered. On the introduction of the Protestant Reformation into Ireland, for example, he recognized that the sociopolitical goal of the introduction of the new faith 'was not to diffuse Protestantism through the land but simply to subvert the R.C. Church'.[33] As Sara noted, the effect of this specific instance of the historical process of 'misrule' had been to destroy the moral foundations of the country and, expressed in deliberately religious terms, to deny the Irish their 'most effective means of grace'.[34] Coleridge's only participation in this debate, as Sara imagines it, was an 1811 article in the *Courier* in which he sided with Ireland by attacking the hateful English commonplace that the Irish were responsible for their poverty and suffering. Sara quoted from the article and summarized:

'Common justice demands that the chief and heaviest blame' (*of the low rank occupied by the main population of Ireland,*) should be taken to itself by the happier and more enlightened country, who having most of the power, had most incurred the obligation, to prevent or to remedy so lamentable a contrast, &c. &c. And again: 'If we have done wrong, *it is iniquitous to urge the effects of that wrong as exempting us from the duty of compensating for it*'.[35]

Her choice of 'obligation' over 'responsibility' displays the moral tenor of her analysis, as she redoubled her father's disdain for the cynical policy of decrying Ireland as a hopeless case and therefore beyond English help. Coleridge emphasized English culpability, Sara moral duty.

In the absence of further analysis by her father, Sara followed de Vere's lead and reconstructed the long history of English misrule, citing Spenser, Berkeley, even Maria Edgeworth on the deformation of the Irish character under English domination. Sara dedicated 'Section VII' of the Introduction to an analysis of the 'Irish Character', which at first blush seems embarrassingly paternalistic, but in historical terms probably represented a relatively enlightened view of the question. No one in England at the time, including de Vere, denied that the Irish character was deformed. Reactionary opinion laid the blame with nature; the Irish were simply lazy and ignorant. More enlightened views did not deny the charges of moral weakness, but held English misrule as their root cause. Sara produced a shocking list of attributes, but not before exempting de Vere and the rest of the Irish gentry in a timely parenthesis: '(the *educated* are citizens of the *world* and very faintly express national character—I refer to the uneducated in Ireland)'.[36] The surprising rhetoric of cosmopolitanism here is probably just an artefact of a necessary distinction. It is unlikely that Sara would have considered members of her own class less English than the peasantry and the working class. Her parenthesis makes honorary Englishmen of the Irish gentry, England understood as the quintessence of the enlightened 'world'. The list of character flaws constructs a familiar English stereotype of the Irish: '1. Confusion of Thought. 2. Levity, Inconstancy or Instability. 3. Untruthfulness. 4. Indolence. 5. Violence, in all its different forms'.[37] Again, Sara's authority for making such harsh judgements was de Vere. She quoted him on the effects of the 'Indolence' produced by generations of English domination, what he termed: 'our Insolent Content and savage Merriment in Misery'.[38] Despite the obvious objections to such stereotyping, this was nonetheless a perceptive piece of social psychology—the victims of colonial domination became listless and transformed their apparently inevitable social condition into a subject of grim humour. Diagnosing such national torpor could potentially rupture the ideological assumptions that 'naturalized' it. 'Merriment in Misery' represented a destructive coping mechanism that left the underlying causes of distress untouched and unquestioned. Understood from the perspective of de Vere's analysis, Sara's list held the potential of constructing an ideological critique of the English colonial politics that created the 'Irish National Character'.

All of Sara's material on the Irish question and its history is interesting, but, in the context of an Introduction to Coleridge's journalism, very nearly irrelevant. To say that the Irish question played a minor role in Coleridge's political thought is an obvious understatement. Why, then, did these sections appear in the Introduction, and how could they possibly serve her central argument for her father's 'consistency'? The cynical response is to assume bad faith, and see the focus on Ireland as a means to displace the more dangerous terrain of an actual account of her father's political views, his hatred of Pitt, for example. This seems too simple, and the length and centrality of the Ireland material suggests something more substantial than evasion. Structurally, the six sections hold the same position as her critique of Newman and Pusey in the Introduction to *Biographia Literaria*. Just as that long disquisition projected Coleridge's theological views into the present moment, simultaneously constructing their continuing relevance and her intellectual authority, her analysis of the current state of Ireland presumably represented her deployment of her father's political principles as the basis for her engagement with the Irish question. The problem is that the structural similarity is utterly facile. Coleridge's rationalism was indeed at the centre of theological debates, as was Sara's; in her analysis of the current state of the Irish question, Coleridge's political views were barely broached beyond recognition of English misrule and general sympathy for the suffering of the Irish. And the evidence of her letter to de Vere during the 1848 Chartist agitation revealed her as isolated and naïve in the face of contemporary politics.

Another reason for the dominance of the Ireland sections may not have been entirely self-conscious—her esteem for de Vere. The passage carefully recapitulates his views, and as we know from her 1848 correspondence she relied on him for both political comfort and political wisdom. Her admiration makes the Introduction, in part, homage to his sagacity and emotional strength. Asserting an absolute accord between de Vere's analysis and her father's political principles (despite a lack of any actual evidence) conflates her father and a man she greatly admires. Without belabouring a Freudian analysis of this transference, the emotional and psychological benefits of the passage are nonetheless obvious. Furthermore, seeing her father in de Vere constructs a highly personal version of another of her rhetorical goals—the establishment of her father's powers of political prophecy. De Vere appears in history as a confirmation of those powers.

That political conditions in contemporary Ireland offer a safer subject than the political upheavals on the continent and home during 1848 seems self-evident. Curiously, Sara created the need for this evasion in the construction of Coleridge's powers of political prophecy, which immediately preceded it. Conditions in England were different because of historical circumstance, an analysis she shared with her father, although one she tended to dress in a religious light. As she argued, Coleridge: 'insisted on the internal stability of the English constitution, and the difference of its condition, in this respect, from that of the continental kingdoms: when he declared that it had no need either of foreign war or measures of arbitrary severity at home, to preserve it from destructive change and convulsion'.[39] The first part of this claim is uncontroversial; the Glorious Revolution, through the establishment of the primacy of parliament, created fundamental institutional differences in England that guaranteed greater political stability. However, this view was hardly unique to Coleridge, and could not be considered prophetic given it was the foundational assumption in Burke's arguments against the Revolution in France. Sara was not necessarily trying to falsify the record and align her father with Burke in the Revolution controversy. For one thing, the success of such a gambit was unlikely despite the passage of a half-century. Coleridge's political commitments of the 1790s could not be simply denied, as she was introducing much of their substance with her edition. The second part of the sentence, however, deliberately distorted the very nature of his political rhetoric by making it appear his arguments against 'foreign wars' and domestic repression, as unnecessary for political stability, followed from his essentially Burkean views. The opposite was true; his opposition to the first Ministerial war with France and denunciation of the Stamp Act, the Gagging Bills, and 'Ministerial treason' in general put him at risk and completely at odds with the strategic hysteria of Burkean evocations of foreign anarchy. The subsequent six sections on Ireland took the place of any further analysis of this historical record, and abruptly concluded the interesting comparison of the political unrest of 1848 and the political upheavals of the 1790s. Had she pursued the comparison an uncomfortable truth would have emerged: Coleridge in the 1790s was in the position of the Chartists, subject to relentless government propaganda and the threat of state violence. His views certainly would not have made him a supporter of the wildly unpopular Duke of Wellington, nor would he have had much sympathy for the self-satisfied, if somewhat hysterical, inhabitants of Regent's Park.

Her religious gloss both exacerbated the problem and made the ideological displacement of history more complete. On the second page heading in the section on 'His Powers of Political Prophecy', she pronounced the 'Moral Superiority of England' arguing that English political stability was divinely ordained. She challenged the reader:

> Not to ascribe the peaceful state of England, in this epoch of change, and her exemption from injurious commotions, to the cause I have indicated [English moral superiority], is to betray want of faith in a moral governor of the World.[40]

At the risk of appearing impious, the execution of Charles I and the arbitrary choice of the Electress of Hanover and her heirs to replace the Stuarts were many things, but they were not acts of providence. Sara conceded that England was not perfect; she was guilty of 'crimes' in 'past ages', the risky terrain of the first Ministerial war, and 'errors and short comings in the present',[41] the much safer matter of misrule in Ireland, the subject that dominated the rest of the Introduction. In the final analysis, it is difficult not to object to Sara's use of providence to efface the very history that made England exceptional, and which her father so carefully analysed. The pattern of forgetting was endemic in her method, and her efforts to isolate an unchanging, self-reflective subjectivity in her father's 'consistency' functioned as an ideological screen through which we were to view his journalism. Whether these subtle rhetorical manoeuvres—the imposition of the Irish question, the confusion of Coleridgean and Burkean views from the 1790s, etc.—were deliberate cannot be definitively established. As I noted above, the possible reasons for the introduction of the Irish material were overdetermined, and Sara herself was clearly an interpolated subject. Growing up in Southey's household, marrying an ultra-Tory who kept her isolated in Regent's Park, it hardly comes as a surprise that Sara succumbed to the retrograde views of her immediate neighbours, her Tory relations, and Coleridge's other executors. In that light, her naïve speculation to de Vere that it could be true that the Duke of Wellington was unpopular indicated both her unworldliness, and the possibility that she might ultimately emerge from the fog. Her premature death at forty-nine two years later cut short an extraordinary process of self-discovery and self-invention, and her friendship with de Vere had the potential to free her from the insidious afterlife of Henry. Freed to live her life by his death, she had become an important theologian and philosopher, potentially an important social figure, and by far the most important figure in the posthumous construction of Coleridge.[42]

8
Collecting Coleridge

In the final weeks of his life Henry Nelson Coleridge became embroiled in an increasingly acrimonious exchange with William Pickering over the publishing future of the Coleridge corpus. Henry had decided, on behalf of the executors, to leave Pickering and move to Edward Moxon. William Wordsworth's deal with Moxon had very attractive financial terms and Henry felt Coleridge's works deserved as generous a deal. Moxon was willing to offer two thirds of all sales to the estate while he kept one third. The deal with Pickering was fifty-fifty with Pickering charging a five per cent annual fee. Henry had completely miscalculated, however, in thinking that Pickering would simply relinquish the publishing rights and unsold stock of the extant editions. Insulted and irritated by Henry's arrogant attitude, Pickering made a counter offer that put the situation in a stark light: they could have the rights if they bought the complete inventory at the 'trade price'. Pickering felt entitled to recoup his half of the total value of the stock, based on his history of risk-taking on Coleridge's behalf, and as compensation for the loss of future profits. The expense of buying the inventory killed any deal, and showed the family who had the upper hand in any future negotiations. Before deciding that Pickering was greedy and the family simply wanted a fair deal, it is important to examine what Henry had failed to acknowledge until too late—Pickering's record as their publisher.

Henry's failing health (he was literally conducting the negotiations from his deathbed) made the situation much more difficult. Even in these circumstances Green wrote to Sara begging off and apologizing for his unsuitability as a negotiator:

My experience with publishers and of business connected with them has been so slight, that I more than distrust my capability of offering any available advice in this very important affair; and though I am quite ready to perform promptly and cheerfully the duty imposed upon me by my lamented friend's will, I should be glad of some better information than I possess at present in order to secure the advantages of the sale of his works to your family. Hitherto the management of the business of publication has been entirely under the more than able direction of Mr Henry Coleridge, that I have had scarcely any intercourse with Pickering on the subject, and circumstances may have escaped my attention which ought perhaps have been noticed.[1]

The 'circumstances' that 'may have escaped his attention' were at the root of the family's dissatisfaction with Pickering; he was constantly late paying the annual Christmas dividend to the estate. The issue had simmered since at least 1840 when Henry wrote to Derwent to report on the state of the overall fund and the expected continuing return on the works then in print. He reported that after he finally got Pickering to pay the trust what he owed ('at Xmas 1838'), and that the fund stood at 'about £3070' and 'stock = £92 per annum or thereabouts'.[2] The two-year delay in payment of the dividend particularly grated, and he attempted to set their relationship with Pickering on a firmer footing or dissolve it. In 1842, he wrote to remind Pickering that the income generated by the fund provided needed income to Coleridge's widow, Sarah Fricker Coleridge, and Hartley:

I am not afraid to speak to you, in a confidential manner, concerning the persons interested in this fund: two of them, my mother-in-law, Mrs S.T. Coleridge, and Mr Hartley Coleridge, are objects of very special care & attention to me and to Mr Green, my Uncle's Executor. The shares which belong to myself, through my wife, and to Mr Derwent Coleridge, are comparatively of less importance under the circumstances; but to Mrs S.T. Coleridge, who has the income of the whole, during her life, the security and the reasonable increase to be expected from the fund has, for a long time, been the subject of much natural interest, both on her own account, as furnishing her with a little ampler means every year, and also, prospectively, on account of her eldest son, who stands & will stand through life more in need of positive help than any other of his family.[3]

The cordial tone here, as he noted their concerns and motives, masked his growing frustration. The draft of this letter in the Harry S. Ransom

Center begins in Sara's hand, as she served as amanuensis as he lay gravely ill, but an earlier version is in Henry's shaky hand, and betrays a tone not present when he was dictating to Sara. The possibility of moving to Moxon under much improved terms had arisen, and coupled with his ongoing anger over late payments and poor accounting, Henry sought to justify dissolving their relationship with Pickering. Recognizing that he had no legal basis on which to proceed (he admitted as much) he attached a hectoring list of demands to clarify and improve their terms, or, he hoped, dissolve their 'whole contract':

1. that from the 1st of January 1843 the net profits shall be divided into 3 parts two of which will be for the estate and one for the publisher.
2. That the publisher shall be at liberty to charge commission of 5 per cent on the copies sold as before.
3. That the accounts of end year to Xmas shall be finally made up & settled by midsummer day the following year & this to be considered a strict condition upon the breach of which the whole contract shall be at an end and the Executor shall be at liberty to transfer the account elsewhere the publisher in that case rendering an account and the balances being paid on one side or another as the case may be.
4. That a statement of the sales during the preceding year shall be made out & rendered to the Executor before end of the month of January following.[4]

He wanted Pickering to voluntarily match Moxon's proposed terms of two thirds/one third, and offered the continuation of Pickering's five per cent commission as a compromise. His anger got the best of him, as he demanded that if Pickering were ever again late with a dividend or in the year-end accounting the contract would be void. That Pickering had never made any of these deadlines in the years Henry had dealt with him both explains the tone, but also reveals the intent—the dissolution of their relationship and the move to Moxon. Part of the intent was to shame Pickering over past offences; he suggested that Pickering had undervalued Coleridge's works and exaggerated the risk in publishing them:

> Now I think you will not yourself say that there is any ultimate risk attending the sale of Coleridge's works—however the case may have appeared some years back it is entirely altered now. You have yourself sold several thousand copies of the poems; and the 'Aids' are now in your hands on the eve of a fifth edition. The other works have also

all had a more or less firm sale, and judging from the note which I have of the number of copies in your hands at Xmas 40—two entire years ago—since which I have seen no account whatever, I shall surmise that several other of his works must by this time be either out of print or very nearly so. In particular, I find by my note that the late[?] work entitled 'the Confessions' had within two months of its first publication in the autumn of 1840 entirely cleared itself of debt excepting a sum of £3 odd shillings and there can be no doubt but that in general every successive year adds & will add to the name fame & notoriety of Mr Coleridge and secure to his works now that they are effectually protected by law a more and more steady & extensive sale.[5]

Barely diplomatic in acknowledging that Pickering had borne considerable risk when he began publishing Coleridge's works, Henry felt fully justified in demanding new terms. His argument was moot; Pickering had the stock and the legal right to publish and sell the works, and could simply stonewall and continue under the terms Henry found so onerous.

What Henry missed in their exchanges, and what made this tone such a blunder, was that Pickering had not taken on publication as a purely commercial enterprise. He felt committed to the work, and to keeping it in print. 'Confessions', as Henry called it, referred to *Confessions of an Enquiring Spirit*, originally intended as an addition to *Aids to Reflection*, and concentrated on Coleridge's method of Biblical interpretation— hardly a title that seemed likely to be profitable. Pickering had produced a handsome edition and it had done well. For this he was given no credit, and, in fact, received disapprobation that he had not sufficiently recognized its success. Clearly aggrieved, Pickering let Henry wait for over five weeks before making his case, choosing a tone of sadness and resignation. He agreed that Henry had the duty to act for 'the benefit of the family', but insisted that their interests had never been competing, nor had his motive for publishing ever been monetary:

Mr Moxon seems to expect that I am to hand over to him all the stock without paying anything & he says that he only engages to print such works as <u>he thinks</u> will answer <u>his purpose</u> mentioning the Poems & Aids. The slower selling books such as Friend, Remains & Church & State the Executor may do. This will of course make great difference to the family & also to the publisher. Take the instance of the Friend—what cost nearly 300£ in 1837 & has now just returned the prime cost. If the family or any publisher had done it—the interest of Capital would be 5 per cent & any expenses of selling—5 per cent & copies & other expenses probably another 5 per cent—The question of whether Mr Moxon would undertake to do these works with the saleable ones & on the same terms.

I have printed every book that the Executor has wished & I now assure you never with the selfish view of making money for myself only, indeed this has not been the motive but a regard for the Author, for his writings & from every one connected with them up to this time I have uniformly experienced kindness. If I had made a large profit I should not for moment hesitate to meet your wishes & of course it will be with regret that I am compelled to give up an interest in a property which I have done somewhat to raise & which I feel assured that the Author himself would not of done. Still I cannot but think that this [hard? MS illegible] measure ought to be well considered & that the terms offered by Mr Moxon should be fairly compared with the present arrangement—he does not keep a large bound stock for the public & the trade, nor does he keep a [? MS illegible] clear, whereby he may save something—I forbear to say more. If he engages to give you 2/3 the profits of 4 vols & only embarks the capital necessary for this—It is very different to taking the risque of 13 Vols & giving one half the profits.[6]

Pickering's pride and dignity had clearly been hurt, but his broader point about his commitment to keeping all of Coleridge's works continually in print and ensuring the production of future volumes out of a 'regard for the Author', was well taken. At such an early stage of negotiation, Moxon's plans for the corpus had yet to be ascertained. By insisting that he was dedicated to Coleridge's memory, he turned the tables and made Henry the party moved by purely, if understandably, commercial interests. He ended by sadly noting the terms under which Moxon could assume publication rights:

If I deliver the Copies of all the Works to Mr Moxon he will of course pay for them & I shall pay one half over to you. I shall only request that he cancel my name in the title pages.

I have to apologize for not writing before, but not being the most agreeable subject to write upon & being for several days engaged in disposing of my old house I have been so occupied that I could not do it.[7]

The tone of resigned reasonableness masked the opposite intention. The uncontroversial statement that Moxon would 'of course pay for' the stock assumed the 'trade price', and was designed to block the transfer—something Moxon quickly recognized.

Having discussed the matter with Pickering the previous week, Moxon wrote to Sara to let her know what to expect:

> I have only <u>just</u> been able to ascertain what Mr Pickering deems would be fair compensation upon his giving up Mr Coleridge's works, which is neither more nor less than this:—that he considers himself part proprietor, and that he would require that the <u>entire</u> stock including the unpublished edition of the Aids to Reflection, should be purchased by me of him, at the <u>full</u> trade price, and that he would then simply account to you for your half share of the profit! This view of the matter satisfies me that there is not the slightest chance of my being able to effect an amicable arrangement with him.[8]

The previous week Moxon had hoped that they could reach a compromise in which Pickering remained the agent for the extant works and, indeed, felt that, 'it would be better that he should continue to sell the old stock'.[9] At issue was the new edition of *Aids to Reflection*, which Moxon felt 'wholly at [Sara's] disposal, Mr Pickering as yet having expended upon it neither time nor capital'.[10] Discovering that Pickering considered the new *Aids to Reflection* part of the existing stock came as a shock, and he assured Sara that he would ask his brother, a lawyer, to find out whether or not 'Mr Pickering will not consider himself entitled to [her] Essay',[11] a reference to 'On Rationalism'. That Sara's important essay was at stake in this tortured process makes it grimly fascinating. As Henry's health rapidly deteriorated (he died on 26 January) Sara's voice became the voice of record in the family's editorial decisions. Moving from fair copyist to amanuensis had already moderated Henry's tone, and in a dramatic letter probably written within a day of his death, her voice suddenly, of necessity, took over. She marked the change with an asterisk: '*So far was dictated by my husband word for word—the rest is the substance of what he added in conversation'. She attempted to ventriloquize 'the substance' of Henry's thought, but the tone of conciliation was hers:

> I have now nothing further to add than my sincere regret at any uneasiness which this affair may have occasioned to you in common with ourselves, and my acknowledgement of your services to

Mr Coleridge's works. In my last letter I expressed, or meant to express, my sense of them and at the same time, my opinion how far our obligation to you upon the score of those services extends.[12]

This was a skilful conclusion for the letter, apologizing for any hurt feelings and personally acknowledging Pickering's contribution to Coleridge's public reputation, but also subtly censuring with the implication that 'this affair' included the final illness and death of Henry. The letter is postmarked 14 February 1843, almost three weeks after the death and enough time to ensure that Pickering had received the news. Sara stopped just short of accusing Pickering of taking advantage of Henry's illness, a charge difficult to deny on Henry's own testimony from his portion of the letter. Physically unable to enter formal 'arbitration' to determine the value of the stock, he hoped to negotiate a settlement by having Pickering name a 'reasonable' price:

Now, my dear Pickering, if you seriously intend to insist upon these latter terms, I shall have nothing more to say than that you must have your way, for I am far too ill to think of trying any point of law, and I would much rather avoid even an arbitration. Nevertheless, if you are not unwilling to condescend to that mode, I believe it would be the proper way to settle the affair pending between us.

What I have to propose, however, is this. In the first place, will you be good enough to name the precise sum which you will finally require on consideration of the delivery of the copies by you to Mr Moxon? It is possible that I may be able to meet your requisition.[13]

Sara sent this reasonable voice from the grave to Pickering, but this last effort to extricate them from Pickering failed, and the matter died with Henry, at least for the time being.

Now in charge of editorial decisions and future negotiations, Sara asked Moxon the question Pickering had broached concerning plans for future editions. She sent him the gist of Pickering's December letter pointing out the considerable difference between the two publishers of offering two thirds of the profits on four volumes, or the continuing commitment to publish thirteen volumes. After concluding that Pickering's terms were designed to ensure that the rights not be transferred, Moxon offered a measured equivocal response to the crucial question:

Mr Pickering is, I can see, angry with me for having accepted your proposal. You say in your note that he says: 'Mr Moxon seems to expect that I am to hand over to him all the stock without paying anything.' I never expected any thing of the kind nor gave him to understand that either you or myself entertained any such expectation; I thought that, in addition to what might be due to him on account of such books as had not paid their expenses, he would most likely require <u>some</u> compensation, but I certainly never imagined that he would contemplate that the entire stock, published and unpublished, should be purchased at the full trade price either by myself or the Executors, and I can only look upon his demand of such terms as an attempt to make the transfer of the books wholly impracticable. He further says: 'Mr M. only engages to print such works as <u>he</u> thinks will answer <u>his</u> purposes.'... Mr Pickering yesterday put this question to me. 'Would you reprint the "Church & State" and the "Friend"?' My answer was; that would depend entirely upon the future sales, and that I had no doubt but that Mr Coleridge [Henry] would allow me the same discretion that had ever been allowed me by Mr Wordsworth & any other Authors for whom I publish.[14]

This was the wrong answer. Sara rightly felt that the deal with Pickering was unfair; he insisted on terms based on the financial risk of publication at the beginning of his relationship with Coleridge, a risk that no longer existed. As she put it:

we cannot help thinking that whatever risk you may then have run has been fully compensated to you by the terms in which for eight years you have published both these and other works of the author not contemplated in the beginning of the connexion: the sale did not long continue to be uncertain, and it seems hardly fair that conditions of publication suited only to a state of things which soon passed away should be continued indefinitely.[15]

However, despite her irritation over unfair financial terms, Pickering's commitment to keeping all of Coleridge's works, those extant, those planned, and those yet to be conceived, in print was unwavering. This was not a commitment Moxon would make, and after Henry's death negotiations with Moxon ceased, and plans to move to another press with more attractive terms went into abeyance. In the end, intellectual considerations outweighed monetary need.[16] As Sara took up her dual task as general editor and volume editor, she operated in an interesting paradox: the more successful she was, the more onerous and unfair the original terms with Pickering became as they 'continued indefinitely'.

Pickering had carried the day by arguing that he was more sensitive to the memory of Coleridge and the mission of publication, and by effectively holding the physical stock hostage. Neither the estate nor Moxon would pay the full 'trade price'; that put the matter at an end.[17]

Their reluctant partnership had an ideal test at the outset. Sara's edition of *Aids to Reflection* had been somewhere between in press and in limbo throughout these protracted, and failed, negotiations. Once it was decided that Pickering would continue as publisher, he wrote with his plan for the edition:

> It was not till this evening that I received from the Printer a copy of the new Aids—I have no time in giving you my opinion of what I think will be best to do, seeing that it is now grown so large. In making the suggestion I do not wish to do any thing that will not be quite agreeable to yourself, but if [it?] is divided into two volumes—the second should contain Mr Marsh's Essay & three Appendices—& in the advertisement simply state the fact it was found too large for one volume & that the second contains as above. If the Appendices are published separately very few would purchase, the Book is known & the Publishers apply for the Aids—& if the Supplement was mentioned they would say we do not want that, it is not ordered, a usual phrase having no relation to the value or importance of the work. I judge you will reluctantly place Mr Marsh's Essay at the end, still as it is not Mr Coleridge's I see no impropriety in doing so & this will nearly equalize the volumes.[18]

The tone and substance of the letter must have gone a long way towards convincing Sara that she had made the right choice. Pickering recognized the value of 'On Rationalism', and suggested a two-volume set to accommodate it. There was risk involved; *Aids to Reflection* was their second most profitable title. Yet, the risk was judged to be worth it to put Sara's essay before the public. Pickering demonstrated the shrewdness necessary to make the edition a success, recognizing that there was no market for Sara's essay on its own, and taking care to indicate that the lack of a ready market had 'no relation to the value or importance of the work'. He also recognized that the likely objection to the scheme would be the removal of Marsh's Introduction, so long a feature of the work, to the second volume. Showing himself sensitive to the issue, but arguing for its 'propriety' nonetheless, also indicated careful deliberation and provided evidence of his intellectual bona fides. In short, if his goal was to win Sara over, it was a perfect letter, and ended with an eloquent acknowledgement of Henry's death and his contribution as an editor: 'I am well aware of the great loss <u>all</u> have sustained in the loving labours of the Editor, altho' your loss is greatest still you must not despond, but bear the trial with cheerfulness'.[19] Offering solace and respecting Henry's memory, despite their recent antagonisms, was crucial if he and Sara were to get on with the dual tasks of editing and republishing the existing works, and determining what would constitute the complete works.

Besides finishing *Aids to Reflection*, they had to plan the new edition of *Biographia Literaria* and determine how best to publish the *Literary Remains*. The latter also required diplomatic skill. Henry's volume of *Literary Remains* had not been successful, either financially or intellectually. Even the circumspect Green had commented to Henry about the randomness of the volume, albeit couched in a compliment about his intellectual prowess:

> Were I to venture any remark on your performance as editor I would say, if you will forgive me, that some of the latter essays appear to have stepped out of their place; but with this exception, I am sure that the friends of Coleridge will be grateful to you for the manner, in which you have performed your task, and may only regret that you have too little tasked your own literary ability, in exercising what you deemed a wise discretion by abstaining from comment or addition.[20]

Pickering suggested that they put the *Literary Remains* on a firmer foundation by dividing them into a series of coherent volumes:

> I suggested to Mr Green that I thought parts of the Remains might be more popular by printing in the smaller size the notes &c. on Shakespeare—in one vol, the notes on Jeremy Taylor & other divines in one or two, perhaps not at the same time—& thus by degrees to get all the works in the same size.[21]

Again, Pickering showed a skilful combination of commercial shrewdness and intellectual rigour. Once the volume size for the complete works was established with the two-volume *Aids to Reflection* serving as the model, the reading public would be eager to receive future editions. Establishing the idea of a forthcoming set of editions all contributing to the overall corpus was excellent marketing. Sara readily adopted this scheme as she began to formulate the complete works, and Pickering helped by exonerating Henry's unsuccessful edition as a product of circumstances:

> The Remains are certainly as valueable, and calculated to be as popular as any of Mr Coleridge's other works—the original idea was to try to get more by the first publication—but making the portions distinct will be the best to adopt hereafter.[22]

The double senses of 'valueable', 'calculated', and 'more', referring at once to intellectual value and commercial potential, make this a good vignette to see the ongoing basis of their professional relationship—both considerations had to be met for agreement to be reached. Pickering's final deliberations on the two-volume *Aids to Reflection* balanced the two criteria perfectly: 'The addition [of "On Rationalism"] will give so much novelty to the Edition that I hope it will more than compensate for the difference [in price between one large volume and two smaller volumes] & as you intended to benefit the work, it would be unreasonable that any loss should be borne by you.'[23] In essence he said that there was risk, and that they should share it, being in agreement about the value of her addition and the commercial sense of offering two volumes at ten shillings instead of one volume at nine. More important, he recognized both values in the 'novelty' of the complex critical apparatus, appendices, and supplementary essay. He became a willing collaborator in the production of a comprehensive scholarly edition, partly because he thought there was a market, partly from his respect for Coleridge and, increasingly, for Sara. Sara's necessarily complex Introduction to *Biographia Literaria* was accepted as a matter of course.

Once *Biographia Literaria* was completed, they could concentrate on how best to 're-arrange' the works already in print. In September 1848 they exchanged letters on organizing the *Literary Remains* into a series of coherent volumes of approximately the same size. Pickering began by suggesting that they remove various poems that were scattered throughout Henry's edition of the *Remains*, including 'The Fall of Robespierre', and 'Poetical fragments' and add them to a new three-volume edition of the poems. That accomplished, they could concentrate on rearranging the prose based on content and genre. For example, he suggested that the criticism on Shakespeare be part of a multiple-volume set of 'Critical Writings', and that it be divided into a volume of 'Notes on Shakespeare and other dramatists' where the 'Lectures' on Shakespeare would only be 'referred to', and another volume dedicated to the 'Lectures'.[24] He had begun to think about an 'Omniana' volume, or perhaps two volumes, but had not yet begun to work out what would be included or how it could be organized. He also agreed to a suggestion by Sara that they add the 'Lay Sermons' to *Confessions of an Inquiring Spirit* to 'equalize' the size of various volumes. Removal of 'Lay Sermons' from the 'Church & State' would reduce that volume's size to a 'proportion' where it would be better priced and easier to sell.[25] Given the overlapping subject matter, this was a good plan, and increased sales did not simply mean more profits, but also wider dissemination of key Coleridge texts. He also sent her a complete copy of Henry's four-volume *Literary Remains* to work from as she 're-arranged'.

Sara responded on 20 September with a long letter and a detailed proposal for a carefully organized eleven-volume set. With the extant volumes before her, she quickly diagnosed the problems with the current arrangement, or lack thereof, and made that part of the rationale for what she recognized was an ambitious scheme:

> I send you a plan partly suggested by yourself, for a new distribution of the Remains & other minor writings of my Father. I know not whether economy will permit its adoption—on account of the copies of Lit. Rem. Vols III & IV & of the thick single vol. (containing Church & State & Lay Sermons) yet to be disposed of. But I think, as regards the advantage of the works—it would be a good one. It makes a number of light vols of nearly equal size, with a more orderly arrangement, as to subject, than hitherto has been possible—as each vol in my scheme is confined to writings of a certain class—and this order would render it easier to find any particular remark, essay, or article. The reader would know where to look for it by subject. Whereas now, religious & political & critical writings are so mingled together, that I myself am often at a loss for some time where to find some passage which in itself I perfectly remember.[26]

Pickering had foreseen the problem of having competing editions in the marketplace, and acknowledged that he would have to 'cancel & destroy the present edition of Lay Sermons'. His letter had included an account of the current stock of the various volumes, so Sara knew that only 122 copies of *Church & State* remained as of 30 December 1847, and that the first two volumes of *Literary Remains* were out of print, leaving 154 copies of volume three and 315 copies of volume four[27] as their potential losses once they decided to supersede Henry's hopelessly 'mingled' edition. With the two of them in agreement that such losses were acceptable given the potential of the new edition, Sara offered a working proposal under the heading: 'Coleridge's "Literary Remains"; "Church & State"; "Confessions"; M.S. Marginalia, and Political articles formerly printed re-arranged'.[28] Using four basic categories: literary and critical, political, theological, and the catchall omniana, she sketched a possible arrangement. However, such category divisions proved slippery, and even in the copy she sent to Pickering she crossed out essays in the critical section that she deemed more 'philosophical'. Nonetheless, her proposal gave an overall shape to Coleridge's corpus by constitut- ing a series of volumes in addition to the established *Aids to Reflection*, *Poems*, and *The Friend*, and the soon to appear new edition of *Biographia Literaria*. This document guided them as they moved forward, and in some cases they made even more ambitious decisions. Notably, they expanded their plans for two volumes of political writing that were to include only '2½ pages' from *The Watchman* and some selections from his writing for *The Morning Post* and *The Courier*. In the end, they decided the political journalism deserved a much more generous selec- tion, and Sara produced the three-volume *Essays On His Own Times*.

The other new feature of Sara's proposal was the organization of the Marginalia into separate volumes *as* Marginalia. She projected three volumes. Most of the material was scattered throughout Henry's edi- tion of *Literary Remains*, and her outline clearly stated the location of each passage. For example, Pickering, according to her note, had the manuscript of the 'Notes on Baxter', and she marked the page numbers in *Literary Remains* '(LR. I. 263–66)'[29] for the 'Notes in Baxter's Life of Himself'. Volumes VIII and IX of the new set would have the most exten- sive and important Marginalia:[30] the Baxter materials, 'Notes on Taylor', Hooker, Leighton, Luther, Pilgrim's Progress, et cetera. She had also begun to divide the 'miscellaneous Marginalia' into categories to make up the final volume of the series. She imagined the volume divided into Historical (including two editions of Pepys's Diary), Political (including Cromwell's Tracts), Physical (including Boerhaave's Chemistry), and Philosophical (including 'one sentence' on Berkeley's Tarwater).[31] This material had not been printed in previous works, and she produced fair copy manuscripts of it. Having gone through the libraries of Gillman, Green, Southey, Lamb[32] and others, she continued to look for and find annotated volumes, and this complicated process provided the founda- tion for the six volumes of *The Marginalia* edited by H. J. Jackson and George Whalley for the Collected Coleridge.[33] Their definitive edition avoided the conceptual nightmare of trying to establish whether material was Philosophical or Political or Theological by organizing the volumes alphabetically by author. Sara's contribution here was the recognition that the Marginalia should be collected in separate volumes rather than interspersed throughout the *Literary Remains* and the other works as supplementary material.

Following the appearance of *Essays On His Own Times*, and after a productive eight-year professional relationship with Pickering, Sara finally completed the move to Edward Moxon in 1850. Moxon wrote in January 1851 to confirm the move: 'You will I am sure be glad to hear that the matter has been finally settled with Pickering. I have received from him the entire stock, and have paid him for half his share £831. As the books have been taken off his hands at the full price, he has every reason to be, & I trust is, satisfied with the arrangement.'[34] We do not hear from Pickering,[35] although I imagine he experienced some sadness. They had put the Coleridge corpus on a strong footing, and completed much of the work that would serve as the foundation for future editors, Derwent and his son Ernest Hartley, and the editors of the Coburn Collected Coleridge. After eight years, Pickering received his original terms, the full 'trade price'. Moxon and Sara felt able to pay the full price in 1850 because of the success of Sara's work as editor. What appeared a risky venture in 1843, and a price Moxon considered 'most exorbitant',[36] now seemed reasonable. The financial pressures that formed the stated justification for their original desire to move to Moxon for his more attractive financial terms, the maintenance of Sarah Fricker Coleridge and Hartley, had ended with Sarah's death in 1845 and Hartley's in 1849, so Sara was in essence securing improved financial terms for future generations, just as the editions themselves had established the conceptual foundation for future family editors. On this last point, Moxon had clearly seen the light, and replaced his over-cautious equivocation of 1843 with genuine enthusiasm for future endeavours in the ongoing construction of Coleridge: 'I need not say that no pains shall be spared on my part either in promoting the sale of the Works, or in the "getting up" of future editions'.[37]

*

Coleridge's sometimes-erratic lifestyle and unusual compositional practices meant that Sara could not hope to recover all the works, the complete Marginalia being an obvious example. For this reason, she and Pickering were not completely in control of the corpus. A notable example occurred in 1848 with the sudden appearance of the 'Idea of Life' attributed to Coleridge and James Gillman. Published by Dr Watson without the permission of the literary executor or Sara, it provoked anger against the publisher and, especially, against James Gillman, junior, whom she had known as a schoolboy. The publisher expressed regret for not gaining permission, but comforted himself with the belief that the work was in some way James Gillman's and thus 'his son's to dispose of as he would'.[38] The work appeared genuine and the obvious inference was that Gillman had served as amanuensis, and the publisher had exploited the ruse of joint authorship to avoid gaining the necessary permissions. Sara heaped scorn on the idea that Gillman could in any way be considered the author. Her disdain for his intellect had been acute since the publication of his memoir of Coleridge, a work she found risible and evidence of 'how long an unwise man may live with a wise one without catching any of his wisdom'.[39] She made Gillman's lack of qualification clear in a letter to Julius Hare, saying that Gillman knew nothing of 'Sir Humphry Davy, of Kant, of Schelling',[40] et cetera. She suspected that the source was either 'from [her] father's dictation or transcribed from his rough manuscript'. Hare agreed that the text was genuine and joined her in speculating on its origins:

> I could not read half a dozen sentences without [persuading? MS illegible] that it was genuine. Still one should much like to know something about its history, how your father came to compose & dictate such a dissertation. Can it have been in any way connected with a course of Lectures which he delivered on philosophy in the year 1820? 1819? I heard two of them at the Crown & Anchor. The Gillmans used to be there with him; & I heard something of the same tone & cast of speculation in one of them.[41]

Evidently written as a philosophical lecture, Hare's conjecture made sense, and the essay is now included in *Lectures 1818–1819: On the History of Philosophy* in the Collected Coleridge.[42]

Coleridge's Notebooks were the major work that Sara chose not to publish. She clearly considered an edition, but demurred under the advice of her friend and adviser, Hare. Posthumous reputation was again at issue, but Hare framed their concerns in stark social terms:

> About the publication of them [the Fly-Catchers] in their totality I feel the strongest scruples, and would earnestly dissuade it. One of my main reasons for this is my conviction, that, in the present state of feeling in England with regard to the Bible, it would entirely destroy the influence of your Father's writings with the persons who at present derive the greatest benefit from them. He would be laid

under the same sort of interdict with Strauss [? MS illegible] & Tom Payne, would be cried up by unbelievers, who would not appreciate the real treasures of his doctrine, for the sake of undermining Christianity; while with the great body of English students, his other writings would be sunk by the weight of these. Now surely, if this were to be the result, as I cannot doubt, of the publication, this would be acting in direct contrariety to the principles which guided his practice through his life, would banish him from those whom he especially desired to teach, & would make him the aider & abetter of principles that he abhorred.[43]

It was not so much fear of possible scandal; there was the risk that his engagement with the Higher Criticism would be misconstrued as unbelief. A complete record of Coleridge's religious views, his vehement attacks on the veracity of the Book of Daniel or the spuriousness of the nativity accounts in the Gospels for example, might make him an 'aider & abetter' of religious sceptics. Hare's anxieties in 1850 seemed even more pronounced than the family pressures exerted on Henry to suppress Coleridge's Biblical philology in *Table Talk*. By 1850 there was more at stake. Hare implies that publishing the 'Fly-Catchers' (the name Coleridge gave the notebooks because they captured the various thoughts buzzing in his head) risked destroying the influence of *Aids to Reflection* on 'those he desired to teach', putting at risk the 'clerisy' project in which Sara was so invested. That they made their decision in response to the inane Biblical literalism that Coleridge found appalling could not be helped—the social stakes were too high. Better to leave the notebooks unpublished than lose Coleridge's influence on those who 'derive[d] the greatest benefit' from it in the 'formation of a Christian character'. This argument proved decisive for Sara as it suggested an unacceptable threat to the patterns of dissemination of Coleridge's religious thought that she had so carefully traced and fostered in her commitment to promoting 'Rational Christianity'. A possible course of action would be to produce a selection from the notebooks, avoiding dangerous religious terrain while providing an accurate portrait of Coleridge's mind, the rationale for publishing. The letter makes it clear that Sara had asked Hare to consider acting as editor in producing a selection. However, he excused himself, pleading lack of time while encouraging her to at least consider the project:

I cannot see any obligation that should preclude you from exercising your discretion in selecting such portions of your father's manuscripts as appear likely to increase his beneficial influence, & to omit what would mar it. Or if you think the exercise of such criticism on him unbecoming your daughterly relation the task of selection might be entrusted to some friend, if you know of any one qualified for the work.[44]

'Exercising your discretion' was a polite phrase for suppressing heretical views, but the potential benefit was the promotion of her father's most influential theological ideas. The problem was that if she could not bring herself to produce this guarded, not to say censored, version, then where would she find 'any one qualified for the work'. Hare, the obvious choice, would not risk any religious association that might jeopardize his own Coleridgean religious project—the Broad Church Movement. This meant that his selection would be necessarily circumscribed:

My own reasons for declining the undertaking are, besides the want of time, that, unless I confined the selection to these parts which would not offend any religious prejudices, the outcry which has already been raised against me would be so increast,—my very position in the Church & the line I have hitherto taken bring incitements to people to join in it,—that whatever influence I may now possess,—& I receive frequent proofs that I do exercise some,—would be entirely destroyed: and this sacrifice would not be compensated by any corresponding good.[45]

Already a target for professing his Coleridgean rationalism, Hare could not see an outcome worth the risk of diminishing his position in the Church. That put the question of Hare's participation at an end, but he nonetheless addressed her 'view of [her] duty to set forth your Father's whole mind' by producing a complete edition. He argued that there was a compromise available:

allow me to observe that, if your father had enjoined the publication of all that is contained in his Fly-catchers, in that case no choice would be left you but either to publish them entirely or to resign the task altogether. But I conceive it is very certain that these observations were not written with any purpose of their being published in the exact state in which they were written. It is no less certain that your Father would not have published them in this state during his life.[46]

If she determined that her father did not intend the publication of the notebooks in their entirety, she would be free to make a selection, which he characterized in cautious terms:

> It seems to me that in all such cases the publisher of posthumous papers is entitled & bound to exercise discretion in selecting that which ought to be published, & that he incurs a heavy responsibility in doing so. He is to select that which is likely to promote truth & righteousness, which may enlarge or inform or edify men's minds, or which may be requisite in order to render the representation of the author's mind correct & ideally completed. But he should only select that which has a permanent value, not that which is fleeting & transitory.[47]

The inference was clear: if publication damaged Coleridge's reputation or influence, or Hare's career, Sara would bear 'a heavy responsibility'. According to Hare, selections should represent 'the author's mind correct & ideally completed', an astonishing suggestion when the mind in question was Coleridge's, and promote ideas of 'permanent value'. Determining which ideas had such value seemed a mysterious, even ominous, enterprise, and it is difficult to accept his implication that Coleridge's lifelong involvement with Biblical scholarship and the Higher Criticism was 'fleeting & transitory'.

This fascinating letter, equal parts kind advice and dire warning, is testament to the intensity of theological debate in 1850. A century later, Kathleen Coburn could take on the life's work of editing the complete notebooks without the same fear of social censure. In response to what must have seemed the nearly intractable problem of organizing the notebook entries, Coburn took an astonishing decision that has benefited Coleridge scholars ever since; she arranged the largely undated entries in chronological order through the sustained concentration and sheer determination of dating entries by internal evidence. The 'Gutch Notebook' was judged coherent enough to be published intact, but the rest of seventy-two notebooks were carefully 'dated' entry by entry in order to tame what she called 'the chaos of notebook after notebook'.[48] Coburn's *The Notebooks of Samuel Taylor Coleridge*[49] demanded comprehensive notes to establish dating, as well as explain entries, identify authors, et cetera. Her four-volume set created easy access for students and active scholars by reproducing a research archive in chronological order, a dated account of the succession of Coleridge's thoughts. The 'Fly-Catchers' as he called them were reorganized to record the buzzing thoughts he experienced over the course of his life in the order he experienced them.

Paul Cheshire reminds us of our debt to Coburn for making it possible to navigate the notebooks,[50] but nonetheless makes an excellent argument that Coburn's editorial policy 'has given rise to unwanted side-effects'.[51] By analysing Notebook 21 in detail, he demonstrates that it is not a random chaos of entries, and that Coleridge's deliberate gaps were often filled in such a way as to create meaning through juxtaposition. Cheshire makes a compelling argument for a variety of specific uses of the individual notebooks. For example, he calls our attention to two adjacent entries in Notebook 21 where Coleridge, in the first, appears to denigrate his artistic works as scattered and 'careless', 'yet no small number crawl forth into life'. The negative formulation, 'no small number', seems a deliberately deflating understatement. The second entry, separated by a horizontal line, praises Wordsworth's diligence in 'devoting himself to his great work',[52] writing *The Recluse*. In Coburn's edition these two entries are separated by ninety pages because of their dates, yet read together as they physically appear in the Notebook they set up a resonant field of possible meaning. It is impossible to believe that their proximity is an accident, and therefore they represent Coleridge's construction of meaning by association. More evocatively, Cheshire points to a series of entries that Coleridge transcribed from an earlier notebook that literally bring Sara Hutchinson forward in time and memory. His description of the results of this procedure as 'Proust-like meditations on memory' proves apt in a beautiful glimpse of Coleridge in his 'noble room' at Greta Hall lost in Proustian reverie of the moment: 'Monday Afternoon, the sun shining in upon the Print, in beautiful Lights—& I just about to take my leave of Mary—& having just before taken leave of Sara'.[53] The recovery of that sequence of moments, pregnant with longing as the ampersands cannot hold them together, reveals something profound about the human condition. By meticulously re-transcribing the passage into Notebook 21, Coleridge redoubled the longing in the very inadequacy of the gesture; memory, evocative as it is, cannot recover the moment before he 'took leave' of Sara. Cheshire's thesis in its entirety includes arguments for re-dating entries in Notebook 21, and he creates a compelling case for a new construction of Coleridge in the publication of *The Notebooks* as notebooks.[54] This is not to quarrel with Coburn's editorial policy, but rather to say that in creating a chronology of his buzzing thoughts she lost a complex and detailed portrait of Coleridge thinking, and that the apparent chaos of the notebooks may sometimes reveal the texture of being as he sat languid in his room awash in light and memory.

Future textual constructions of Coleridge seem inevitable. A new edition of the letters seems a possibility, with the ongoing electronic edition of the Southey letters on the *Romantic Circles* site as a model. I would make a case for negative creation, based on chapter 3 above, and declare that *Table Talk* is not part of the *Collected Works of Samuel Taylor Coleridge*—to put it bluntly, he was not the author. The most recent 'new' work presents a fascinating case of how such works come into being, and how they might change 'Coleridge'. Sara Coleridge did not publish *Opus Maximum* for the simple, if mistaken, reason that she believed it to be an unfinished joint work by her father and Joseph Henry Green. She naturally deferred to Green, who, furthermore, was entrusted with the 'work-in-progress' in Coleridge's will. Those disciples of Coleridge who knew of the manuscript felt confident that Green would do a creditable job of bringing it forward and publishing in some form. In section XXI of his 'Prolegomena', 'Why the existing Fragments of the *Opus Maximum* Were Not Published', Thomas McFarland quotes a representative posthumous view from F. D. Maurice about the fate of the manuscript. He believed that it was safe 'in the hands of Green, from whom it will of course, receive every justice'.[55] John Sterling had hoped to receive permission to publish the 'theological manuscripts', but deferred to Green who seemed ideally qualified. Sara was unaware that Green was Coleridge's amanuensis, not his co-author. In her Introduction to *Biographia Literaria* she referred to a 'philosophical work by his friend and fellow student Mr. Green' which would address many of the philosophical questions pursued in chapter twelve, perhaps including the long deferred deduction of the imagination.[56] Had she not died when she did, she may well have reached the inevitable conclusion that that work was not forthcoming for the simple reason that Green was incapable of producing it. Psychologically, Green had played a crucial role in developing the manuscript fragments—he provided Coleridge with the ideal audience to develop his ideas, and the intellectual stimulation involved naturally enough produced a sense of shared enterprise. In the end this co-dependence proved paralysing for Green; he misrecognized the scale of his role, and could not fulfil the self-imposed burden of completing his friend's magnum opus. McFarland describes the growing agitation among intellectuals that the family should make good and publish the much-rumoured *Logosophia*, a demand that simply could not be met. In the end, Green responded to the pressure by publishing not *Opus Maximum*, but an unsatisfactory derivative work: *Spiritual Philosophy; Founded on the Teaching of the Late Samuel Taylor Coleridge* in 1865.[57]

From Sara's perspective, she may eventually have realized that Green was not the co-author of the missing treatise, a treatise that held the promise of further securing Coleridge's reputation as a philosopher and theologian. She had recognized straight away that Gillman lacked the mental capacity to be a co-author of anything with Coleridge, and, therefore, her deference to Green suggests real respect for his intellect, as well as the necessary respect for his role of literary executor established by Coleridge's will. However, Green had established a pattern of promising important philosophical contributions to the various editions Sara produced, and failing to deliver on them. In her outline for the 're-arrangement' of the works that she sent to Pickering, she included a sidebar to *Confessions of an Inquiring Spirit*: 'Mr Green's Introduction will be <u>I hope</u> 100 or 120 pages certainly 40'.[58] Her emphasis on '<u>I hope</u>' was telling. The long Introduction could equalize a two-volume edition, part of their general rationale for re-organizing the works, but they could not wait indefinitely as Sara made clear in the body of her letter:

> I wrote to Mr Green about the <u>Confessions</u>—asking if we might hope for an Introduction from him. He came to talk with me on the subject, and brought a beginning of an Introduction, which I am anxious that he should finish. After reading what he has already produced I have written again to him on the subject, saying that at present it looks like a <u>torso</u>, a fine head & bust, but truncated. He gave me hope that he would finish it, if 8 or ten weeks were allowed him. I certainly think the <u>Confessions</u> ought not to remain much longer out of print. Regret has been expressed on the subject—still it could be worthwhile to wait a few weeks in order to obtain what may be a great help to readers to a clear comprehension of the object of the Letters & my Father's religious philosophy in general.[59]

Her confidence that Green had a contribution to make in helping 'readers to a clear comprehension of the object of the Letters & my Father's religious philosophy in general', was tinged with scepticism that the 'truncated' version was an unfinished whole, rather than what it was— a record of Green's complete effort at comprehension. In the end, he contributed nothing, and his letter to Sara acknowledging that they had to proceed with publication without him was both resigned and sad:

> I am not sorry that you have decided against publishing any part of the MS, which I submitted to you. The whole essay, which I sent, is a part only of a larger work on the grounds of religion, and when

you have read that portion, I shall have great pleasure in sending for your perusal & judgement the remain[der] [MS torn]:—and indeed I should be very desirous to obtain your opinion on all my MSS with a view to publication. But of this more hereafter.[60]

His implication that the work he had thus far put into the Introduction for *Confessions* was part of 'a larger work on the grounds of religion', his arrangement and projected commentary on the *Opus Maximum* fragments, can but produce pathos in retrospect. He had already disappointed Sara by promising an extensive philosophical essay for *Biographia Literaria*, which had never progressed beyond the outline he sent her in an enthusiastic letter.[61] His enthusiasm had doubtless been fired by Sara's impassioned immersion in German philosophy as she prepared for her great task. Green had a prospective new companion in the pursuit of the logical truth of Christianity that Coleridge had promised. He was not a fantasist; he hoped to do his best in reverence for the memory of his friend. It is a sign of the seductive power of Coleridge's personality and the force of his rhetoric that Green came to believe himself capable of a task he could not perform. John Sterling might well have produced a creditable work from the fragments, or Sara herself, had she lived longer. In the end, over a century later, the labour fell to Thomas McFarland as a key part of Kathleen Coburn's vision of the *Collected Works of Samuel Taylor Coleridge*.

Coda

While the appearance of a *new* major work by Coleridge in 2002, one hundred and sixty-eight years after his death, has to be recognized as an extraordinary event, the history of textual production I have described above makes it less surprising. The addition of Thomas McFarland's 'Prolegomena', and his organization of the 'Four Fragments' to form *Opus Maximum* follows in the tradition of Sara Coleridge's Introductions and creative reconstruction of her father's career through her editions of the *Literary Remains*. In the few years since the appearance of *Opus Maximum*, another phenomenon has occurred for which Sara also serves as harbinger—the creation of ad hoc communities to study the text and to disseminate its influence in their own historical moment. The 2010 Coleridge Summer Conference has sent out a call for papers for a special session on *Opus Maximum* to be organized by Murray Evans. In 2003 Douglas Hedley led a seminar dedicated to *Opus Maximum* at Cambridge that drew members from around the world. Jeffery Barbeau acknowledges the influence of that seminar on his work in the Introduction to his recently published study of *Confessions of an Inquiring Spirit* and Coleridge's methodical reading of the Bible, *Coleridge, the Bible, and Religion*. It is difficult not to see Hedley's Cambridge seminar as a tableau. The historical echo of Julius Hare, F. D. Maurice, and John Sterling forming the 'Cambridge Apostles' to read, and eventually disseminate, *Aids to Reflection*, sounds as we picture scholars gathered around *Opus Maximum* intently engaged in the construction of Coleridge.

Notes

Introduction

1 Louis Althusser's famous formulation of 'interpolated subjects' 'subjected' to deterministic social formations does not need rehearsing here. For the key texts see: 'Ideology and Ideological State Apparatuses' in *Lenin and Philosophy and Other Essays*, trans. Ben Brewster (New York: Monthly Review Press, 2001), and 'Contradiction and overdetermination' in *For Marx*, trans. Ben Brewster (London: Verso, 1996).

2 I recognize that this is easier said than done, but the hope is that by keeping moral judgement in abeyance I can better understand the motives for those constructing Coleridge by not over-investing in any particular Coleridge. As a matter of full disclosure, I should say that my preferred Coleridge is a democrat and reformer, albeit a gradualist, never a Tory in the reactionary anti-reform sense, not an adherent of any religious orthodoxy, one of the finest English poets in terms of representing consciousness and lyric subjectivity, and the finest neo-Kantian philosopher in English letters.

3 Notable examples of the Historicist turn in Coleridge studies are Nicholas Roe's *Wordsworth and Coleridge: the Radical Years* (Oxford: Clarendon Press, 2003). The influence of Roe's book is reflected in the Oxford University Press decision to republish it in 2003. An excellent early Historicist account is Paul Magnuson's *Coleridge and Wordsworth: a Lyrical Dialogue* (Princeton: Princeton University Press, 1988), and his *Reading Public Romanticism* (Princeton: Princeton University Press, 1998) offers important readings of Coleridge's various published 'paratexts'. More recently there has been a conservative response to the Historicist accounts of Coleridge in the 1790s, notably Pamela Edwards's *The Statesman's Science: History, Nature, Law in the Political Thought of Samuel Taylor Coleridge* (New York: Columbia University Press, 2004).

4 An argument can be made for Kathleen Coburn, but my analysis suggests that many of her volume decisions, not to mention attitude to constructing and enhancing Coleridge's reputation, were derived from Sara's lead. Ernest Hartley Coleridge, another candidate, was clearly repeating Sara's conceptual work. Henry Nelson Coleridge was once considered the key figure, and this book will rigorously argue against that view, showing it to be a simple series of reading mistakes, confusing Sara's wifely deference for actual work, and that his Coleridge was a strange parody of himself. Philosophically, Henry's lack of self-awareness should disqualify him as a candidate on the grounds of a distinct lack of Coleridgean sensibility.

5 Commissioning Julius Hare to refute De Quincey's plagiarism charge in the *British Critic*, for example.

6 All of the personal sketches in *Biographia Literaria* can be read in the way I'm suggesting, but given that the focus of the book is on the posthumous Coleridge, I have limited myself to a single instance that exemplifies the general pattern.

7 The success of *Aids* is a very complex subject taken up in earnest in chapter 5, and Marsh's American edition is central to that discussion. His Introduction to the American edition was foundational in the development of Coleridge's thought in America, and became the standard Introduction in both countries once Henry adopted it for the third edition.

8 Unlike Sara he did not know that Coleridge had completed the arrangement of Schelling's ideas that later became chapter twelve in a notebook entry. Her argument proved successful as Ferrier wrote to a friend years later that Coleridge's offence: 'should be attributed to forgetfulness rather than wilful plagiarism'. Cited by his biographer Arthur Thomson in *Ferrier of St Andrews: an Academic Tragedy* (Edinburgh: Scottish Academical, 1985). Crucially, Sara did not insult his intelligence by claiming that there was no plagiarism. Her view was much closer to De Quincey's than to Henry's.

1 'Once a Jacobin Always a Jacobin'

1 *Essays on His Times*, ed. David V. Erdman (London: Routledge & Kegan Paul, 1978), pp.11–12. To avoid confusion with Sara Coleridge's edition, references to the Erdman edition will be cited as Erdman. Sara Coleridge judiciously edited this piece of forthright radical provocation out of her edition.

2 Erdman, p.21. This phrase demonstrates the rhetorical use of bodily sensation by describing the political malaise in Switzerland as symptoms of a diseased and suffering body.

3 *Anti-Jacobin, or Weekly Examiner*, fourth edition, 2 vols. vol. 1 (London: J. Wright, 1799), pp.7–8.

4 *Anti-Jacobin Review and Magazine*, July 1800, p.594. Coleridge probably saw this essay as evidenced by his adopting its title, 'the Literati and Literature of Germany', in his own history of his German travels and interests in No. 18, the 21 December 1809 issue of *The Friend*. *The Friend*, ed. Barbara E. Rooke, vol. 2 (London: Routledge & Kegan Paul, 1969), p.239.

5 As evidenced by his self-justifications in 'France: An Ode'.

6 Erdman, p.368.

7 Erdman, pp.372–3.

8 In fact, a disagreement over the extent of the levelling implications of the plan contributed to its failure. Coleridge was shocked when he discovered that Southey did not recognize the basic contradiction of taking servants with them to America.

9 For an excellent brief account of the still ongoing critical controversy surrounding Coleridge's dissembling on the issue of property, see the headnote and notes for 'Once a Jacobin Always a Jacobin' in *Coleridge's Poetry and Prose*, eds. Nicholas Halmi, Paul Magnuson and Raimonda Modiano (New York and London: Norton, 2004), pp.299–306.

10 *The Sublime Object of Ideology* (London: Verso, 1989). See especially the section 'The Ideological Quilt', pp.87–9. Žižek employs deconstruction and Lacanian psychoanalysis to describe ideological desire as the need to provide the fiction of certainty both at the level of indeterminable 'floating signifiers' and overdetermined social forces.

11   *The Friend*, vol. 2, p.147. 'Fanaticism' is another term that cuts both ways: on the one hand denoting an excessively narrow ideological framework, while on the other denoting the capacity of overzealous feeling to overwhelm rational judgement.

12   See *Complete Works of William Hazlitt*, ed. P. P. Howe, vol. 19 (London: J. M. Dent & Sons, 1933), p.203. Hazlitt was incensed by Coleridge's betrayal of the cause of reform, and attacked this political apostasy by recalling Coleridge's former revolutionary idealism. Byron used a similar device in attacking Southey when he referred to him as the author of *Wat Tyler*, Southey's long suppressed Jacobin drama.

13   *The Friend*, vol. 1, pp.328–9.

14   *The Friend*, vol. 1, pp.334–5.

15   *The Friend*, vol. 1, p.326 and p.331.

16   Cited in *Coleridge: The Critical Heritage*, ed. J. R. de J. Jackson (New York: Barnes & Noble, 1970), p.343. Hereafter cited as Wilson.

17   Wilson, p.343.

18   Wilson, p.343.

19   Cited in *Coleridge: The Critical Heritage*, ed. J. R. de J. Jackson (New York: Barnes & Noble, 1970), p.309. Hereafter cited as Hazlitt.

20   Hazlitt, p.304.

21   Hazlitt, p.305.

22   Hazlitt, p.320.

23   Wilson, p.349.

24   Wilson, p.348.

25   Cited by Grevel Lindop in his biography of De Quincey, *The Opium-Eater* (Oxford: Oxford University Press, 1985), p.239.

26   Hazlitt, p.309.

27   Hazlitt, p.309.

28   Hazlitt, p.299.

29   *Early recollections; chiefly relating to the late Samuel Taylor Coleridge, during his long stay in Bristol* (London: Longman, Rees & Co., 1837). The full title makes the focus on Bristol clear. I have used the expanded and revised 1848 editon *Reminiscences of Samuel Taylor Coleridge and Robert Southey* (London: Houlston and Stoneman, 1848). The entries I cite are largely unchanged from the first edition, the real differences coming in his expansion of the Southey material and some score settling against critics of the first edition. If anything, his vehemence in defending Bristol intellectual history is more fierce. Passages will be cited as *Reminiscences*.

30   *Biographia Literaria*, ed. James Engell and W. Jackson Bate (London: Routledge & Kegan Paul, 1983), p.246. Hereafter cited as *BL* (CC), for Collected Coleridge, to differentiate it from Sara Coleridge's edition to be discussed in detail in chapter 6.

31   *BL* (CC), p.248.

32   *BL* (CC), p.248.

33   *BL* (CC), p.250.

34   *BL* (CC), p.250.

35   *Reminiscences*, p.76.

36   *Reminiscences*, p.93.

37   *Reminiscences*, p.77.
38   *Reminiscences*, p.77.
39   *Reminiscences*, p.85.
40   *Reminiscences*, p.85.
41   *Reminiscences*, p.85.
42   *Reminiscences*, p.90.
43   *Reminiscences*, p.93.
44   *BL* (CC), p.249. Coleridge quoted the passage from the tenth issue of the 1809 version of *The Friend*, which in turn echoed the 'Introductory Address' from *Conciones ad Populum*, another example of his strategic redeployment of passages in different historical moments. The 1795 original descibed his political strategy in working for reform, while the *Biographia* restatement intended to suggest he had never been a radical Democrat.
45   *Reminiscences*, p.79.
46   *BL* (CC), p.249.
47   *BL* (CC), p.249.
48   *Reminiscences*, p.95.
49   *Reminiscences*, p.96.

2 'Ungentlemanly Productions': De Quincey and Scandal

1   'Letter to Henry Nelson Coleridge [hereafter HNC], 11–12 September 1834', Harry S. Ransom Center MS. The archive at the Harry S. Ransom Center at the University of Texas in Austin was organized by Carl L. Grantz as an unpublished Ph.D. Dissertation, *Letters of Sara Coleridge: A Calendar and Index of Her Manuscript Correspondence in the University of Texas Library* (June, 1968). It includes brief descriptions of the letters, and maintains a good chronology; much of his folio numbering is still intact. Nonetheless, because there are some folio discrepancies, I will use addressee and date to identify the individual letters, and HRC to identify the archive. The Ransom Center archives use 'Recip.' to designate recipient letters, and includes them in a separate 'Recip. file' at the end of the individual archive. I have adopted that notation.
2   *Tait's Edinburgh Magazine*, September 1834.
3   *Tait's Edinburgh Magazine*, September 1834.
4   'Letter to HNC, 11–12 September 1834', HRC.
5   *Tait's Edinburgh Magazine*, September 1834.
6   *Confessions of an English Opium-Eater* (London: Walter Scott, 1886), p.79.
7   'Letter to HNC, 14–15 September 1834', HRC.
8   *Tait's Edinburgh Magazine*, September 1834.
9   'Letter from Cottle to Poole, 15 June 1836'. Emphasis in the original. Pratt Library, Victoria College, University of Toronto, BT 13, vol. 3 (item 939), Fol. 732–8. Cited hereafter as Pratt.
10   'Letter from Cottle to Poole', 15 June 1836. Emphasis in the original. Pratt, BT 13, vol. 3 (item 939), Fol. 727–9.
11   'Letter from Cottle to Poole', 15 June 1836. Emphasis in the original; the words 'rude' and 'ungentlemanly' are over twice the size of the others, signalling the magnitude of his anger to Poole. Pratt, Fol. 727–9.

12 'Letter from Gillman to Cottle, 8 June 1836', Pratt, Fol. 730–2.
13 'Letter from Cottle to Poole, 15 June 1836'. Emphasis in the original. Pratt, Fol. 732–8.
14 'Letter from Gillman to Cottle, 8 June 1836', Pratt, Fol. 730–2.
15 'Letter from Cottle to Poole, 15 June 1836'. Emphasis in the original. Pratt, Fol. 73–28.
16 Warren E. Gibb carefully reconstructs the correspondence in 'Unpublished Letters concerning Cottle's Coleridge', *PMLA*, Vol. 49, No. 1 (March 1934), pp.208–28 (see especially pp.214–18). Gibb gives The Thomas Poole Collection, British Museum, Add. MS. 35344 as his source, but the letters have since been purchased by the Pratt Library as I've noted above.
17 See Chapter 4 below.
18 Gibb, p.208.
19 Norman Fruman, *Coleridge, the Damaged Archangel* (New York: George Braziller, 1971).
20 'Letter to HNC, 6 September 1834', HRC.
21 'Letter to HNC, 7 September 1834', HRC.
22 'Letter to HNC, 31 August 1834', HRC.
23 'Letter to HNC, 11–12 September 1834', HRC.
24 De Quincey had even more trouble with Blackwood's sons, Robert and Alexander, after old William died in 1834. By the end of the decade financial necessity meant he was often writing for both magazines at the same time.
25 'Letter to HNC, 11–12 September 1834', HRC.
26 'Letter to HNC, [?] September 1834', HRC.
27 'Letter to HNC, 13–15 September', HRC.
28 'Letter to HNC, [?] September 1834', HRC.
29 'To HNC, 31 December 1834', HRC.
30 'Letter to Sara, 3 January 1835', HRC.
31 Hartley's lack of authority within the family had serious consequences for the vision of the *Literary Remains* they pursued. Political differences with Henry, for example, were always to be decided in the latter's favour so far as they affected editorial decisions. See my discussion of these issues in light of Henry's *Table Talk* in chapter 3.
32 'Letter to HNC, 29 March 1837', HRC.
33 Henry's Introduction to the second edition of *Table Talk*, including Hare's essay, appears in vol. 2 of Woodring's *Table Talk* as 'Appendix H'. This passage is on p.23.
34 Woodring 2, p.23.
35 Woodring 2, p.23.
36 It is entirely possible that De Quincey made his obscure reference to Schelling's *Philosophische Schriften* deliberately, sparing Coleridge's chapter a damning section by section exposé. Determining De Quincey's motives is a fruitless endeavour, unknowable probably even to himself, but it would be a mistake to assume that Hare and Henry Nelson were correct in calling them 'malicious' (Woodring 2, p.23).
37 Woodring 2, p.23. Hare admits the worst here; Coleridge simply took Schelling's work, and any additions are trivial, thus rendering a defence impossible. While he is right about the lack of 'additions', Coleridge's contribution, in the form of arranging disparate points from Schelling's works

(many not drawn from *The System of Transcendental Idealism*) was complex and significant. See Chapter 4.

38   *Tait's Edinburgh Magazine*, September 1834.
39   Woodring 2, p.24.
40   Woodring 2, pp.24–5, Coleridge's italics.
41   *Tait's Edinburgh Magazine*, September 1834.
42   In many ways the presence of the note makes the offence worse by suggesting possible deliberate subterfuge. See my account of Ferrier's pursuit of this argument in chapter 4.
43   See chapter 6 below.
44   Woodring 2, p.25.
45   Woodring 2, p.26.
46   The pervasiveness of this defence, beginning here, made more sophisticated by Sara, and especially spirited in reaction to the publication of Fruman's *Coleridge, the Damaged Archangel*, points to an understandable desire to defend the author. My point is that the defence is counter-productive as Ferrier first made clear.
47   *Tait's Edinburgh Magazine*, September 1834.
48   *Tait's Edinburgh Magazine*, September 1834.
49   Woodring 2, p.26.
50   *Tait's Edinburgh Magazine*, September 1834.
51   *The Sublime Object of Ideology* (London: Verso, 1989), pp.87–9.
52   Henry was probably blind to the ideological parameters of his project, taking its ideological shape as 'natural' and given. Notions of 'propriety', 'respectablity', and 'reputation' were all subsumed into the same ideological blindness.

3 'Henry's Book'

1   'Recip. letter from Derwent, 18 October 1835', HRC. The Harry S. Ransom Center archive was organized by Frances Anne Stephens as an unpublished Ph.D. Dissertation, *The Hartley Coleridge Letters at the University of Texas: A Calendar and Index*, January, 1970, and includes brief descriptions of the contents of the letters. However, while her chronology is intact, her folio numbering has been partially replaced by another series (probably Griggs's), and the whole of the archive is interpolated with (often inaccurate) transcriptions by Griggs. To avoid confusion all references to Hartley's letters, including the Recip. file, will be by letter date.
2   'Letter to HNC, 11 January 1836', HRC.
3   See my discussions of Cottle's 'Reminiscences' in chapters 1 and 2.
4   'Letter to Hartley, 21 January 1836', HRC.
5   *Table Talk*, ed. Carl Woodring (London: Routledge, 1990), 2 vols., p.cx.
6   Quoted in Woodring, p.cxv.
7   Quoted in Woodring, p.cx.
8   'Letter to Hartley, 21 January 1836'.
9   'Letter to HNC, 31 December 1834'. See discussion in chapter 2.
10   Quoted in Woodring, pp.cx–cxi.

11 'Letter to HNC, 8 May 1836'.
12 Henry's inabilty to judge De Quincey's plagiarism charges makes this clear. He deferred to Hartley and left the defence to family friend, and qualified Germanist, Julius Hare.
13 This letter is unfortunately lost.
14 Griggs inserts a phantom 'not' in his transcription here, definitely not in the MS, that confuses the letter by making it state the opposite!
15 Woodring provides the publication history, including the size of print runs, throughout the 19th century. Murray held the rights until 1884, with their 1882 run numbering an astonishing 1250. Woodring, p.c.
16 Woodring details only three occasions (1 June 1824, 4 April 1832, 8 June 1833) where anyone other than Henry was present for conversations he recorded. In addition, of all the MS entires only five fall on Thursdays (the night of Gillman's famous dinner parties) and there is no evidence of an audience beyond Henry on those dates. Woodring, pp.lxxxiv–v.
17 Woodring, p.lxxxv.
18 *Quarterly Review* LIII (February 1835), p.103.
19 Woodring, p.cx.
20 Woodring, p.lxxxvii.
21 Woodring somewhat ominously suggests that Henry 'considered himself superior as a popular stylist to Coleridge—and he proved to be so'. p.lxxxviii. The 19th-century popularity of *Table Talk* ensured that this stylistic misrepresentation paradoxically became recognized as Coleridge's style.
22 Quoted in Woodring, p.cix.
23 *A Book of Memories* (2nd edn., 1871), p.43. Quoted in Woodring, n.235, p.cix.
24 *Literary Reminiscences* (Boston and New York: Houghton, Mifflin, 1876), pp.169–70.
25 'Letter to Sara, 24 September 1834'.
26 Indeed, it was the subject of the first article in the first number of *The Analytic Review*.
27 These are items 289 and 290 in the Samuel Taylor Coleridge archive at the Pratt Library of Victoria College at the University of Toronto.
28 HNC's *Table Talk* MS is located in the back pages of a red-spined notebook titled 'HNC's Letters from France', and is housed under: Coleridge, Henry Nelson, Letters, To Coleridge, James, and family at the Ransom Center. The notebook is the MS material for vol. 1 of *Table Talk*, pp.1–55 (dated 29 December 1822 to 10 June 1824). This is entry number 11.
29 *Table Talk*, p.24. The first entry in the volume, dated 29 January 1822.
30 Woodring has included the scraps as MS F in Appendix C of *Table Talk*, pp.525–37. This entry is on p.528. The scraps are part of the Coleridge archive at the Pratt Library, and the loose strips of paper make a striking visual impression confirming Henry's censorship.
31 *Table Talk*, p.530. This scrap was part of number 73 in the original notebook, and dateable to 8 October 1830 by its original placement.
32 *Table Talk*, p.531. Notebook entry number 83.
33 *Table Talk*, p.531.
34 *Table Talk*, p.531.

4 Coleridge the Plagiarist

1   *Tait's Edinburgh Magazine*, September 1834. For the sake of complete citation, I will use David Mason's reprint of the article in his edition of *The Collected Writings of Thomas De Quincey*, Vol. 2, Edinburgh: A. and C. Black, 1889. This edition includes De Quincey's long footnote on the contoversy; this passage occurs on p.147.

2   Mason, p.143.

3   Mason, p.142.

4   Mason, p.143.

5   Mason, p.143.

6   Mason, p.146.

7   'Letter to HNC, September 1834', HRC.

8   James Frederick Ferrier, 'The Plagiarisms of S. T. Coleridge', *Blackwood's Edinburgh Magazine*, March 1840, p.288.

9   'Plagiarisms', p.288.

10   'Plagiarisms', p.288.

11   Mason, p.146.

12   'Plagiarisms', p.288.

13   'Plagiarisms', p.293.

14   'Plagiarisms', p.288.

15   'Plagiarisms', p.289.

16   'Plagiarisms', p.289.

17   Quoted in 'Plagiarisms', p.289.

18   'Plagiarisms', p.289.

19   'Plagiarisms', p.289.

20   'Plagiarisms', p.290.

21   'Plagiarisms', p.290.

22   'Plagiarisms', p.290.

23   'Plagiarisms', p.293.

24   *BL* (CC) pp.279–80.

25   'Plagiarisms', p.296.

26   'Plagiarisms', p.296.

27   Quoted in Arthur Thomson's biography, *Ferrier of St Andrews: An Academic Tragedy* (Edinburgh: Scottish Academical, 1985), p.47.

28   Thomson, p.47.

29   'Letter to HNC, 10 July 1840', HRC

30   *BL* (CC), p.cxv

31   Thomas McFarland, *Coleridge and the Pantheist Tradition* (Oxford: Oxford University Press), 1969.

32   *BL* (CC), p.cxv.

33   Hamilton charged Coleridge with having plagiarized Maas in chapters five and six of *BL*. William Hamilton, 'Supplementary Dissertation' to *The Works of Thomas Reid* (Edinburgh: Longman Brown, 1846). See especially note 1 on p.333.

34   Quoted in James Buchan, *Crowded with Genius* (New York: Haper Collins, 2003), p.123. Buchan continues this venerable tradition. In describing the first impressions of Adam Smith upon his arrival at Balliol College in 1740, fresh from studying with Francis Hutcheson at Glasgow, Buchan

quips that he found a milieu 'in contrast, sunk in wine and Jacobite sloth', p.123.

35 McFarland, p.6. In fact the Hamilton charge was nothing new. It was a reca-pitulation of the identical charge (chapter five of *BL* relied entirely on Maas) detailed in Ferrier's essay, p.296. Listing it as a separate charge gives scope to the Scottish conspiracy, whereas it probably more clearly demonstrates the influence of Ferrier's attack in Scottish philosophical circles.

36 McFarland, p.7.

37 *Coleridge's Poetry and Prose*, eds. Nicolas Halmi, Paul Magnuson and Raimonda Modiano (Norton: New York and London, 2004), p.555.

38 *The Friend*, excerpted in Norton, p.555.

39 *Aids to Reflection*, excerpted in Norton, p.572.

40 Thomson, p.44.

41 'An Introduction to the Philosophy of Consciousness', *Blackwood's Edinburgh Magazine*, February 1838, p.190.

42 'Philosophy of Consciousness', p.191.

43 *Blackwood's Edinburgh Magazine*, 1838. Summarized by Thomson, p.48.

44 Thomson's concise summary, p.48.

45 Samuel Bailey, 'A Review of Berkeley's Theory of Vision', in *Essays on the Formation and Publication of Opinions* (London, 1842).

46 'Proposition I: The primary law or condition of all knowledge', *The Institutes of Metaphysic*, 3rd edition (Edinburgh, 1875). This edition has been recently republished as volume 1 of *The Philosophical Works of James Frederick Ferrier*, ed. John Haldane (Bristol: Thoemmes Press, 2001). This work is Ferrier's opus and his final attempt to complete the arduous project he shared with Coleridge. It is arranged in three sections: 'Section I, The Epistemology, or Theory of Kowledge', 'Section II, The Agniology, or Theory of Ignorance', and 'Section III, The Ontology, or Theory of Being'. 'Epistemology' is Ferrier's coinage. In this extraordinary work, Ferrier attempts to complete Schelling's deduction using only the laws of contradiction and identity. The second section works by an entirely negative method, using the laws of logic to reveal errors in traditional conceptions of knowledge. In his 'Introduction' to *Works*, Haldane argues that in the end Ferrier's ideas and method, including the early 'An Introduction to the Philosophy of Consciousness', are less suggestive of Coleridge and more 'suggestive of the sort of linguistic analytical "phenomenology" assocociated with Husserl and Wittgenstein', p.x.

47 F. W. Schelling, *Vom Ich als Prinzip der Philosophie* in *Philosophische Schriften*, Landshut 1809. This is the volume Coleridge owned. J. G. Fichte, *Grundlage der gesammten Wissenschaftslehre*, Jena and Leipzig, 1794. For a detailed account of the sources see the Bate and Engel notes, *BL*, pp.272–3.

48 *BL*, p.274, n.2.

49 F. W. Schelling, *System des transscendentalen Idealismus*, Tübingen, 1800. Coleridge owned this edition.

50 F. W. Schelling, *Abhandlungen zur Erläuterung des Idealismus*, also in *Philosophische Schriften*, Landshut 1809.

51 'Plagiarisms', p.293.

52 Quoted in 'Plagiarisms', p.289.

53 Mason, p.227.

54 'Letter to John Thelwall, 14 October 1797', excerpted in *Romanticism: An Anthology*, ed. Duncan Wu, 2nd edition (Oxford: Blackwell, 2000), p.460.
55 Peter Larkin, 'Repetition, Difference and Liturgical Participation in Coleridge's 'The Ancient Mariner''. An offprint of this essay was kindly provided by the author, p.14.
56 Larkin, p.12.
57 Thomson, p.48.

5 Her Father's 'Remains': Editing and Filial Love

1 Bradford Mudge, *Sara Coleridge: A Victorian Daughter* (New Haven: Yale University Press, 1989), p.108. Mudge offers the best account of Sara's career, focusing on the interrelated issues of Victorian gender roles and female authorship. His astute analysis of how Sara was confined by social expectations, but nonetheless found the means to resist them, offers a detailed account of her coming into writing. His hypothesis that Sara gained intellectual authority for her philosophical and theological ideas through the reflected authority of her father shows how she paradoxically accepted her prescribed social role while nonetheless becoming an important voice in contemporary religious debates. She appeared to remain in a woman's 'sphere of action' (her phrase) while nonetheless effecting ongoing debates through her acts of authorship (p.139). I share Mudge's interest in this social phenomenon and am indebted to his work. My interest, however, is limited to how Sara's acts of authorial self-creation conditioned the version of Coleridge that emerged in the Introductions, notes, and appendices to her editions.
2 'Letter to Emily Trevenen, 9 April 1838'. Cited in Mudge, p.102.
3 Green provided a possible outline for his Appendix in a letter to Sara of 25 October 1844, 'Recip. letter from J. H. Green', HRC:

> With respect to the appendix to the B.L. my hope is to be able to exhibit S.T.C's system under the following heads:
>
> 1. The essential character of his philosophy is that of a <u>Spiritual Philosophy</u>, as that which is grounded, not merely in the intellect—which is but a fragment of the whole man—but in the whole nature of man, head and heart, and as essentially inwoven with his moral interests.
> 2. Its character compared with the schemes of the Sensualists, with Reid, with Hume, Kant, Fichte, Schelling, and Hegel; and its originality vindicated.
> 3. Its prolegomena those of rational psychology. The great facts of Conscience and Consciousness—the fundamental distinction of Reason and Understanding, and the instruction of Will. Hume's and Kant's opinion's that we have no knowledge of the soul except as a <u>phenomenon</u> (i.e. as thoughts, feelings, volitions) and the question discussed of our knowledge of a <u>Noumenon</u> to Metaphysics or Speculative Philosophy. Ideas. The Absolute. The Will as the universal and common ground of mind and nature. Essentially moral character of speculative philosophy—its three great Ideas.
> a. <u>Idea of God</u>; the ideal of Reason, the idea of the Absolute Good as absolute will causative of all reality. The Trinity as a truth of Reason.

b. <u>Idea of the Universe</u> as a system of Moral Order. [Pleroma? MS illegible]. Fall. Origin of Evil. Redemptive Process. Connexion of this Idea with Science, and with the principles of Dynamics.
c. <u>Idea of the Soul</u>, spiritual man, or humanity in contradistinction to natural man. Man's duties and destination. Spiritual Philosophy resolves itself into Christianity.

To bring the exposition of these heads into a brief, lucid and comprehensive statement is a task of no small difficulty; but still I think the attempt ought to be made, and may perhaps succeed by avoiding controversy [future charges of plagiarism] and by a plain statement of the truths in their grand bold and distinctive lineaments.

4 'Recip. Letter from J. H. Green 6 March 1845', HRC.
5 'Letter to Hartley, October 1845?'. Only the last two sheets of an apparently long letter on editing *BL* survive, and can be conjecturally dated to October 1845.
6 Mudge, p.76. Sara erred in the opposite direction making Henry the nominal editor of the works she prepared. The new edition of *Aids to Reflection*, published in 1843 and republished in 1848, serves as a good example. Henry is listed as the editor, but his illness and death ensured that he played no role in either. This work in particular is interesting because Sara's editorial apparatus (the Introduction and her masterful 'Essay on Rationalism' that served as the Appendix) mark it as highly original in its application of Coleridgean philosophy to contemporary theological controversy.
7 'Letter to Sara, 12 September 1834', HRC. Quoted in Mudge, p.76.
8 See Chapter 3.
9 'Letter to Henry, 21 September 1837', HRC.
10 'Letter to Henry, 16 September 1834', HRC.
11 This strategic illness kept her isolated from her family for over two months, and alowed her time to intellectually take stock despite suffering from hysteria and probably loss of control of her opium habit. See Mudge, pp.89–93.
12 'Letter to Henry, 13 November 1836', HRC.
13 Mudge is excellent on the paradox of intellectual opportunity and social constraint that defined Sara's life in the Southey household and the Southey/Wordsworth circle. See chapter 2, 'Castles in the Air', especially pp.25–7 and pp.37–9 for her early publication anxieties.
14 'Letter to Charlotte Brontë, March 1837'. Quoted in Mudge, p.38.
15 'Letter to Joseph Cottle, 26 April 1814'. *The Collected Letters of Samuel Taylor Coleridge*, Vol. 3, ed. Earl Leslie Griggs (Oxford: Clarendon Press, 1959), p.476. This is from Letter 919 in Griggs's counting, but I will use volume and page numbers for the purposes of identification.
16 'Letter to Cottle, 26 April 1814'. Griggs, Vol. 3, p.478.
17 Despite the severity of his depression, Coleridge was encouraged by Cottle's scheme to get up a subscription to pay for Coleridge to be confined under a physician's care in an effort to break the addiction. Coleridge suggested Dr Fox as the most knowledgeable choice. The plan came to nothing when Cottle consulted with Southey and sent him Coleridge's letters. Convinced that Coleridge was lying in the 26 April letter when he claimed that he had not indulged out of 'any temptation of Pleasure, or expectation or desire of

exciting pleasureable Sensation', Southey argued that it would be a mistake to place him under restraint when it was a lack of self-restraint that remained at the root of the problem. Griggs, Vol. 3, p.477. Southey saw Coleridge as a weak sensualist whose motives were 'inclination and indulgence'. He believed that Coleridge should simply show self-restraint and stop, then take his place at Keswick and throw himself into the care of his family. See note 2 in Griggs, Vol. 3, pp.279–80 for the text of Southey's return letter to Cottle. While it is anachronistic to pillory Southey for not understanding opium addiction (as Griggs is quick to do), it is nonetheless the case that his attitude exacerbated the problem and undoubtedly caused his friend much pain and suffering, both physical and psychological, given the vapid moralizing at its heart.

18   'Letter to Cottle, 27 April 1814', Griggs, Vol. 3, pp.478–9. The letter is undated and Griggs' conjecture of 27 April makes sense. The letter clearly follows the despairing letter of 26 April and precedes the long letter on Socinianism and the Trinity of a few days later. The quoted paragraph presents the opening salvo in his argument for a 'rational' understanding of the Trinity as necessary to faith.

19   'Letter to Cottle, late April 1814', Griggs, Vol. 3, pp.481 and 484. This letter is undated, but clearly follows closely on the 26 April letter.

20   Griggs, p.486.

21   Robert Leighton, *The Expository Works and Other Remains of Archbishop Leighton, some of which were never before printed. Revised by Philip Doddridge, D.D. With a Preface by the Doctor* (Edinburgh, 1748). For the details of Coleridge's relationship with Elwyn and the provenance of the annotations see: *Marginalia*, Vol. 3, eds. H. J. Jackson and George Whalley, with the 'Leighton' coeditor John Beer (Princeton: Princeton Univerity Press, 1993), pp.507–8

22   *Marginalia*, Vol. 3, p.509.

23   *The Genuine Works of R. Leighton, D.D. Archbishop of Glasgow*, 4 Vols (London, 1819). See *Marginalia*, Vol. 3, p.514 for details.

24   *Marginalia*, Vol. 3, pp. 522–3.

25   The editors of the Norton *Coleridge's Poetry and Prose* provide an excellent summary of this developmental history. For a detailed account, see John Beer's 'Editor's Introduction' to the Collected Coleridge edition (London: Routledge & Kegan Paul, 1993).

26   *Aids to Reflection, Fourth Edition with the Author's Last Corrections*, edited Henry Nelson Coleridge (London: William Pickering, 1839), pp.110–313. I've used the 1839 edition here as the edition over which Sara Coleridge first had any control, although her name does not appear and Henry Nelson is the nominal editor. Her influence over the edition is difficult to ascertain, but her role in all the late 1830s editions was extensive. Regardless, the arrangement of this volume is the one she completely inherited for her 1843 and 1848 reworkings. This passage is substantively the same as in the 1825 edition. Henry Nelson Coleridge's editing debut, the 1831 edition, has many problems. The editors of the Norton Critical Edition, *Coleridge's Poetry and Prose*, offer a concise summary of those problems in explaining their decision to use the 1825 edition as their copy text: '... the omission of several passages

from the early part of the book and of the designations "LEIGHTON" and "EDITOR" throughout. The result of this last omission was to obscure the distinction between Coleridge's own contributions and the texts by Leighton and others. Neither the printed errata nor Coleridge's holograph annotations in various copies of the first edition were systematically incorporated into the second, and the reduced capitalization of nouns in the second edition does not conform to Coleridge's usual practice in his manuscripts', p.570. How Sara Coleridge responded to these blunders is developed in the next section of this chapter.

27 *Aids* (1839), pp.157–72.
28 *Aids* (1839), p.169.
29 'Introductory Aphorism V', *Aids* (1839), p.2.
30 *Aids* (1839), p.172.
31 *Aids* (1839), p.172.
32 For a detailed account of these problems, see John Beer's Introduction to the Collected Coleridge edition, pp.cxxviii–cxxxiii.
33 Mudge, p.89.
34 She is noticeably absent from the official account. John Beer does not mention her work on the 1839 edition in the Collected Coleridge, 'Appendix H' on the chronolgical history of the various editions. More troubling, he names Derwent Coleridge responsible for seeing the 1843 and 1848 editions 'through the press'. Henry Nelson remained the nominal editor of both volumes, primarily because of Sara's sense of devotion to his memory. There is little to suggest that Henry had any influence on either volume. The arrangement of the materials was hers: the James Marsh Introduction shifted to an appendix, she commisioned Green's essay on 'Instinct', her 'Essay on Rationalism' comprised the bulk of the second volume, a volume she convinced Pickering to include. Furthermore, there is no evidence Derwent played any role in editing until after Sara's death. For Beer's summaries see 'Appendix H', pp.545–7.
35 Mudge, p.89.
36 For a detailed account of the influence of *Aids to Reflection* in America, see John Beer's 'Editor's Introduction', pp.cxvi–cxxviii.
37 Quoted in Beer, pp.cxxiv–v.
38 Quoted in Beer, p.cxxv.
39 James Marsh, 'Preliminary Essay', *Aids* (1839), p.xv.
40 *Aids* (1839), p.viii.
41 *Aids to Reflection*, Vol. 2. (London: William Pickering, 1848), pp.5–12. I have used the 1848 edition, but there were no changes in organization between the 1843 and 1848 volumes.
42 See Beer's detailed summary in his 'Editor's Introduction'.
43 'On Rationalism', *Aids* (1848), Vol. 2, footnote on p.13.
44 'On Rationalism,' *Aids* (1848), Vol. 2, footnote on p.14. Quoted from her and Henry's edition of *The Literary Remains of S. T. Coleridge*, vol. 3. p.272.
45 'On Rationalism', p.15.
46 'On Rationalism', p.15.
47 'On Rationalism', pp.15–16.
48 'On Rationalism', p.16.

49 'On Rationalism', pp.21–2.
50 'On Rationalism', p.29.
51 'On Rationalism', p.30.

6 *Biographia Literaria*, Sara Coleridge, and Self-Creation

1   *Biographia Literaria*, Second Edition Prepared for Publication in Part by the Late Henry Nelson Coleridge and Completed by his Widow (London: William Pickering, 1847), p.xxxvii. Typically the editor's note nearly erases Sara despite the fact that the work is entirely hers; Henry's contribution was asserting that a new edition was needed to answer the charges, and utter despair that anyone could produce it.
2   *BL* (1847), p.xxxviii.
3   *BL* (1847), p.v.
4   *BL* (1847), p.xlviii. This discussion is crucial for Sara's posthumous project of using her father's ideas to engage contemporary religious controversies that she began with 'On Rationalism', and I'll return to it in detail.
5   *BL* (1847), p.v.
6   *BL* (1847), p.vi.
7   *BL* (1847), p.vii.
8   *BL* (1847), pp.vii–viii.
9   *BL* (1847), p.viii.
10 *BL* (1847), pp.viii and ix.
11 *BL* (1847), p.viii.
12 *BL* (1847), p.viii.
13 *BL* (1847), p.xv.
14 *BL* (1847), p.xiv.
15 I'll develop this point when I turn to Sara's critique of Pusey and Newman in the second part of her Introduction.
16 *BL* (1847), p.xv.
17 *BL* (1847), p.xviii.
18 *BL* (1847), p.xviii.
19 *BL* (1847), pp.xviii–ix.
20 *BL* (1847), p.xix.
21 *BL* (1847), p.xix.
22 *BL* (1847), p.xxi.
23 *BL* (1847), p.xxi.
24 Sara's brilliant psychological analysis is disingenuous on two points. First, she suggests that the opposition of his friends to his interest in and growing reliance on German ideas contributed to his physical languor, and served as a drag on his body. However, he wrote the 'letter from a friend', so even if he is ventriloquizing Wordsworth, Southey, et al. he nonetheless stages the breakdown. The second point is more serious. She deliberately misconstrues Ferrier's essay, mocking him with her mastery of Schelling. She complains that nowhere in Schelling is this 'stupendous theory of the imagination' to be found, and thus he must be either inept or a fantasist. But of course the lack of the theory is precisely Ferrier's point, and Sara is much too gifted a reader to have misunderstood his intent.

25 Mudge, p.201, n.1. 'Nervousness' was written during Fall 1834, following her father's death that July.
26 Mudge, p.203.
27 Sara's symptoms would likely have been diagnosed as post partum depression were she our contemporary, and one can only wonder whether the pregnancies, miscarriages, still births, etc. felt like bodily betrayal—a loss of control over whether one can be 'gladsome or gloomy'.
28 Mudge, p.203.
29 *BL* (1847), p.xix.
30 *BL* (1847), p.xxxix.
31 *BL* (1847), p.clxviii.
32 *BL* (1847), p.lvii.
33 *BL* (1847), p.lvii.
34 *BL* (1847), p.lxi.
35 *BL* (1847), p.lxxi.
36 *BL* (1847), p.lxxi.
37 *BL* (1847), pp.lxxviii–ix.
38 *BL* (1847), p.lxxix.
39 *BL* (1847), p.lxxv.
40 *BL* (1847), p.lxxx. Italics hers.
41 *BL* (1847), pp.lxxx–xxxi. Italics hers.
42 *BL* (1847), p.lxxxv.
43 *BL* (1847), pp.cxiv–xv. See footnote 53.
44 *BL* (1847), pp.cxix–xx.
45 *BL* (1847), p.cxxv.
46 *BL* (1847), p.cxxxi.
47 *BL* (1847), p.cxxxi.
48 *BL* (1847), p.cxxxiii.
49 *BL* (1847), p.cxxxvi–vii.
50 *BL* (1847), p.cxxxviii–ix.
51 This edition, the labour of Thomas McFarland, assited by Nicholas Halmi, finally has made available to a wide audience Coleridge's dictations to Green over the last fifteen years of his life. Sara refers to this material both as her father's late unpublished thinking on these subjects and as Green's work that he undertook as Coleridge's colleague. McFarland demonstrates in his 'Prolegomena' that the ideas are Coleridge's and that Green served as amanuensis. See her reference to a forthcoming 'philosophical work by his friend and fellow student Mr. Green' on p.xxiii.
52 *BL* (1847), p.cxlii.
53 *BL* (1847), p.cxlviii.
54 *BL* (1847), p.cxliv.
55 Bate and Engell p.284, n.3. This is a good indication of Sara's continuing influence in Coleridge studies. Her translation is used for the crucial passage from Schelling's *System of Transcendental Idealism* that serves as the basis for Thesis X of chapter twelve. It argues for the primacy of 'self-consciousness' as the only means by which 'the absolute identity of the subjective and objective' can occur.
56 *BL* (1847), p.clxxxii.
57 *BL* (1847), p.clxxxii–iv.
58 *BL* (1847), p.clxxxiii.

7 'Posterity and Writing 'for the Day''

1   This late appearance of the Jacobinism charge in the debate almost feels like the return of the repressed, given its centrality in Coleridge's self-representations. Avoided in her Introduction to *Biographia Literaria*, she must face it here because of the political focus of the volume.

2   *The Times*, 4 September 1850, p.7.

3   *The Times*, 9 September 1850, p.6.

4   *Essays on his Own Times Forming a Second Series of the Friend* (London: William Pickering, 1850), p.xix. References hereafter as *EOT* are to this edition unless otherwise noted.

5   *EOT*, p.xiii. Italics hers.

6   *EOT*, p.xiii. Italics hers.

7   *EOT*, p.xiii. Italics hers.

8   *EOT*, p.xxiii.

9   *EOT*, p.xxiii.

10 *EOT*, p.xxv.

11 Suspicion is more than warranted here; it is inevitable given the effacement of history explicit in her method. Žižek's formulation seems particularly apt.

12 *EOT*, pp.xxv–xxxi.

13 *EOT*, p.xxxi.

14 'Patriot' was a fiercely contested term. Those who opposed the war were, legally speaking, 'unpatriotic', but radicals were quick to invert the term and use it to denote their own 'true patriotism' answering to a higher moral authority than the corrupt Pittites. Sara introduced the term at the outset when she included establishing 'his claim to the praise of patriotism' (p.xix) as one of her goals. The obvious inference, that her father had always been a 'patriot' 'in essence', suggests that the historical triumph of the Pittite view of the term was irrelevant. That this rhetorical manoeuvre turns the facts of the case on their head, reversing and/or denying Coleridge's definition of the term as he deployed it during the revolution debate, demonstrates how Sara's method produces historical forgetfulness in the service of ideological certainty.

15 'Letter to Aubrey de Vere, 14 April 1848', in *Memoir and Letters of Sara Coleridge,* ed. Her Daughter [Edith Coleridge], 2 vols (London: Henry S. King & Co., 1873), vol. 2, pp.161–5.

16 *Memoir and Letters*, vol. 2, p.162.

17 *EOT*, p.xxii.

18 'Letter to Aubrey de Vere, 14 April 1848', *Memoir and Letters*, vol. 2, p.164.

19 'Letter to Aubrey de Vere, 14 April 1848', *Memoir and Letters*, vol. 2, p.164.

20 'Letter to Aubrey de Vere, 14 April 1848', *Memoir and Letters*, vol. 2, p.165.

21 *The Times*, 11 April 1848, p.4.

22 *EOT*, vol. 1, p.108.

23 *EOT*, vol. 1, p.108. Coleridge's italics.

24 *Burke, Paine, Godwin, and the Revolution Controversy*, ed. Marilyn Butler (Cambridge: Cambridge University Press, 1984), p.50.

25 *EOT*, vol. 1, pp.119–20. Coleridge's italics.

26 *The Watchman*, ed. Lewis Patton (London: Routledge & Kegan Paul), 1970, pp.43–5.

27 See chapter 1.
28 For an excellent discussion of this issue see Paul Magnuson's 'The Politics of 'Frost at Midnight'', *The Wordsworth Circle*, Winter 1991, pp.3–11.
29 *EOT*, vol. 1, p.xxxv. Sections V–XI concern contemporary problems and events in Ireland, pp.xxxv–lxxiii.
30 *EOT*, vol. 1, pp.xxxvii–viii.
31 It is interesting to speculate about how history might have been different had Sara accepted de Vere's overtures. A high profile Catholic convert in 1851, de Vere lent significant impetus to Newman's movement. It is difficult to imagine this conversion occuring had he remained under Sara's intellectual influence. Her premature death the following year makes further conjecture impossible, but it appears likely, from his interactions with Sara on the Irish question, that the impetus for his conversion was a commitment to Irish nationalist politics. Nonetheless he titled the relevant chapter in his *Recollections of Aubrey de Vere* (reprinted by Bibliobazaar, 2008) 'My Submission to the Roman Catholic Church'.
32 *EOT*, vol. 1, p.xxxvi.
33 *EOT*, vol. 1, p.xxxvi.
34 *EOT*, vol. 1, p.xxxvi.
35 *EOT*, vol. 1, p.xli. Sara's parenthetical italics, Coleridge's within the quotation. The passage is from the *Courier*, 13 September 1811.
36 *EOT*, vol. 1, p.xlvii.
37 *EOT*, vol. 1, pp.xlvii–viii.
38 *EOT*, vol. 1, p.xlviii.
39 *EOT*, vol. 1, p.xxxii.
40 *EOT*, vol. 1, p.xxxiii.
41 *EOT*, vol. 1, p.xxxiii.
42 An argument can be made for Kathleen Coburn, and I take up that possibility in the final chapter.

8 Collecting Coleridge

1 'Recip. letter from Joseph Henry Green, 22 December 1842', Harry S. Ransom Center Manuscript, hereafter cited as HRC.
2 'Letter to Derwent, 5 January 1840', HRC.
3 'Letter to William Pickering, 12 December 1842', HRC. Notably, the family's continuing infantilization of Hartley extended to the terms of Coleridge's will.
4 'Letter to William Pickering, 12 December 1842', HRC.
5 'Letter to William Pickering, 12 December 1842', HRC.
6 'Recip. letter from William Pickering, 20 January 1843', HRC.
7 'Recip. letter from William Pickering, 20 January 1843', HRC.
8 'Recip. letter from Edward Moxon, 19 January 1843', HRC.
9 'Recip. letter from Edward Moxon, 11 January 1843', HRC.
10 'Recip. letter from Edward Moxon, 11 January 1843', HRC.
11 'Recip. letter from Edward Moxon, undated', but the reference to 'sell the present stock' makes it after 11 January 1843 and before the 19 January letter where Pickering's intention had become clear, HRC.

12 'Letter to William Pickering, postmarked 14 February 1843,' almost three weeks after his death on 26 January! HRC.
13 'Letter to William Pickering, postmarked 14 February 1843', HRC.
14 'Recip. letter from Edward Moxon, 21 January 1843', HRC.
15 'Letter to William Pickering, January 1843', dated only as January, but clearly before Henry's death, HRC.
16 The desire for better terms was based on 'real necessities' as she reminded Pickering in the late January letter; both Sarah Fricker Coleridge and Hartley depended on the income generated by sales. She could never be completely satisfied with Pickering so long as the fifty/fifty arrangement was in place.
17 After careful consideration, Green, acting as executor, advised against pursuing the move to Moxon under Pickering's terms: 'I am disposed to recommend to you to abstain from the purchase of the remaining stock'. 'Recip. letter from J. H. Green, 23 February 1843', HRC.
18 'Recip. letter from William Pickering, 9 March 1843', HRC.
19 'Recip. letter from William Pickering, 9 March 1843', HRC.
20 'Recip. letter from Joseph Henry Green, 8 November 1836', HRC.
21 'Recip. letter from William Pickering, 11 March 1843', HRC.
22 'Recip. letter from William Pickering, 18 March 1843', HRC.
23 'Recip. letter from William Pickering, 29 March 1843', HRC.
24 'Recip. letter from William Pickering, 6 September 1848', HRC.
25 'Recip. letter from William Pickering, 6 September 1848', HRC.
26 'Letter to William Pickering, 20 September 1848', HRC.
27 'Recip. letter from William Pickering, 6 September 1848', HRC.
28 'Letter to William Pickering, 20 September 1848', HRC.
29 'Letter to William Pickering, 20 September 1848', HRC.
30 The Leighton, Hooker, and Taylor Marginalia represented the starting point of *Aids to Reflection*, and the Luther material had played a major role in her attack on Newman in her Introduction to *Biographia Literaria*.
31 'Letter to William Pickering, 20 September 1848', HRC.
32 The value of the Marginalia had been clear to the ostensible owners of the volumes from the beginning. Writing in 1820 as Elia in the *London Magazine*, Lamb cautioned readers to avoid lending books, with the singular exception of 'S.T.C.' Describing some of the volumes that formed Sara's proposed edition, Lamb wrote: 'he [Coleridge] will return them ... with usury; enriched with annotations, tripling their value. I have had experience. Many of these special MSS. of his—(in *matter* oftentimes, and almost in *quantity* not infrequently, vying with the originals)—in no clerkly hand—legible in my Daniel; in old Burton; in Sir Thomas Browne; and those abstruser cogitations of Greville, now, alas! wandering in Pagan lands—I counsel thee, shut not thy heart, nor thy library, against S.T.C.' 'The Two Races of Men', *The Essays of Elia* (London: Taylor and Hessey, 1823).
33 *Marginalia* (CC), edited by H. J. Jackson and George Whalley (London: Routledge & Kegan Paul, 2001).
34 'Recip. letter from Edward Moxon, 8 January 1851', HRC.
35 There is no extant letter in the Sara letter MSS at the Harry S. Ransom Center.
36 'Recip. letter from Edward Moxon, 20 January 1843', HRC.
37 'Recip. letter from Edward Moxon, 8 January 1851', HRC.

38 'Letter to Julius Hare', undated, but probably October or early November 1848 on the basis of the return letter from Hare dated 10 November 1848, Victoria Library Pratt Library S MS F13.7. Hereafter, Pratt.

39 'Letter to Emily Trevenen', 9 April 1838. Cited in Mudge, p.102.

40 'Letter to Julius Hare' [November ?] 1848, Pratt S MS Fol. 13.7.

41 'Letter from Julius Hare, 10 November 1848', Pratt S MS Fol. 13.16 (item 999).

42 *Lectures 1818–1819: On the History of Philosophy* (CC), edited by J. R. de J. Jackson (London: Routledge & Kegan Paul, 1969).

43 'Recip. letter from Julius Hare, 26 April 1850', HRC.

44 'Recip. letter from Julius Hare, 26 April 1850', HRC.

45 'Recip. letter from Julius Hare, 26 April 1850', HRC.

46 'Recip. letter from Julius Hare, 26 April 1850', HRC.

47 'Recip. letter from Julius Hare, 26 April 1850', HRC.

48 Cited by Paul Cheshire in his essay, 'From Infant's Soul to Black Book: Coleridge's Use of Notebook 21', *The Coleridge Bulletin*, Summer 2008, p.19. Hereafter cited as Cheshire. Also see his chapter on the *Notebooks* in *The Oxford Companion to Samuel Taylor Coleridge*, ed. Frederick Burwick (Oxford: Oxford University Press, 2009), pp.288–306.

49 *The Notebooks of Samuel Taylor Coleridge*, 4 Vols. edited Kathleen Coburn and Merton Christensen (Vol. 4) (Princeton: Princeton University Press, 1957). Volumes 1 and 2 were originally published by Pantheon Books in New York, and volume 5 has been completed by Anthony John Harding since Coburn's death.

50 Cheshire describes how he used Coburn's 'appendices, tables and notes' to get a clear map of [Notebook 21's] contents and trace Coleridge's movements through the book', p.20.

51 Cheshire, p.20.

52 Cheshire, p.25.

53 Cheshire, p.24.

54 Cheshire's work makes an excellent case for Notebook 21 to be published, and doubtless other candidates can be found among the rest.

55 *Opus Maximum*, ed. Thomas McFarland with the assistance of Nicholas Halmi (Princeton: Princeton University Press, 2002), p.cxliv. McFarland gives a definitive account of the reasons for not publishing, including Green's role and the anxiety of how such a fragmentary work could be presented or how it might be received. See his section, 'Why the existing Fragments of the *Opus Maximum* Were Not Published' in his 'Prolegomena', pp.cxliii–clvii. I am primarily interested in Sara Coleridge's decision not to list it among Coleridge's *Literary Remains*.

56 *Biographia Literaria*, p.xxiii.

57 See McFarland, pp.clii–clvii. This tortured history accounts for the four fragments not being published until McFarland took up the task at Kathleen Coburn's suggestion, and Nicholas Halmi assisted in its final completion.

58 'Letter to William Pickering, 20 September 1848', HRC.

59 'Letter to William Pickering, 20 September 1848', HRC.

60 'Recip. Letter from J. H. Green, 27 May 1849', HRC.

61 See Chapter 5, n.3 above.

Works Cited

Editions of Coleridge's works are listed chronologically. The Collected Coleridge edition of *Table Talk* is listed here because of Carl Woodring's addition of other Coleridge materials to the volume. As the book makes clear, Henry Nelson Coleridge was the author of the original *Table Talk*, and it is listed accordingly.

Coleridge, Samuel Taylor, *Aids to Reflection, Fourth Edition with the Author's Last Corrections*, ed. Henry Nelson Coleridge (London: William Pickering, 1839).

——, *Aids to Reflection*, 2 vols, ed. Sara Coleridge. vol. 2 (London: William Pickering, 1848).

——, *Aids to Reflection*, ed. John Beer (Princeton: Princeton University Press, 1993).

——, *Biographia Literaria, Second Edition Prepared for Publication in Part by the Late Henry Nelson Coleridge and Completed by his Widow*, 2 vols (London: William Pickering, 1847).

——, *Biographia Literaria*. 2 vols, eds. James Engell and W. Jackson Bate (London: Routledge & Kegan Paul, 1983).

——, *Coleridge's Poetry and Prose*, eds. Nicolas Halmi, Paul Magnuson and Raimonda Modiano (Norton: New York and London, 2005).

——, 'Letter to Joseph Cottle', 26 April 1814, *The Collected Letters of Samuel Taylor Coleridge*, 6 vols, ed. Earl Leslie Griggs, vol. 3 (Oxford: Clarendon Press, 1959). 476.

——, 'Letter to Joseph Cottle', 27 April 1814, 478–9.

——, 'Letter to Joseph Cottle', April 1814, 481, 484.

——, *Confessions of an Enquiring Spirit*, ed. Henry Nelson Coleridge (London: William Pickering, 1840).

——, *Essays on His Own Times Forming a Second Series of the Friend*, 3 vols, ed. Sara Coleridge (London: William Pickering, 1850).

——, *Essays on His Own Times*, 3 vols, ed. David V. Erdman (London: Routledge & Kegan Paul, 1978).

——, *Lectures 1818–1819: On the History of Philosophy*, ed. J. R. de J. Jackson (London: Routledge & Kegan Paul, 1969).

——, 'The Literati and Literature of Germany', *The Friend*, 2 vols, ed. Barbara E. Rooke, vol. 1 (London: Routledge & Kegan Paul, 1969).

——, *The Literary Remains of Samuel Taylor Coleridge*, ed. Henry Nelson Coleridge, 4 vols (London: William Pickering, 1836–9).

——, *Marginalia*, 6 vols, eds. H. J. Jackson and George Whalley (London: Routledge & Kegan Paul, 2001).

——, *The Notebooks of Samuel Taylor Coleridge*, 5 vols, eds. Merton Christensen, Kathleen Coburn and Anthony John Harding, vol. 4 (Princeton: Princeton University Press, 1957–2002).

——, *Opus Maximum*, ed. Thomas McFarland and Nicholas Halmi (Princeton: Princeton University Press, 2002).

Coleridge, Samuel Taylor, 'Once a Jacobin Always a Jacobin', *Coleridge's Poetry and Prose*, eds. Nicholas Hamli, Paul Magnuson and Raimonda Modiano (New York and London: Norton, 2004). 299–306.
——, *Table Talk*, ed. Carl Woodring (London and Princeton: Princeton University Press, 1990).
——, *The Watchman*, ed. Lewis Patton (London: Routledge & Kegan Paul, 1970).

Other works cited

Althusser, Louis, 'Contradiction and Overdetermination', *For Marx*, trans. Ben Brewster (London: Verso, 1996).
——, 'Ideology and Ideological State Apparatuses', *Lenin and Philosophy and Other Essays*, trans. Ben Brewster (New York: Monthly Review Press, 2001).
Bailey, Samuel, 'A Review of Berkeley's Theory of Vision', *Essays on the Formation and Publication of Opinions* (London, 1842).
Barbeau, Jeffrey, *Coleridge, the Bible, and Religion* (Basingstoke: Palgrave Macmillan, 2008).
Beer, John, 'Editor's Introduction', *Aids to Reflection* (London: Routledge & Kegan Paul, 1993).
Buchan, James, *Crowded with Genius: The Scottish Enlightenment: Edinburgh's Moment of the Mind* (New York: Harper Collins, 2003). 123.
Butler, Marilyn, ed. *Burke, Paine, Godwin, and the Revolution Controversy* (Cambridge: Cambridge University Press, 1984). 50.
'The Chartist Demonstrations', *The Times* (11 April 1848), 4.
Cheshire, Paul, 'From Infant's Soul to Black Book: Coleridge's Use of Notebook 21', *The Coleridge Bulletin* n.s. 31 (Summer 2008), 19.
——, 'Coleridge's Notebooks', *The Oxford Handbook of Samuel Taylor Coleridge*, ed. Frederick Burwick (Oxford: Oxford University Press, 2009). 288–306.
Coleridge, Derwent, 'Letter', *The Times* (9 September 1850), 6.
Coleridge, Henry Nelson, *Specimens of the Table Talk of the late Samuel Taylor Coleridge*, 2 vols, vol. 1 (London: John Murray, 1835).
Coleridge, Sara, 'On Rationalism', *Aids to Reflection*, 2 vols, vol. 2 (London: William Pickering, 1848).
——, *Memoir and Letters of Sara Coleridge*, 2 vols, ed. Edith Coleridge, vol. 2 (London: Henry S. King & Co., 1873).
Cottle, Joseph, *Early Recollections; Chiefly Relating to the Late Samuel Taylor Coleridge, During His Long Stay in Bristol* (London: Longman, Rees & Co., 1837).
——, *Reminiscences of Samuel Taylor Coleridge and Robert Southey* (London: Houlston and Stoneman, 1848).
De Quincey, Thomas, 'Coleridge', *Tait's Edinburgh Magazine*, September 1834.
——, *Literary Reminiscences: From the Autobiography of an English Opium-Eater* (Boston and New York: Houghton Mifflin, 1876). 169–70.
——, *Confessions of an English Opium-Eater* (London: Walter Scott, 1886), 79.
——, *The Collected Writings of Thomas De Quincey*, 14 vols, ed. David Mason, vol 2 (Edinburgh: A. and C. Black, 1889). 147.
de Vere, Aubrey, 'My Submission to the Roman Catholic Church', *Recollections of Aubrey de Vere* (Bibliobazaar, 2008). 307–321.

Edwards, Pamela, *The Statesman's Science: History, Nature, Law in the Political Thought of Samuel Taylor Coleridge* (New York: Columbia University Press, 2004).

Ferrier, James Frederick, 'An Introduction to the Philosophy of Consciousness', *Blackwood's Edinburgh Magazine* (February 1838), 190.

——, 'The Plagiarisms of S. T. Coleridge', *Blackwood's Edinburgh Magazine* (March 1840), 287–99.

——, 'Proposition I: The Primary Law or Condition of All Knowledge', *The Institutes of Metaphysic*, 3rd edn (Edinburgh: William Blackwood and Sons, 1875).

——, *The Philosophical Works of James Frederick Ferrier*, 3 vols, ed. John Haldane, vol. 1 (Bristol: Thoemmes Press, 2001).

Fichte, J. G., *Grundlage der gesammten Wissenschaftslehre* (Jena and Leipzig, 1794).

Fruman, Norman, *Coleridge, the Damaged Archangel* (New York: George Braziller, 1971).

Gibbs, Warren E., 'Unpublished Letters Concerning Cottle's Coleridge', *PMLA*, 49 (March 1934), 202–28.

Grantz, Carl L., 'Letters of Sara Coleridge: A Calendar and Index of Her Manuscript Correspondence in the University of Texas Library', Dissertation, University of Texas, (June 1986).

Green, J. H., *Spiritual Philosophy: Founded on the Teaching of the Late Samuel Taylor Coleridge*, ed. John Simon, 2 vols (London: Macmillan, 1865).

Hall, S. C., *A Book of Memories of Great Men and Women* (London: Virtue and Co., 1871).

Hare, Julius, 'Samuel Coleridge and the English Opium-Eater', *British Magazine and Monthly Register of Religion and Ecclesiastical Information*, vol. 7 (January, 1835), 15–27.

Hazlitt, William, *Complete Works of William Hazlitt*, 21 vols, ed. P. P. Howe, vol. 19 (London: J. M. Dent & Sons, 1933), 203.

Jackson, J. R.. de J., ed., *Coleridge: The Critical Heritage*, 2 vols, vol. 1 (London: Routledge & Kegan Paul, 1970; 1991), 343.

Lamb, Charles, 'The Two Races of Men', *The Essays of Elia* (London: Taylor and Hessey, 1823).

Larkin, Peter, 'Repetition, Difference and Liturgical Participation in Coleridge's "The Ancient Mariner",' *Literature and Theology* 21.2 (June 2007), 146–159.

Leighton, Robert, *The Expository Works and Other Remains of Archbishop Leighton, Some of Which Were Never Before Printed. Revised by Philip Doddridge, D.D. With a Preface by the Doctor*, 2 vols (Edinburgh: 1748).

——, *The Genuine Works of R. Leighton, D.D. Archbishop of Glasgow*, 4 vols (London: 1819).

Lindop, Grevel, *The Opium-Eater* (Oxford: Oxford University Press, 1985), 239.

'The Literati and Literature of Germany', *Anti-Jacobin Review and Magazine* (London: J. Wright, July 1800), 594.

Lockhart, John Gibson, 'Review of *Specimens of the Table Talk of the late Samuel Taylor Coleridge*', *Quarterly Review*, 53 (February 1835), 103.

Magnuson, Paul, *Coleridge and Wordsworth: A Lyrical Dialogue* (Princeton: Princeton University Press, 1988).

——, 'The Politics of "Frost at Midnight",' *The Wordsworth Circle* 22.1 (Winter 1991), 3–11.

——, *Reading Public Romanticism* (Princeton: Princeton University Press, 1998).

Marsh, James, 'Preliminary Essay', *Aids to Reflection* (Port Washington, NY: Kennikat, 1971).

McFarland, Thomas, *Coleridge and the Pantheist Tradition* (Oxford: Oxford University Press, 1969).

'Misrepresentations', *Anti-Jacobin, or Weekly Examiner*, 5 March 1798, 4th edn, vol. 1 (London: J. Wright, 1799), 7–8.

Mudge, Bradford, *Sara Coleridge: A Victorian Daughter* (New Haven: Yale University Press, 1989).

Reid, Thomas, *The Works of Thomas Reid, D.D., Now Fully Collected, with Selections from His Unpublished Letters. Preface, Notes and Supplementary Dissertations*, 2 vols, ed. William Hamilton (Edinburgh: Longman Brown, 1846).

'Review of *The Autobiography of Leigh Hunt*', *The Times* (4 September 1850), 7.

Roe, Nicholas, *Wordsworth and Coleridge: The Radical Years* (Oxford: Clarendon Press, 2003).

Schelling, F. W., 'Abhandlungen zur Erläuterung des Idealismus', *Philosophische Schriften* (Landshut, 1809).

——, 'Vom Ich als Prinzip der Philosophie', *Philosophische Schriften* (Landshut, 1809).

——, *System des transscendentalen Idealismus* (Tübingen, 1800).

Stephens, Frances Anne, 'The Hartley Coleridge Letters at the University of Texas: A Calendar and Index', Dissertation, University of Texas (January 1970).

Thomson, Arthur, *Ferrier of St. Andrews: An Academic Tragedy* (Edinburgh: Scottish Academical, 1985).

Wu, Duncan, ed. *Romanticism: An Anthology*, 2nd edn (Oxford: Blackwell, 2000). 460.

Žižek, Slavoj, *The Sublime Object of Ideology* (London: Verso, 1989).

Index

moralistic criticism of Coleridge, 123–4
  and Derwent Coleridge's response to, 124
Morning Post, and Coleridge's involvement with, 10
Moxon, Edward, 9
  and becomes publisher of Coleridge's works, 155
  and negotiations with Sara Coleridge, 148–9
  and negotiations with William Pickering, 147
  and publishing terms offered by, 142
Mudge, Bradford, 83, 93, 109, 136
Murray, John, 91

Newman, John Henry, 96–7
  and Sara Coleridge's attack on, 112, 114–16
North, Christopher, *see* Wilson, John
Notebooks of Samuel Taylor Coleridge
  and Coburn's edition, 159–60; side-effects of chronological order, 160
  and Sara Coleridge's decision not to publish, 156–9

'Once a Jacobin Always a Jacobin'
  and Coleridge's defence against accusations of Jacobinism, 4, 13–14
  and republication of, 5
opium addiction
  and attempts to suppress publication of Coleridge's letter, 31, 32, 33–4
  and Coleridge on sufferings of, 86–7
  and De Quincey's essays on Coleridge, 35
  and Hartley Coleridge, 36, 37
  and Sara Coleridge, 92, 109
Opus Maximum
  and contemporary study of, 163–4
  and impact on Coleridge's reputation, 1, 2
  and misplaced charge of idleness, 124
  and publication history, 163
Oxford Movement, 60, 96, 113, 114

Pantisocracy, 13, 14–15
Pickering, William, 7, 84
  and *Aids to Reflection*, 150–1, 152
  and commitment to keeping works in print, 150
  and late payment of dividends, 143
  and *Literary Remains*, 151–2, 152–3
  and motives for publishing Coleridge, 145–6
  and negotiations with Henry Nelson Coleridge, 142, 143–5, 148; response to, 145–7
  and negotiations with Sara Coleridge, 9, 147–8, 150–1; organization of works, 153–4
  and publishing terms, 142; unfairness of, 150
Pitt, William, 15, 16, 17, 21, 23, 128, 133, 138
plagiarism by Coleridge, 2
  and Coleridge's defence against accusations of, 67–8; as confession, 78–9; Ferrier's analysis of, 67–9, 76–7, 78; qualified readers, 79, 80
  and De Quincey's accusations of, 5, 26, 31, 64, 65; Hare's rebuttal of, 39–43, 67; as 'literary curiosity', 42, 43; motives for, 64, 72, 79; self-dramatization, 65–6
  and Ferrier's 'The Plagiarisms of S T Coleridge', 6, 34, 41, 66–7; analysis of Coleridge's defence, 67–9, 76–7, 78; explanation of variations, 69–70; Hartley Coleridge's response, 71–2; lack of apparent motive, 71–2; motives for, 72–3, 74–5, 76–7; philosophical context of, 74–7; regrets over, 80; Sara Coleridge's response to, 41–2, 101–12; 'verbatim translation' charge, 77–8
  and Hare's rebuttal of charges, 39–43
  as improvisational plagiarism, 77–8
political opinions, and Coleridge
  and accusations of Jacobinism: *Anti-Jacobin, or Weekly Examiner*, 11;